Teaching and Learning Secondary Science

Science education has changed radically in recent years, both as a result of debates within the subject itself and because of external influences such as curriculum legislation and changes in society and technology. In this book Jerry Wellington (with Mick Nott and Jon Scaife) discusses the major issues in science education today – questions such as the place of practical work, the role of information and communication technology (ICT), and the nature of science as a subject – and uses this discussion to support a very practical resource for teachers in training, practising teachers, and mentors. The book covers the major aspects of science teaching and learning, including:

- planning and managing
- differentiation and special needs
- practical work . . . and what it is for
- investigations
- ICT in science teaching and learning
- building on children's prior learning
- handling controversial issues
- language in science education
- the nature of science
- why teach science . . . and why learn it?

Throughout the book chapters are accompanied by activities and annotated lists of further reading aimed at helping readers to follow up their interests in depth and explore topics in more detail.

Jerry Wellington taught science in Tower Hamlets, East London, before joining the University of Sheffield where he is now Reader in Education. He is the author of many publications including the precursor to this book for Routledge entitled *Secondary Science*.

Teaching and Learning Secondary Science

Contemporary issues and practical approaches

Jerry Wellington

London and New York

First published 2000
by Routledge
11 New Fetter Lane, London EC4P 4EE

Simultaneously published in the USA and Canada
by Routledge
29 West 35th Street, New York, NY 10001

Routledge is an imprint of the Taylor & Francis Group

Selection and editorial matter © 2000 Jerry Wellington and © contributed chapters the
contributors

Some of the material in this book was first published as part of *Secondary Science*, published in
1994 by Routledge

Typeset in Goudy by Exe Valley Dataset Ltd, Exeter, Devon
Printed and bound in Great Britain by Biddles Ltd, Guildford and King's Lynn

British Library Cataloguing in Publication Data
A catalogue record for this book is available fom the British Library

Library of Congress Cataloging in Publication Data
Wellington, J. J. (Jerry J.)
    Teaching and learning secondary science: contemporary issues and
practical approaches / Jerry Wellington.
        p.   cm.
    Includes bibliographical references and index.
    1. Science—Study and teaching (Secondary)   I. Title.
Q181.W4416   1999
507'. 1'2—dc21   99–16842
                                                              CIP

ISBN 0–415–21403–3

We dedicate this book to the memory of the late Ros Driver, a major contributor to our understanding of children's learning.

Contents

Figures

Tables

Contributors

Mick Nott is a Principal Lecturer in science education at Sheffield Hallam University. His curriculum development interests are in using the history, philosophy and sociology of science to teach science. His current research interests are in teachers' understandings of the nature of science, the professional development of teachers of science and the history, philosophy and sociology of the school science curriculum.

Jon Scaife is a lecturer in Education at the University of Sheffield in England. His background is in mathematical physics. He has taught physics and maths to A-level and undergraduate students, but found it just as interesting and rewarding teaching 'elementary' science, woodwork and music. He has worked in the Physics and Education departments at the University of Sheffield, where his main study interest is in learning and how people do it.

Preface

There is no substitute for teaching experience and classroom observation. On the other hand, time is often needed to stand back and reflect upon this experience. The aim of this book is to encourage and assist teachers (both in training and in service), mentors and others involved in science education with that process of reflection in the hope that it will improve and enrich practice.

A lot has happened in recent years. This book is partly based on *Secondary Science: Contemporary Issues and Practical Approaches*, but it is rather more than a new edition of the 1994 book. It has been written with new standards for initial teacher training in mind but is not geared specifically to any particular statements of standards or competencies, nor to a specific curriculum. It should therefore be of value to students, teachers and mentors in the UK, USA, Australasia and other countries.

The book aims both to cover contemporary issues in science education which will have a direct bearing on science teaching in the new century, and to present and discuss practical approaches in science education. Contemporary issues such as the role of practical work, the nature of science, the place of information and communication technology (ICT), children's prior learning, the importance of language in science education, the need for differentiation, the handling of controversial issues, and the role of 'informal' learning are all considered. In parallel with those discussions, practical approaches for teaching and learning are offered which, I hope, will be of value in the classroom and the laboratory.

Space is limited, so none of the discussions or suggestions goes into the depth that could be achieved if a single book were written on just one of the areas. Consequently, ample references and suggestions for further reading are given throughout. This book, like science teaching for all, is designed for a mixed-ability, mixed-attainment and mixed-motivation audience, so it provides for the possibility of special needs and interests and offers ample scope for extension work. Some readers may not have the time or the inclination to follow up the references and further reading but we hope that others will.

Finally, readers are bound to find something missing – not every issue or practical approach could possibly be covered in a book of this kind. The main aim here is to introduce readers to the basic questions of *why*, *what* and *how* that occur so frequently in the teaching and learning of science.

Comments and feedback on any points either in, or not in, the book are welcome – either by post to Jerry Wellington at the University of Sheffield or by e-mail to: j.wellington@sheffield.ac.uk.

Acknowledgements

I would like to acknowledge the contribution of Mick Nott to several parts of this book and to my own thinking and reflection on many of the issues in it over a number of years. I would also like to thank Jon Scaife for his new chapter on learning in science. Three of my colleagues (Jenny Henderson, Vic Lally and Stephen Knutton) contributed to the 1994 book on which this one is partly based and I would like to thank them for their chapters in that forerunner. The excellent drawings in Chapters 2 and 5 were done by David Houchin who is a year 11 pupil at Silverdale Comprehensive School in Sheffield. I would like to thank David, and also Ruth Lawless for organising these drawings. I am very grateful to Tina Cartwright once again with all her help in supporting the research on which this is based, in helping with the manuscript and assisting with the other tasks which are needed in producing a book. Last but not least, I would like to thank my family (Wendy, Daniel, Rebecca and Hannah) for their encouragement and support.

The authors and publisher would like to thank the following for permission to include tables or figures:

Mick Nott for the Venn diagrams on teacher development in Chapter 2.
Robin Millar for Table 2.1.
Richard White for Figure 4.9 and Table 4.1.
Crown Copyright for Figures 4.6, 4.10 and 4.11 (all reproduced with the permission of the Controller of HMSO).
Heinemann for Figures 4.4, 4.5, 4.7 and 10.4(b); also Table 4.3.
Oxford University Press for Figure 9.3.
New Media for Figures 10.3(a) and (b).
CAPEDIA Ltd for Figure 10.2.
Roger Frost for Figures 10.4(a) and 10.5.
Cambridge University Press for Figure 11.1.
Thomas Nelson for Figures 11.7, 11.8 and 11.9.
The *Sheffield Star* for Figure 12.3.
The *Manchester Evening News* for Figure 12.4.
The concept map was provided anonymously by a student at Bath University.

Science teaching, the science curriculum and the nature of science

Chapter 1

The art and craft of science teaching

Meeting high standards – a tall order

One of the premises of this book is that science teaching is an extremely demanding occupation. No other subject teacher has to cope with such a range of situations, with such a conceptually difficult subject and a group of learners who bring all kinds of prior learning and preconceptions to it. Teaching science is a tall order. In this first chapter, we identify ten key aspects of science teaching and begin to outline some of the questions they raise and to offer some practical ways forward. Each area is developed later in the book.

Ten key areas of science teaching are summarised: using language, questioning, explaining, practical work, using resources, presenting the nature of science, assessing learning, developing progression and continuity, planning and managing – and lastly, but most importantly, generating motivation and enthusiasm.

1 Using language carefully

Learning science is, in many ways, like learning a new language. In some ways it presents more difficulty in that many of the hard, conceptual words of science – such as energy, work, power – have a precise meaning in science and sometimes an exact science definition, but a very different meaning in everyday life. Equally, many of the naming words of our lives have been commandeered by science. Consider: element, conductor, cell, field, circuit, compound. This is made worse because many of the terms of science are metaphors. For example, a field in science is not really a field.

Another category of language which science teachers (and many other teachers) use, has been christened the 'language of secondary education'. The list includes: modify, compare, evaluate, hypothesise, infer, recapitulate . . . and so on. These are words used by teachers and exam papers but rarely heard in playgrounds, pubs or at football matches.

What should science teachers do about their specialist language and the language of secondary education? Well, they cannot avoid it, skirt round it, or constantly translate it into the 'vernacular'. This would do a disservice to their pupils who will eventually be confronted by science language, certainly in test papers and examinations. The general answer is to treat language with care, to be aware of its difficulties, and to bear in mind that although pupils can and do use scientific terms in speech and writing this does not imply that they understand them (this is equally true of journalists, other writers and radio or TV pundits of course).

More specifically, a later chapter is devoted to language in science and discusses: directed or structured *reading*; note-taking and note-making; pupils' *writing* in science; and discussion and debating. Of course, communication in science involves far more than just the spoken and the written word and this is also discussed in Chapter 9.

2 Questioning

One of the most difficult arts (or is it a science?) of teaching which involves judicious use of language is the activity of *questioning*, which goes on in so many classrooms. Research shows that most of the questions are asked by teachers and that most pupil responses are short answers to *closed* questions, involving factual recall:

> Teacher: Which element has an atomic number of 6?
> Pupil: Carbon.

At another end of the spectrum is the art of Socratic questioning. A classic book called *The Meno* describes how Socrates 'pulled out' or literally educed (from the Latin *educare*: to educate) the principle of Pythagoras from a 'mere slave'. He did this purely by questioning-eliciting and building upon the slave's existing ideas and knowledge. This is the highest form of questioning. Cynics may argue that this may have worked for a genius like Socrates in a one-to-one with a lowly slave – but try doing this with 24 adolescents on a wet Friday afternoon. I have sympathy with the cynics. But it is still worth examining the questioning techniques used by teachers and how they can be improved. The best teachers are often the best questioners.

What types of question are there and what purposes do they serve?

- *closed* questions, which have only one acceptable answer, e.g. a name, a piece of information, a specific line of reasoning (or argument);
- *open* questions – a number of different answers could be accepted e.g. an opinion, an evaluation, a belief, a pupil's own line of reasoning.

Research indicates that most teachers' questions are closed, partly because the responses are (not surprisingly) easier to handle. Also, closed questions are useful in controlling and shaping a lesson, not least in ensuring that a whole class is paying attention. Many questions can be used by a teacher to either focus, guide or redirect a lesson. These are generally *diagnostic* questions, e.g. eliciting what pupils already know, checking that pupils are 'on the right lines'.

One type of question which teachers use, but need to be wary of, is the 'guess what's in my head' or pseudo-question. This type of question was caricatured humorously by Peter Ustinov:

> Teacher: Who is the greatest composer?
> Pupil: Beethoven.
> Teacher: Wrong, Bach.
> Teacher: Name me one Russian composer.
> Pupil: Tchaikovsky.
> Teacher: Wrong. Rimsky-Korsakov.
>
> (*Printed in Edwards and Westgate, 1994: 100*)

In Chapter 5 we look again at the art of questioning, as part of the business of planning and managing teaching.

3 The art of explaining

One of the great arts of teaching is to be able to explain things, i.e. to put difficult ideas into terms which pupils can understand. As teachers develop, they learn a range of different ways of representing and formulating the ideas of science which make them comprehensible to pupils. Through observation, practice and experience teachers develop a repertoire of explanations and different ways of explaining things. If one doesn't work, then perhaps another will. This 'wisdom of practice' (Shulman, 1986: 9) develops over time – teachers acquire a whole armoury of examples, illustrations, explanations and analogies.

The art of explaining involves the ability to convey difficult scientific ideas without distorting their meaning or telling lies. This often requires considerable intellectual effort and sound subject knowledge. It involves breaking down a complex idea, or a process, into its smaller component steps. Processes such as photosynthesis, cooling by evaporation, melting or boiling, and fractional distillation can only be understood if the simpler ideas they rely on are first identified then put into a sequence, then explained. The business of *identifying* the underlying or prerequisite ideas, then *sequencing* them is the basis of *concept mapping*. Box One (shown below) gives a few of the key ideas behind concept mapping and some suggested steps in making them for oneself. Figure 1.1 shows an example of a concept map produced by a new science teacher.

It requires considerable mental effort. Just try doing it for any of the above processes. Similarly with a complex idea such as momentum or acceleration. 'Momentum' depends on an understanding of 'mass' and 'velocity'. Velocity requires an understanding of speed and direction. Speed is understood by . . . and so on. Explaining momentum requires a lot more effort than simply defining it as mass times velocity. One way to aid understanding is to use lots and lots of examples, from many different contexts. Moving objects with a large or a small momentum could be shown or talked about: a lorry, a train, a bee, the *Titanic*. Examples help.

Box I Concept mapping

What is a concept map?

A concept map is a special kind of thinking (metacognitive) tool. Its purpose is to relate concepts to one another as a hierarchy which, at the same time, should display their relationships in a scientifically valid form. (Note: the word 'concept' in this case is taken to mean any word or phrase which has a scientific meaning.)

There are three very specific features that characterise a concept map.

1. *It must represent a hierarchy of ideas ranging from the most general idea at the apex to the most specific ideas at the base.*
2. *The link between any two ideas must have a word or phrase which describes the relationship and is scientifically valid.*
3. *The concept map must be revised each time new information is included and when incorrect relationships are discovered.*

Creating concept maps

The concept map is rooted in this idea of *relationships* and that is why the hierarchy and the statements of relationship are essential if the map is to function. If you cannot find words to describe the scientific relationship between two ideas then it is not valid to make the link.

Links should not be made if they cannot be justified. The relationship should be researched more deeply through texts or consultation, until either a suitable connecting phrase is found or the idea is rejected.

One danger with the process is that the map can end up as a topic web, in which case it will have neither hierarchy nor statements or relationships and will do nothing to promote understanding of the subject matter.

Concept mapping is a dynamic process and the map should be constantly revised. The first map is merely a starting point which may contain errors and/or misconceptions. Its value, however, is that it not only challenges the author's understanding but also opens up the thinking to other people in a highly visible and accessible way.

Steps in Concept Mapping

1. Choose the concepts, i.e. key words or very short phrases, you wish to use in your map. Don't choose too many at this stage. Write them out on small separate pieces of paper.
2. Rank the list of concepts from the most abstract and inclusive to the most concrete and specific to establish a hierarchy.
3. Group the concepts according to two criteria:
   (i) concepts that seem to be at similar levels of generality or specificity;
   (ii) concepts that are closely related.
4. Arrange the concepts as a two-dimensional array rather like a family tree with the most general concepts at the top.
5. Try to think of words or phrases that could link the concepts together so that it makes scientific sense. If you can't make a link at this point leave out the concept for the time being.
6. When you are satisfied that the map now reflects your current understanding, draw it out on a sheeet of A4 paper.
7. Link the related concepts with lines and label them with the connecting phrase or word which describes the logical connections and which makes sense when read in conjunction with the concepts.
8. Be prepared to revise your map. A concept map should allow the reorganisation and reconstruction of ideas in order to create a dynamic framework for knowledge and understanding.

Source: this is based on a set of guidelines produced by Keith Bishop of the University of Bath, partly derived from Novak and Gowin (1984).

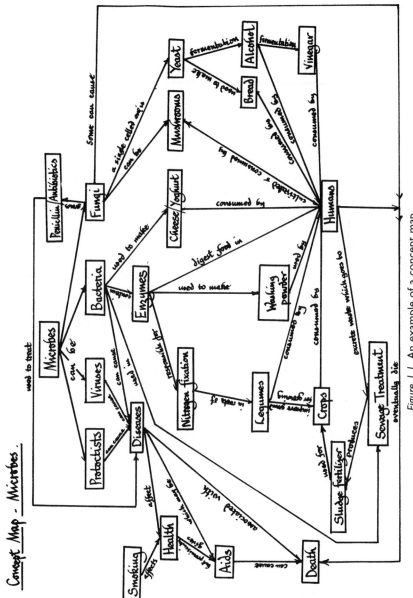

Figure 1.1 An example of a concept map.

Equally, analogies and metaphors are an integral part of science. Many explanations involve describing the unfamiliar in familiar terms, or explaining unfamiliar events by comparing them with familiar occurrences. Thus, electric current is like the flow of water in a pipe (the water analogy). Fractional distillation is like sorting out a pack of cards into Kings, Queens, Jacks and so on. Global warming is, in some ways, like the effect of a greenhouse on its contents. Respiration is like burning. Light is sometimes like a stream of particles, sometimes more like the waves in a tank of water. But all analogies and comparisons have their limits. If a water pipe is cut, the water leaks out – but electricity does not 'leak out' of a wall socket or a cut wire (although we often talk of 'leakage' in an electrical context). Thus, analogies are valuable but must not be taken too far: this message has to be conveyed to pupils.

Similarly with both multimedia images and physical models in teaching science. Multimedia can be a powerful tool in teaching science, especially in showing the normally invisible entities which scientific explanations rely on, e.g. particles in a melting block of ice; electrons in a wire; electrons 'orbiting' the nucleus. But there is a danger if pupils take these images too literally or too seriously (see Chapter 5 of Collins, Hammond and Wellington 1997).

Similarly, physical models can be used to show things which are either very small, e.g. atoms and their bonds, the helix of DNA, or particles as marbles in a tray; and things which are very large, e.g. plate tectonics. But, like analogies, models have their limitations. Atoms, and bonds between them, are not really like balls and lengths of string.

In summary, good explanations often require illustrations, models and analogies but teachers need to be careful to:

- point out their limitations, i.e. where the analogy breaks down;
- use illustrations and examples which *are* familiar to pupils and take account of their own environment and personal circumstances (when I started my teaching career in East London I always used insulation in house lofts in discussing heat loss, until I realised that 95 per cent of the school population lived in blocks of flats);
- avoid examples, illustrations or analogies which may be gender, culturally or religiously biased (see Gilbert 1998, for a good discussion of explanations and models).

4 Making best use of practical work

Science is about language. But it is also about doing things, seeing things happen, measuring and controlling things. This is all part of practical work – something which pupils have come to expect in secondary science ('when are we getting the Bunsens out?') and which (unfortunately) many teachers now often take for granted.

On the positive side of the balance sheet, practical work can excite, motivate, illustrate and clarify. But on the other hand it can also confuse, turn off, complicate and demotivate. Teachers need to be clear about which practicals to do, *when* and *why*, i.e. what is the purpose of each piece of practical work? So many practicals in school science have been 'passed on' from one teacher or textbook to the next and have become 'institutionalised' into school schemes of work. They are here (and done) because they're here because they're here . . .

Returning to a positive note, practical activity in science can have several important purposes:

- to illustrate a scientific law, e.g. the connection between pressure and volume of a gas;
- to demonstrate a phenomenon, e.g. expansion; or a process, e.g. rusting, photosynthesis;
- to interest and motivate pupils;
- to aid memory of events and processes;
- to develop and teach specific scientific skills and techniques, e.g. using a Bunsen; reading from meters; adjusting a microscope; taking measurements;
- to show potential dangers and safety hazards;
- to stimulate discussion, e.g. with a Predict-Observe-Explain (POE) activity.

The art (or science) of good science teaching is to match the learning objective(s) of a lesson to an activity, whether it be practical work or not. For example, theories and theoretical ideas are not best learnt by doing practical work, especially if they involve abstract, invisible entities such as particles, atoms, electrons, fields or waves.

In short, practical work is valuable in showing *what* happens (phenomena, events) and sometimes[1] *how* (processes) but rarely in explaining *why* things happen (theories). Science as a subject is as much theoretical as it is practical (see Millar 1998: 29 and other chapters in Wellington 1998), and therefore hands-on work alone is not enough. 'Minds-on' are needed too.

A full chapter (7) later in this book is devoted to practical work, its value and its drawbacks, with another chapter (8) on Investigations.

5 Choosing and using resources

One key aspect of planning and managing learning is the skill of selecting the right resources for the right teaching and learning objectives. Picture a dream world where science teachers have a range of teaching resources at their disposal: videos, a class set of textbooks, differentiated worksheets, an overhead projector (OHP) and transparencies, a class set of equipment for each pupil practical, a helpful and supportive technician, ready access to computers and software in labs and a bookable computer suite, the Internet, a library/resource centre stocked with science materials, funding for field-trips and visits to museums or interactive science centres . . .

Now wake up. In a real school, *most* teachers will have access to *some* of the above wish-list. *None* will have access to *all* of them. Even Ofsted admit that reality is far from perfect and that class teachers are not always at fault. The Ofsted (1998) review of the nineties reports that the level of resources in 'a significant number of schools' adversely affects subject teaching, commonly in the 'teaching of practical subjects' (Ofsted 1998: 12). This is often beyond the control of the science teacher, since it is due to 'major weaknesses in the management of resources' such as 'the library and IT facilities'.

ICT, which both new and long-serving teachers are constantly being counselled to use in supporting learning and teaching, is a classic case. Many science teachers would love to use ICT given half the chance – they may well appreciate the power of spreadsheets and databases, the value of computer simulations, the benefits of data-logging, the potential of multimedia to animate and make the invisible visible, and the new horizons opened up by the Internet. But they have to work in classrooms which are located in institutions called schools. Access to ICT resources – *when* and *where* they want them – and to technical support for ICT in *science* teaching is a major problem for most teachers. The same Ofsted review (1998) reported that in only one-third of schools has careful management ensured 'adequacy of IT resources' and even in many schools in this small minority the available IT is not put to 'good use' (page 148) often for lack of technical support.

So, in the real world, the task of choosing resources to match learning objectives, i.e. horses for courses, is a messy and complex business. Given their availability we can say, however, that:

- *videos* and multimedia can capture interest and demonstrate events, pro-cesses or experiments which cannot be shown in the school lab – from volcanoes erupting to babies being born;
- the *OHP* (if the bulb is working) can be one of the best visual aids ever invented: for demonstrating, e.g. ripples in a see-through tank or iron filings round a magnet; for showing animation; or simply for giving notes while actually looking at a class;
- *visits* to factories, power-stations, museums or science centres can be a memorable part of a pupil's curriculum and relate lab science to the world outside.

Finally, ICT (if you can get your hands on it) is valuable in teaching and learning science. A chapter (10) later in this book is devoted to ICT use in science. Using other resources (such as newspaper cuttings and interactive centres) to support school science teaching is discussed in the last chapter.

6 Presenting and portraying the 'nature' of science

The job of science teachers is a tough one. Not only do they have to teach scientific knowledge, develop the skills of science and foster scientific attitudes –

they also have to convey messages about the nature of science and the work of scientists. These messages have to be conveyed either overtly and explicitly, i.e. by planned activities or prepared teaching; or covertly and implicitly, i.e. by the teachers' actions during practical work or by their reactions to pupils' work or practical data.

We all know that practical work in science does not always go according to plan. Nature, especially in science labs, sometimes does not behave itself. What should teachers do when their practicals go wrong? There is evidence that some teachers 'talk their way through it', some know crafty ways of rigging or tweaking experiments, while some just cheat (see Nott and Wellington 1997). What messages do teachers' actions convey about science and scientists?

Later, a whole chapter (11) is devoted to this issue and to practical ideas for teaching, or conveying messages, about the nature of science, i.e. the how. But here, in this introduction, we consider briefly: what are the key messages about science and scientific activity that we wish to convey?

This, in itself, is highly debatable. Hence the summary below is presented in (what I call) 'Yes . . . but' format:

- Science is *Contextualised*? Science and scientists operate in a spiritual, moral and political context.
  Yes . . . but it does cross boundaries. Viagra works on both sides of the Atlantic (not that I've tried to verify or falsify this). Genetically modified food can be imported and exported.

- Science is *Provisional*? Its ideas and theories change over time.
  Yes . . . but Newton's laws are centuries old and they got us to the moon and back. Theories may be tentative, but many laws are *not* (e.g. Ohm's, Boyle's, Charles'), nor are facts, e.g. expansion of metals. Copper will still conduct electricity in 100 years time.

- Science is not *Value-free*?
  Agreed . . . but some scientific facts, laws and theories are independent of people and society. Newton's Second Law works in Iran as well as it does in North America. The kinetic theory of particles can be applied globally.

- Science is *Limited*? It cannot explain everything.
  Yes . . . but surely it deserves at least 8/10?

- Science is a *Double-edged sword*?
  Yes . . . it does have its drawbacks. **But** would you like to live (except as an aristocrat) in pre-science days?

- Science deals in *Relative, not Absolute truth*?
  Yes . . . but an iron bar will expand when it is heated. This is *absolutely* true: any place, any time.

- Science is *Determined by reality*? (see Ogborn, J. (1995) on 'Recovering reality').

Yes . . . reality (not just people and their construction of it) does determine science. **But** a lot of good scientific theories have come from creative thinking, hunches and leaps of the imagination. Many scientific explanations depend on entities and ideas that are *not* real or observable, e.g. point masses, fields, frictionless surfaces.

- Science is *Theory-laden*?
  Mostly . . . but some research at the 'frontiers of science' may not be, e.g. on BSE, GM Foods.

- Science is an *Objective, rational* activity.
  Yes . . . but science is not a totally objective pursuit of the truth, and not totally guided by the natural world. It is a *human* activity, driven by personalities, egos and funding; often done in the context of large institutions, driven by social movements; even driven by the media and public opinion; often driven by politicians and other decision-makers. Science involves competition as well as co-operation.

- Science is *Tentative*?
  Yes . . . but some scientific knowledge is pretty *reliable*. We ride in planes, we drive over suspension bridges. We take antibiotics. People, quite rightly, have some faith in science.

We look in more depth at the nature of science in Chapters 2 and 11.

7 Assessing and evaluating learning (and teaching)

What is assessment for?

Experienced teachers are constantly assessing pupils in classrooms – whether it be from oral questioning, from overhearing their conversations during small group work, from reading their written work or from closely observing their actions during practical sessions. Assessing or (more harshly) judging people occurs inevitably.

Teachers might decide to assess pupils, or be forced to assess them, for a wide variety of reasons. For example, teachers might assess their students in order to:

- enable teachers to set targets for individual pupils
- boost the self-esteem of pupils (equally, it can dampen it)
- inform higher education or employers about attainment
- give feedback to pupils and parents on progress
- maintain standards
- rank pupils
- entertain, for example, with a quiz
- sort pupils into different sets or groups
- motivate pupils and give incentives for learning (a stick and a carrot)

- give feedback on their own teaching effectiveness
- identify individual weaknesses and problems
- assist pupils in subject/career choice
- diagnose errors and misconceptions

Some of these purposes involve *looking forward*; some involve *looking back*; and some, perhaps the most important, are intended to *guide action* (see Knutton 1994: 73–4, for a full discussion). Some of the above examples are *summative*, some *formative* and some *diagnostic*.

Types of assessment

Summative assessment of pupils, e.g. at the end of a unit, a module or a key stage in order to give them a 'mark', is the area we often focus upon. This form of assessment also receives the most publicity in terms of media coverage (the 'league tables'), political debate and discussion on 'standards'. But summative assessment comes, in a sense, too late. For the classroom teacher the two forms of assessment most valuable in identifying needs, planning for learning, and organising differentiation are:

- *diagnostic* assessment: to identify pupils' preconceptions or learning difficulties so that future teaching can be guided and pitched appropriately or tailored to individuals' needs;
- *formative* assessment: to assess learning as it proceeds, recognising positive achievements, and making decisions about (forming) future steps and targets.

The main purposes of both are to improve teaching and learning. Day-to-day assessment can be used: to identify very able or gifted pupils' difficulties in spoken or written English; and to become aware of the wide range of special educational needs (SEN) which a large group of learners inevitably has.

Strictly speaking, summative assessment comes at the *end* of a course or a teaching scheme and has no influence on the teaching and learning process. In contrast, diagnostic and formative assessment of individual pupils is, quite simply, the only sound basis for good teaching. To paraphrase Ausubel (discussed later), you cannot teach pupils unless you know them and 'start from where they are'. *Self-assessment* can also be valuable to pupils in assessing where they are.

Class teachers will also inevitably be involved in *summative* assessment, e.g. an end-of-unit test, or end-of-year exam. Marking and monitoring pupils' work regularly, providing pupils with helpful oral and written feedback, and setting sensible targets for future progress are all important skills for the science teacher.

How can teachers become 'good assessors' and use assessment as a *positive*, motivating tool? Thorp (1991: 101) suggested five important principles for good assessment which still apply. He argues that good assessment should:

- influence and inform future teaching and learning
- show what pupils know, understand and can do
- measure pupil progress
- provide feedback for pupils, teachers and parents
- give pupils a positive sense of achievement and therefore empower them

These principles can be put into practice through three different media: what the teacher *sees*, what the teacher *reads* and what the teacher *hears*.

The need for variety and differentiation in assessment

Thus, teachers can assess and evaluate their pupils' progression in three different ways:

(a) *By observation*, i.e. by observing them during classwork whether it be written work, discussion work or practical work. A teacher's observations of their actions and procedures can be an important part of assessing practical skills or the ability to investigate.

(b) From their *oral work*, i.e. by listening to what pupils say in either whole class discussion (e.g. question and answer sessions); by listening to and observing small-group work; by arranging time for oral presentation of their work, e.g. on a project or a report-back on a homework.

(c) From *written work*, i.e. from written tests or examinations; from written classwork or homework; from written reports on practical work and investigations.

In practice, assessment has depended far too heavily on the written word. Teachers have, often for justifiable practical reasons in a busy classroom, been unable to use observation and oral work to assess learners. Even when they have done this informally and internally, it has not been encouraged or accepted formally and externally. This is unfortunate because the almost total emphasis on the written word has disadvantaged many pupils – many may be good at speaking and doing science but poor at writing science. There is still a huge need for differentiated assessment.

The important activities of differentiation, questioning, feedback, marking and setting homework are discussed in later chapters.

8 Ensuring continuity and progression in learning and teaching

One of the key aims in teaching, given more publicity (if not prominence) by the advent of a National Curriculum, is to develop continuity and progression in children's learning. The two terms have become buzz words for something which is good and desirable. But in reality they are hard to define and even harder to put into practice.

Although the words 'continuity' and 'progression' are usually spoken or written together, they do *not* denote the same thing. Continuity is to do with organising and planning a curriculum or a programme of study, whereas progression is more about an individual's development or increasing complexity in a pupil's scientific ideas. Driver *et al.* (1994) expressed it well:

> The term progression is applied to something that happens inside a learner's head: thinking about experience and ideas, children develop their ideas. Some aspects of their learning may happen quite quickly and easily, whereas others happen in very small steps over a number of years.
>
> Continuity on the other hand is something organised by the teacher: it describes the relationship between experiences, activities and ideas which pupils meet over a period of time, in a curriculum which is structured to support learning. Curriculum continuity cannot guarantee progression. Its role is to structure ideas and experiences for learners in a way which will help them to move their conceptual understanding forward in scientific terms.

On the face of it, continuity might appear easier to develop since it is somehow more 'external', 'written down' and open to checking. But research (especially the extensive work by Ruth Jarman) has shown that, except in a few outstanding cases, it is not happening. As Jarman (1999) points out, there are difficulties about *what* continuity is, *why* it is needed and *how* it should be achieved. Teachers offer a range of interpretations and metaphors for the term continuity, for example: 'building upon', 'the next rung of the ladder', 'not repeating', 'not leaving a gap', 'maintaining momentum', 'no gaps, no overlaps', 'not duplicating', 'picking up where "they" left off', 'a gradual transition', 'a common thread'. These terms are used by teachers in Jarman's research and in curriculum documents, both local and national.

However, in reality teachers have found it hard to put these ideas into practice, particularly at the interface between primary and secondary education (in the UK, key stages 2 to 3). Some teachers treat new pupils in the secondary school as a blank slate or *tabula rasa*, imagining (as some have put it) that they are 'building on a greenfield site'. This often occurs because primary pupils come from such a variety of backgrounds (with huge differences in teaching approach, level of treatment of topics, knowledge 'input') and a wide diversity of feeder schools. True liaison and continuity require a huge investment in time and energy by teachers in both phases – teachers in the secondary phase especially question whether the benefits outweigh the costs. Not surprisingly, many prefer to start from scratch. In addition, a minority of secondary science teachers simply do not *trust* what their primary predecessors have done.

Progression

Progression in children's scientific ideas needs to be built in to curriculum documents, schemes of work and, for the individual teachers, lesson plans. Genuine progression will:

- *build on* the learner's previous ideas, whether they be from outside experience or formal education;
- *extend* children's understanding from a narrow range of *contexts*, e.g. the school lab, to a *broad* range, e.g. the home, other planets, industrial processes;
- enable learners to move from explaining *simple* events and phenomena, e.g. magnets attracting, falling objects, to explaining more *complicated* events and processes, e.g. electromagnetic induction, planetary motion;
- proceed from explaining things in *qualitative* terms, e.g. heat lost through single and double glazing, to explanations using numbers and symbols, e.g. the equation for heat 'flow' across a boundary;
- develop from explanations using things which can be seen, e.g. water in a pipe, to explanations based on entities which are *not* observable, e.g. electrons in a wire, particles in a liquid, frictionless bodies.

Table 1.1 sums up some of the main features of progression

Table 1.1 Dimensions of progression in a person's knowledge and understanding

From	To
From *narrow* . . . experiences and understanding in a small number of examples in a narrow range of contexts.	. . . to *broad* knowledge of many examples in a broad range of situations.
From *simple* . . . understanding simple events.	. . . to *complex* knowing and explaining complicated situations.
From using *everyday ideas* . . .	. . . to using *scientific ideas*
From knowledge *that* . . .	. . . to knowledge *how and why* things happen
From *qualitative explanation* . . .	. . . to *explanations using numbers, formulae and equations*
From explanations based only on *observable entities* . . .	. . . to explanations using *unobservable, idealised entities*, e.g. point masses, rigid bodies.

These are the key elements of progression in knowledge and understanding. Asoko and Squires (1998) offer a useful example of progression in ideas which gives the principles above some meaning:

puddles disappear
↓
puddles disappear faster when it is windy
↓
when puddles disappear the water evaporates into the air
↓
puddles disappear faster when it is windy because the air above them does not become saturated with water vapour

(Asoko and Squires 1998: 176)

Knowledge of evaporation could also progress by:

(a) seeing or discussing it in a wider range of contexts, e.g. petrol on a forecourt or another volatile liquid in the lab; the Dead Sea, the school pond;
(b) bringing in the *unobservable* entities, i.e. liquid particles, to explain why it occurs and how (for example) wind affects it;
(c) bringing in *quantitative* elements, e.g. the kinetic energy ($\frac{1}{2} mv^2$) of particles; the reasons for cooling by evaporation.

The skill of the teacher is, first, to examine the scientific ideas being taught to consider the progression in *them*. How can ideas or processes such as photosynthesis, nuclear fission, digestion, chemical reactions or electromagnetic induction be sequenced in the same way as evaporation above? Second, this progression in ideas must be related to the *learner*, e.g. at what stage are learners 'ready' for a numeric, quantitative explanation? These ideas are explored more fully in Scaife's Chapter 4 on learning in science.

Progression in investigations

Progression can also occur, and be built into, practical and investigational work. This will occur as:

- pupils learn to deal with, or control, more than one variable at a time;
- *scientific* ideas, rather than their own everyday ideas, are brought into their *predictions* and their *evaluations*;
- the business of analysing their data and evaluating its strengths and limitations is based more and more on scientific ideas and knowledge;
- their range of instruments and techniques for data collection is extended, as is their ability to make informed choices on how and what to measure, and what instruments and methods to use;
- their presentation of results or data becomes more refined and employs diagrams, tables or graphs using accepted scientific conventions;
- written work employs more and more scientific language and terminology.

The issue of progression in investigations and other practical work is discussed more fully later in Chapter 8.

The final message for this section is a challenging one. Centrally imposed curricula have not ensured either continuity or progression. This is still the teacher's job. It requires not only hard work, e.g. liaising with others, looking at previous work, studying others' schemes of work, but also intellectual effort. Sequencing scientific ideas and concepts into a progressive order is not easy – just try it on a few examples.

9 Planning and managing lessons and schemes

At the heart of good teaching lies good planning and good management. Individual lessons need to be well planned and structured, and to some extent be self-contained. But they must also relate to previous lessons, previous knowledge and previous understanding – and connect to future lessons and future learning. This is why individual lessons need to be planned and sequenced into a *scheme of work*. A scheme of work covering a period of several weeks has exactly the same requirements as an individual lesson plan. Both should have:

- clear *aims and objectives*
- clearly identified *keywords* and *key scientific ideas*
- *variety*, in terms of activities, resources and teaching or learning styles
- *connections* with previous knowledge and links to future teaching and learning
- *links* to other areas of science, other parts of the curriculum (where possible) and to everyday life

As for an individual lesson, there is some measure of agreement about the main components needed for 'good practice':

- a clear *introduction* including these elements: gaining attention; stating the purpose of the lesson, i.e. why are you teaching this?; reviewing and relating back to previous learning and teaching;
- a *variety* of activities, e.g. perhaps some listening, some questioning, some group work, some writing, but not an entire lesson of all the same thing;
- appropriate supervision, *intervention and guidance* during classwork, i.e. knowing when to leave groups alone, when to challenge them, when to move them on; providing appropriate remedial help where needed; keeping pupils on task;
- a *summary* or 'recap' at the end of a lesson: reviewing and consolidating what's been learnt, looking forward to the next lesson in the scheme, and setting follow-up work when appropriate.

Most teachers would agree that these are the main components of a 'good lesson'. They certainly do not apply to every situation or circumstance nor is it always practically possible to include them all – but they offer a useful frame-work or *aide-mémoire* when lesson planning.

One of the bonuses, but at the same time one of the drawbacks, of being a science teacher is the sheer range of classroom and laboratory situations that one is able, but also expected, to manage successfully. Situations range from didactic teaching, investigational work, teacher demonstration and class prac-ticals to small group discussion, note-taking, fieldwork and the use of computers. *No other subject teacher has to plan for and manage such a range of situations.*

Chapter 5 is devoted to the business of planning and managing. One situ-ation which science teachers increasingly have to deal with is the presentation and discussion of *controversial or sensitive issues* (see Chapter 11). Curriculum planners and textbook writers have (rather belatedly) come to realise that science is as much about *values* as it is about *facts*. Indeed, in modern science, facts and values are often inseparable. Recent issues such as cloning, BSE and genetically modified (GM) food have made this obvious – not least to the pupils themselves, thanks to extensive media coverage. Other controversial issues – the nuclear debate, evolution versus creationism, and the origin of the universe – have been around for decades. Presenting controversial issues in a *balanced* way (which is a legal requirement) and handling subsequent discussion is a skill which science teachers must now add to their repertoire. A later section puts forward practical ideas.

10 Generating motivation and enthusiasm for science

Probably the most important, but sometimes the most neglected, aspect of science teaching is the ability to interest a wide range of pupils in science. This is the *affective* domain of educational aims, underlying the entire *cognitive* domain: without motivation, interest and engagement there will be little achieve-ment. For the broad range of pupils, science has a poor track record in this, the affective, domain. Up to the age of 16, all pupils have to study science in some form so there is no obvious problem. But post-16, the lack of interest in and enthusiasm for science subjects shines clearly through the statistics. DfEE figures show a steady decline in the numbers taking physical sciences at Advanced Level. More worryingly, boys in the 1990s were three times more likely to opt for physical sciences than girls. Girls have been more likely than boys to choose life sciences, though the gender gap in this direction is less marked.

The simple statement of the Ofsted review (1998) is low key but damning: 'Post-16, the teaching of science subjects compares unfavourably with that of most other subjects' (page 133). The report talks of 'spoon feeding', and an over-reliance on dictated notes and duplicated hand-outs. The introduction of GNVQ Science at Advanced Level (in 1993) did extend the range and style of study available in science post-16. But there is clearly a lot more work to be done in order to interest and enthuse learners of all abilities and both sexes in science education, both pre- and post-16.

What can be done, especially in the context of a fairly rigid national curriculum and the dominant view of the teacher as a 'deliverer' of knowledge (see later)? Teachers can adopt a number of strategies in planning and managing lessons:

- using a variety of teaching methods
- increasing their awareness of both sexes and all abilities
- using topical and controversial issues as a context for teaching content and processes
- planning for a range of learning styles and interests
- broadening science education and connecting it with other areas and everyday experiences (i.e. making it *relevant*)

In terms of their own classroom behaviour, teachers can convey enthusiasm and increase motivation in the following ways:

- The greatest possible use of praise and rewards: punishment may be unavoidable but it certainly demotivates, as does sarcasm or humiliation.
- 'Success breeds success': ensuring some success, however small, can be a huge motivator for pupils. Continuing failure, and excessive criticism, are not.
- *Self-presentation*: a teacher's own body language and posture can convey enthusiasm e.g. gestures, facial expression, posture or stance – similarly with teaching voice.

These are hard principles to live up to, especially every day of the week. But remember that *teachers do have an impact* – a learner's enthusiasm (or dislike) for a subject is retained long after their memory of its facts or content. The way that science teachers present their subject is far more important than what they teach. Praise, encouragement and reward will have long-term benefits: excessive criticism, ridicule and sarcasm will ultimately rebound.

> *Children learn what they live*
>
> If a child lives with criticism,
>   he learns to condemn,
> If a child lives with hostility,
>   he learns to fight,
> If a child lives with ridicule,
>   he learns to be shy,
> If a child lives with shame,
>   he learns to feel guilty,
> If a child lives with tolerance,
>   he learns to be patient,
> If a child lives with encouragement,
>   he learns confidence,

If a child lives with praise,
    he learns to appreciate,
If a child lives with fairness,
    he learns justice,
If a child lives with security,
    he learns to have faith,
If a child lives with approval,
    he learns to like himself,
If a child lives with acceptance and friendship,
    he learns to find love in the world.

        Dorothy Law Nolta (date unknown)

Notes

1   Processes which are either too fast, too slow, too risky or too costly for the school lab are often best shown with video or multimedia.

References and further reading

This list is short and very selective. Longer suggestions for further reading are given at the end of the later chapters which cover in depth the ten aspects of teaching introduced here.

Language

Language barriers, and some practical ideas for tackling them, are discussed in:

Edwards, A. and Westgate, D. (1994) *Investigating Classroom Talk*, London: Falmer Press.
Henderson, J. and Wellington, J. (1998) 'Lowering the language barrier in learning and teaching science', *School Science Review*, March 1998, vol. 79, no. 288, pp. 35–46.

Questioning

A very useful short article, focusing on the work of one science department, is:

Carr, D. (1998) 'The art of asking questions in the teaching of science', *School Science Review*, June 1998, vol. 79, no. 289, pp. 47–50.

The other source of questions, the learners, is explored in:

Watts, M., Gould, G. and Alsop, S. (1997), 'Questions of understanding: categorising pupils' questions in science', *School Science Review*, vol. 79, no. 286, pp. 57–63.

Explaining

Gilbert, J. (1998) 'Explaining with models', in Ratcliffe, M. (ed.) (1998) *ASE Guide to Secondary Education*, pp. 159–67.
Ogborn, J., Kress, G., Martins, I. and McGillicuddy, K. (1996) *Explaining Science in the Classroom*, Buckingham: Open University Press.

Shulman, L. (1986) 'Those who understand: knowledge growth in teaching', *Educational Researcher*, vol. 15, no. 2, pp. 3–14.

Practical work

Although I cite it myself, one useful book containing 16 different perspectives on practical work, and what it is for, is:

Wellington, J. (ed.) (1998) *Practical Work in School Science: Which Way Now?*, London: Routledge.
Millar, R. (1998) 'Rhetoric and reality: what practical work is really for', in Wellington, J. (ed.) *Practical Work in School Science: Which Way Now?*, pp. 16–31.

The nature of science

Nott, M. and Wellington, J. (1997) 'Producing the evidence', *Research in Science Education*, vol. 27, no. 3, pp. 395–409.
Ogborn, J. (1995) 'Recovering reality', *Studies in Science Education*, vol. 25 (1995), pp. 3–38.
Osborne, J. (1998) 'Learning and teaching about the nature of science', in Ratcliffe, M. (ed.) (1998), pp. 100–9.
Thorp, S. (ed.) (1991) *Race, Equality and Science Teaching*, Hatfield: ASE.

Assessment

Black, P. (1998) 'Formative assessment: raising standards inside the classroom', *School Science Review*, vol. 80, no. 291, pp. 39–46.
Black, P. and William, D. (1998) 'Assessment and classroom learning', *Assessment in Education*, vol. 5, no. 1, pp. 7–71.
Hayes, P. (1998) 'Assessment in the classroom', in Ratcliffe, M. (ed.) *ASE Guide to Secondary Science Education*, Hatfield: ASE/Stanley Thornes, pp. 138–45.
Knutton, S. (1994) 'Assessing children's learning in science', in Wellington, J. (ed.) *Secondary Science: Contemporary Issues and Practical Approaches*, London: Routledge.

Continuity and progression

Ruth Jarman's work stands out in this area and has resulted in a number of publications. One useful summary appears in *Education in Science*, February 1999 issue, which includes practical examples from teachers.

Adey, P. (1997) 'Dimensions of progression in a curriculum', *The Curriculum Journal*, vol. 8, no. 3, pp. 367–391.
Asoko, H. and Squires, A. (1998) 'Progression and continuity', in Ratcliffe, M. (ed.) *ASE Guide To Secondary Science Education*, Hatfield: ASE/Stanley Thornes.
Driver, R., Squires, A., Rushworth, P. and Wood-Robinson, V. (1994) *Making Sense of Secondary Science*, London: Routledge.

Planning and managing

Kyriacou, C. (1992) *Effective Teaching in Schools*, Hemel Hempstead: Simon and Schuster.

Generating motivation

Driver, R., Leach, J., Millar, R. and Scott, P. (1996) *Young People's Images of Science*, Buckingham: Open University Press.
Osborne, J., Driver, R. and Simon, S. (1998) 'Attitudes to science: issues and concerns', *School Science Review*, vol. 79, no. 288, pp. 27–33.

General

Claxton, G. (1990) *Teaching to Learn*, London: Cassell.
Collins, J., Hammond, M. and Wellington, J. (1997) *Teaching and Learning with Multimedia*, London: Routledge.
An excellent range of 27 chapters under one cover can be found in:

Ratcliffe, M. (ed.) (1998) *ASE Guide to Secondary Education*, Hatfield: ASE/Stanley Thornes (this is referred to many times in later chapters).

For an overview of science education in the 1990s in the UK see:

Ofsted (1998) *Secondary Education: A Review of Secondary Schools in England*, London: The Stationery Office.

A useful source of general ideas on many aspects of teaching is:

Capel, S., Leask, M. and Turner, T. (eds) (1995) *Learning to Teach in the Secondary School*, London: Routledge.

One of the best books on learning and concept mapping, which is still valuable now, is:

Novak, J. and Gowin, D. (1984) *Learning How to Learn*, Cambridge: Cambridge University Press.

Other valuable, well-written sources on science teaching and learning are:

Bishop, K. and Denley, P. (1997) *Effective Learning in Science*, Stafford: Network Educational Press.
Hodson, D. (1998) *Teaching and Learning Science: Towards a Personalised Approach*, Buckingham: Open University Press.
Levinson, R. (ed.) (1994) *Teaching Science*, London: Routledge/Open University Press.
Parkinson, J. (1994) *The Effective Teaching of Secondary Science*, Harlow: Longman.
Whitelegg, E., Thomas, J. and Tresman, S. (eds) (1993) *Challenges and Opportunities for Scienced Education*, London: Paul Chapman/Open University Press.

A series of books on science teaching and learning was published in the 1990s (series editor: Brian Woolnough). These are still useful, for example:

Reiss, M. (1995) *Science Education for a Pluralist Society*, Buckingham: Open University Press.
Woolnough, B. (1996) *The Effective Teaching of Science*, Buckingham: Open University Press.

(Other books in this series are referred to in later chapters.)

Finally, a useful and very practical source of ideas for new teachers is:

Turner, T. and DiMarco, W. (1998) *Learning to Teach Science in the Secondary School*, London: Routledge.

Chapter 2

Becoming a teacher

Metaphors for the teacher

One of the difficulties in becoming a teacher, and continuing to develop as a teacher, is in deciding what counts as a 'good teacher'. What works for one person may not 'work' for another. What one person believes is good teaching may not accord with another's beliefs or principles.

There is certainly a significant amount of research evidence on 'good teaching', reported by authors such as David Reynolds (in several publications) and others. A crude summary of some of the common features of the 'effective teacher' could be listed as follows:

- thoughtful planning
- clear, restricted goals in a lesson
- lesson clarity
- strong structuring of lessons
- careful and effective time management
- use of pupils' own ideas
- high percentage of time-on-task for the pupils
- appropriate, varied questions, directed at a range of pupils
- variety of teaching methods
- frequent feedback to pupils (on their spoken and written answers)
- high expectations of pupils

These are helpful, if a little bit daunting and certainly hard to live up to. But a list such as this does not really explore what it means to be a teacher, and what a teacher's guiding values, beliefs and principles might be.

One way of reflecting upon this is to consider what *metaphors* we might use for teachers and for learners. This idea was first publicised widely by some of the excellent Children's Learning in Science (CLIS) materials in the early 1990s. Consider the following:

- the teacher as a postal worker (Postman Pat)
- the teacher as an air-traffic controller (or an airline pilot) or a navigator

- the teacher as an actor
- the teacher as a caterer, providing either self-service or waiter-service meals
- the teacher as a barman or barmaid
- the teacher as a bricklayer . . . or maybe an architect.

Figure 2.1 illustrates some of these models or metaphors.

Metaphors like these provoke all kinds of thought and discussion. The teacher can be seen as: a potter, moulding clay; a guide in hilly terrain with the pupil as traveller; a petrol pump attendant filling a car; a gardener, tending plants and giving them nutrients, and in many other ways. It is interesting to note that different models relate to different industries: the construction industry, retail and catering, agriculture, the travel industry and others.

When people reflect on their own teaching they may subscribe to more than one of these metaphors. Indeed, moving from one model to another is part of what is meant by 'a variety of teaching approaches'. Perhaps the biggest danger in educational policy and practice has been to rely (perhaps unknowingly) on one dominant metaphor. The all-pervasive model of the 1990s has been 'the teacher as deliverer' – the Postman Pat model of education. The language of teachers 'delivering' things has dominated the discourse of curriculum documents, staffroom chat, parents' evenings and formal staff meetings. The metaphor of teachers delivering 'items', commodities or packages to learners has permeated our thinking to such an extent that the word 'deliver' is almost impossible to avoid in discussions about teaching.

Surely a better way forward is to recognise that teaching and learning can be likened to many different situations, from different industries. A number of metaphors can be employed, for different situations. Some models or metaphors work best for one set of circumstances, ages, abilities and aims – some work best for others.

Developing, and continuing to develop, as a science teacher

As already mentioned, science must be one of the most (if not *the* most) difficult subjects to teach in the secondary school. Not only do science teachers need to be able to manage and control all kinds of situations such as lab work, demonstrations, small group activities, didactic teaching, discussion work, 'circuses' of experiments: they also need to be aware of, and able to handle, all kinds of health and safety issues in their daily teaching. Their job is at stake in safely organising rooms containing gas, electricity, glass and chemicals.

In addition, their subject is a conceptually difficult one. Just having and maintaining one's own *subject* knowledge is a prerequisite for good science teaching but is in itself a tough requirement. Many science teachers have a subject specialism, e.g. physics or biology, and just keeping this up to date and rust-free is a tall order. But most scientists, especially in lower secondary, are also required to teach outside their own specialism. This makes additional demands on planning, preparation and thinking time.

Actor

Deliverer

Bartender

Gardener

Guide/navigator

Figure 2.1 Cartoons showing different models or metaphors of teaching.
Source: Drawn for the author by David Houchin.

Finally, science teachers are dealing with learners who may not only find science difficult and uninteresting but also bring into the classroom precon-ceived ideas about many 'science' topics: energy, force, heat flow and plant growth are just a few examples. Their preconceptions (sometimes misconcep-tions) need to be considered and occasionally challenged. There is sometimes a gap between 'common sense' and scientific ideas. Indeed, some scientific ideas, e.g. Newton's laws, centrifugal force being 'fictitious', plant mass coming mainly from carbon dioxide in the air, run *contrary* to common sense.

In short, science teachers face considerable challenges:

- getting to grips with their own subject, sometimes outside their own specia-lism;
- managing and controlling a range of situations, some involving difficult safety issues;
- enthusing and motivating their pupils;
- handling pupils' prior conceptions about the natural world and presenting them with new ideas and explanations which will appear contrary to common sense.

Perhaps science teachers should be paid more than other subject specialists?

Models of 'becoming a teacher'

Two models of teacher development and the art of teaching have been widely used in the last two decades. Like any models, they are over-simplifications and are open to criticism, but they can be useful in conceptualising what it means to become a teacher. One is from Shulman, the other from Schön.

(a) Subject knowledge and pedagogical knowledge

Teachers have a set of knowledge which they bring to the classroom and a set of knowledge which is developed and learned from their classroom experience. These two ways of knowing our subject have been called respectively, *subject content knowledge* and *pedagogical content knowledge* (Shulman 1986 and 1987). The two sets of knowledge interact and inform each other. At the start of a teacher's career the pedagogical content knowledge is fairly thin, but studies have shown that new teachers undergo a rapid acquisition of this knowledge (Wilson, Shulman and Richert 1987). As teachers progress through their careers the pedagogical content knowledge increases in size and importance in relationship to the subject content knowledge, and the two inform each other.

Through teaching experience, and by working with mentors and learning alongside teaching colleagues, we develop new tactics and approaches. Teachers learn new explanations for difficult concepts, and new metaphors or analogies to help them explain. As they learn this 'pedagogical knowledge' their understanding of their own subject improves – hence the old adage: 'You don't know your subject until you teach it!' The diagrams below show crudely how these two types of knowledge might change over time:

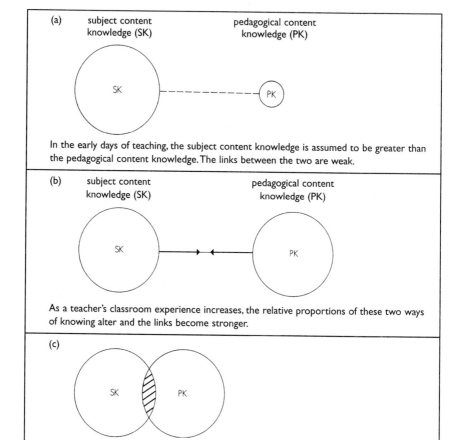

(a)   subject content   pedagogical content
         knowledge (SK)   knowledge (PK)

SK   - - - - - - - - - -   PK

In the early days of teaching, the subject content knowledge is assumed to be greater than the pedagogical content knowledge. The links between the two are weak.

(b)   subject content   pedagogical content
         knowledge (SK)   knowledge (PK)

SK   ———►◄———   PK

As a teacher's classroom experience increases, the relative proportions of these two ways of knowing alter and the links become stronger.

(c)

SK   PK

As teachers become more experienced the two categories may overlap so that some elements are common to both areas.

(d)

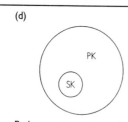

PK
SK

Perhaps some very experienced teachers have all the elements of their subject knowledge identical with some elements of their pedagogical knowledge?

Figure 2.2 Development of subject knowledge and pedagogical knowledge in teaching. (Source: Mick Nott.)

Of course, the relative sizes of these elements, and their positions relative to each other, are open to some debate. However, one would hope that knowledge of science (SK) does grow as a result of teaching, i.e. it is both brought *to* the classroom and developed *by* classroom experience. Similarly, knowledge of teaching (PK) must surely develop through observing others, coaching and mentoring, reading books like this and *reflecting* on one's own practice.

(b) Reflective practice

The second model sees the effective teacher as a reflective practitioner, capable of reflecting upon and analysing his or her own teaching practices, even though they cannot always be formulated, made explicit or put into words. Schön claims (1983: 54) that teachers possess a type of knowledge called 'knowing-in-action', which is a form of practical knowledge (akin to Shulman's PK). This knowledge is personal and tacit in that 'we are usually unable to describe the knowing which our action reveals' (page 54) – hence the notion that teaching is an art and a craft as well as a science.

Teachers develop by reflecting back on their own practice, especially when everyday teaching throws up 'surprises' (Schön, 1987) which they have to respond to (we discuss these in Chapter 11, calling them 'Critical Incidents'). Teachers also reflect during the actual practice of teaching, which Schön calls 'reflection-in-action' (which relates to what we might call 'thinking on your feet'). This model has its critics. Some say that 'reflective practice' has just become a well-worn slogan, empty of meaning (Gilroy 1993: 140). It is not always clear what reflection in teaching involves, nor is there agreement about the word's meaning. Gilroy (1993: 126) cites Lucas' work in Sheffield where he reported that reflection can mean several things: 'ripping oneself to shreds', critical feedback and evaluation, a guiding principle for teaching, or a 'tough mode of active learning'.

My own view is that the model of the teacher as a 'reflective practitioner' (and it is only a *model*) is a valuable one. Schön's work deserves to be read. It would be a strange thing if a good teacher did not reflect on his or her own practice. However, simply being a reflective practitioner is not a *sufficient* condition for being a 'good' teacher. A reflective practitioner could be an incompetent teacher. Similarly, plenty of historical figures from the past have been reflective practitioners and have not always been good people. Hitler was a reflective practitioner.

Mentoring and the role of a mentor

What Shulman's and Schön's models partly neglect is that 'becoming a teacher' should not be, and rarely is, a *lone process*. Teachers may often be alone in the classroom but they are always part of a departmental team and a school staff. Teachers (new and old) can learn from the teaching of others as much as they can from reflecting on their own teaching.

New teachers will often have a mentor whose job it is to support, help and guide them, much as a craftsman did with an apprentice in the old apprentice-ship model. The mentor is often said to be a critical friend, offering help and guidance, but also setting up *challenges* to allow the novice to develop and extend their teaching ability. Successful mentors will begin by acting as a role model and then as a coach, i.e. by agreeing to be observed, by giving direct assistance in planning, and classroom support during teaching. But then mentors will move on to giving feedback on teaching, suggesting new teaching strategies to try out, and encouraging new teachers to analyse and reflect upon their own teaching. Good mentors will recognise these stages in a new teacher's development and take account of them. For instance, to launch into extensive criticism and analysis of lessons in the early days would be poor mentoring. On the other hand, in the later stages, the new or student teacher should start to become more independent and autonomous, and grow into the role of reflective practitioner.

Mentoring is clearly an important and complex process in the professional development of teachers and deserves a lot more space than this book has room for. For further reading, Brooks and Sikes (1997) makes an excellent start. They argue that 'a mentor's personal characteristics and interpersonal skills are . . . important', that it is a skilled role and requires something more than the offering of general friendship. Among the personal qualities cited are, 'honesty, openness, sensitivity, enthusiasm, sense of humour, organisation, self-awareness and reflectiveness'; and the interpersonal skills of 'the ability to listen effec-tively, to give criticism constructively and to empathise'.

Brooks and Sikes (1997: 35) conclude that:

- mentoring is a collection of strategies used flexibly and sensitively in response to changing needs;
- mentoring is an individualised form of training, often conducted on a one-to-one basis, which needs to be tailored to the needs of the individual;
- mentoring is a dynamic process, aimed at propelling students forward, which needs to combine support with challenge.

In short, mentoring is an extremely difficult and greatly underestimated job.

My own observations and experiences in schools over the last 27 years indicate that the practice of mentoring varies enormously in both quantity and quality. Some are 'born mentors', some develop into good mentors through reflective practice, while those who have mentoring thrust upon them are often the worst in practising it.

Why should anyone learn science ... and therefore why teach it?

It is important for teachers to be able to articulate an answer to the question 'why teach science?', especially when pupils pose it. This can always be a slightly embarrassing question for any subject specialist teacher in a secondary school: 'Why teach French if most pupils go to Spain for their holidays . . . let alone Florida?' 'Why teach History . . . it's all in the past?' 'Why teach about "old" literature or Shakespeare's plays?'

We start this section with an activity devised by Robin Millar (Table 2.1). It lists twelve specific areas or topics which are taught in most science curricula around the world. On what grounds can we justify their inclusion in the secondary science curriculum? Before reading on, try the activity:

Table 2.1 What should be in the science curriculum, and why?

Consider each of the 'pieces' of scientific knowledge and understanding in the list below. For each, decide which of the following categories you think it should be placed in:

U Everyone ought to understand this at an appropriate level – for *utilitarian* reasons (i.e. it is practically useful).

D Everyone ought to understand this at an appropriate level – for *democratic* reasons (i.e. it is necessary knowledge for participation in decision-making).

C Everyone ought to understand this at an appropriate level – for *cultural* reasons (i.e. it is a necessary component of an appreciation of science as a human enterprise).

X It is *not necessary* that everyone know this. It need not be included in a science curriculum the aim of which is public understanding of science.

'Pieces' of scientific knowledge

	Science topic	Your classification
1	The germ theory of disease	
2	The heliocentric model of the solar system	
3	The carbon cycle	
4	The reactivity series for metals	
5	The electromagnetic spectrum	
6	Radioactivity and ionising radiation	
7	Newton's laws of motion	
8	Energy: its conservation and dissipation	
9	An understanding of simple series and parallel electric circuits	
10	The theory of plate tectonics	
11	Darwin's theory of evolution	
12	Acids and bases	

Source: Robin Millar 1993.

If we applied a *crude criterion of relevance* to the curriculum we could be left with nothing except reading and writing and perhaps some number work, though even this can be replaced by a cheap calculator. Even ICT skills boil down to reading, writing and the manipulative skill of using a 'mouse'. So if we wield 'relevance' like a huge axe to hack away any element of the curriculum which is *neither* practically useful *nor* of vocational significance, i.e. gets people jobs, there is little left standing in the secondary timetable.

Take science. What specific knowledge or skill from secondary science is of *practical* value to us? How many examples can you list? Wiring a plug is an obvious example (though this is hardly a *science* skill). It is far easier to list counter-examples. When did you last *use* Faraday's laws of electrolysis, the particle theory of matter, or the ability to carry out a titration? In short, justifications for teaching science based on crude, utilitarian grounds, i.e. its subsequent *usefulness*, are limited. This is especially true when we remember that only a small minority of our pupils will go on to use *science* in their working lives (they are more likely to use technology) and an even tinier minority will become working scientists.

For most learners then, teachers will need to be able to justify why they are teaching them science on other grounds. My own attempt to articulate some justifications is given below. Whether they will cut any ice with cynical, disaffected pupils in science is debatable. I will divide them up crudely into three areas: the *intrinsic* worth of learning science; its extrinsic or *utility* value; and the citizenship argument.

I The intrinsic value of science education

First, learning science can help us to *make sense* of the universe we live in – and of ourselves. It can help people to understand some of the events and phenomena which we see happening – either on television, the Internet, or in everyday life. We see: fossils, avalanches, droughts, thunderstorms, volcanoes erupting, oil films on puddles, tidal waves, leaves falling in Autumn, skin cancer, condensation, frost and dew, blue sky (occasionally), fog, frogs and tadpoles, obesity, famine, orbiting comets, 'shooting stars' and the occasional eclipse.

I could write two more pages of examples, and any reader could add to the list. Science can help people to make sense of all these events. It may not have definitive answers on all their *causes*, e.g. the alleged causal connection between global warming and drought, famine or flood. But surely it is better to know that the two very bright objects which 'came together' in the evening sky in February 1999 were Venus and Jupiter rather than two UFOs making a rendezvous; or that the eclipse on 11 August 1999 was not a message from God? We can understand a lot more about the world if we add *scientific sense* to *common sense*. The latter is limited.

Second, science can actually be interesting and exciting. Not everything has to be 'relevant'. Teachers and curriculum developers have suffered under the cloud of relevance for about 25 years (I personally blame James Callaghan's famous education speech, when he was Labour PM in 1976, for launching the relevance bandwagon). Many events in science, e.g. caesium reacting with water, and many explanations, e.g. why a needle floats on the surface of water, can be interesting and intellectually stimulating in their own right. Many young (and old) people have hobbies or pastimes which are totally 'irrelevant' – except to them. Please can we have a break from the relevance criterion?

Finally, in this first category, we have the culture and heritage argument. This is an important one, even if it cuts little ice with 15–year-olds. Science is part of our past culture, and a big chunk of our contemporary culture. It is also a global activity, even if it may differ from one culture or nation to another. Our heritage, our history and many of the important stories of the past are based on science and scientists. Part of science education is about science stories or stories about scientists. Knowing these stories, and understanding science, is part of what it means to be a cultured and educated person.

2 The citizenship argument

(a) The need for scientific knowledge: for individuals and key decision-makers

Participants in a democracy, it is argued, cannot make decisions and important choices without scientific knowledge and understanding. This argument becomes of clear importance when we consider past and current issues such as nuclear energy and nuclear weapons, traffic pollution, the use of drugs, animal testing, and not least many of the debates about the food we consume. (Should we eat genetically modified (GM) foods, beef from the bone or any meat at all?)

Our individual decisions on these issues (as democrats) can be informed by our knowledge of the science behind them. *However, there are two limitations to this*. First, the *amount* of science we need to know on each issue may not need to be that great. For example, with GM foods we need to know what they are, how they are created, their dangers (or advantages) and how far their pollen might spread – but detailed knowledge of DNA or genetic theory is probably not necessary. Nor is in-depth, mathematical knowledge of nuclear fission or fusion needed for all citizens in the nuclear debate, although knowledge of nuclear waste, radiation, and half-life might be useful.

Second, ultimately scientific knowledge will not make the decision for us. Knowledge of science is a necessary but *not sufficient* basis for a decision. In the final analysis, decisions are made on the basis of *values* as well as knowledge and understanding of science.

A scientifically literate society would not necessarily be a 'good society'. However, some knowledge of science is essential in order for individuals to make decisions and become citizens in a democracy. Knowledge of science is even more important for those who are the key *decision-makers* in a democracy. This is plainly true but in practice few key politicians or other decision-makers in the past have been scientifically literate.

(b) The need for knowledge about scientists, their work, 'scientific evidence' and the nature of science

As well as knowing some science, citizens in a democracy need to understand something about science itself and how scientists work. They need to know that scientific evidence is not always conclusive. Evidence is messy as often as it is clear cut. This was shown throughout the 1990s with issues such as global warming, BSE, GM foods, cloning and debates over sources of energy. The days of certainty, proof and simple causality (chains of cause and effect) have long gone. We live in an age where risk, probability and correlation are more important ideas than proof, and certainty and causality.

Learners (and indeed all citizens) need to know that:

- science has *limits* (it cannot predict and explain everything; there are other ways of understanding the world);
- science is done by people, or by groups and networks of people – it is a human activity and therefore not 100% infallible;
- scientific evidence is not always conclusive – decisions are not made on scientific grounds alone. Most decisions have to be made by weighing up benefits, risks and probabilities;
- science does change over time (albeit slowly) and across cultures or nations;
- above all, science proceeds in a social, moral, spiritual and cultural context.

3 Utilitarian arguments

Actually, elements of science education *can* be useful, even if not to everybody. Some arguments relate to individuals, some to the economy.

(a) Many students will not go on to follow careers in science, but *some* will. This minority should not determine the shape or content of the entire science curriculum for the majority (as may well have happened in the past). But, like any minority, they should not be forgotten – either for their own sake or for the good of the economy.

Similarly, we must not forget that a significant number of people do use science in their own work, even if very occasionally, inadvertently or unknowingly. Certainly, some civil servants and politicians (who almost seem to take pride in being scientifically illiterate) *should* use it.

(b) The generic skills argument: science may well develop certain general, transferable skills in people which can be of direct value in life or in the workplace. Skills such as 'problem-solving' are often quoted, though exactly what this is and whether it is really transferable is debatable. However, certain lesser skills do develop in science education and are of direct utility: measuring accurately, recording results, tabulating and analysing data, estimating, forming hypotheses, predicting, evaluating what went wrong, handling apparatus, 'troubleshooting', using a range of measuring instruments, and so on. All of these are enhanced by science education, some are central to it. All are of utilitarian value, either in everyday life or the workplace.

(c) Attitudes: science education can also help to develop attitudes or 'dispositions' which can be of direct value to life and to work: an enquiring mind, curiosity and wonder, a sense of healthy scepticism, a critical and analytical approach.

Table 2.2 What is science education for? A summary of justifications

1. *Intrinsic value*

1.1   Making sense of natural phenomena; demystifying them.
1.2   Understanding our own bodies, our own selves.
1.3   Interesting, exciting and intellectually stimulating.
1.4   Part of our culture, our heritage.

2. *Citizenship arguments*

2.1   Science knowledge and knowledge of scientists' work are needed for *all* citizens to make informed decisions in a democracy.
2.2   Key decision-makers (e.g. civil servants, politicians) need knowledge of science, scientists' work and the limitations of scientific evidence, to make key decisions, e.g. on foods, energy resources.

3. *Utilitarian arguments*

3.1   Developing generic skills which are of value to *all*, e.g. measuring, estimating, evaluating.
3.2   Preparing *some* for careers and jobs which involve *some* science.
3.3   Preparing a smaller number for careers using science or as 'scientists'.
3.4   Developing important attitudes/dispositions: curiosity, wonder, scepticism . . .

In summary, there are plenty of good reasons for teaching science, some of which can (and certainly should) be conveyed to learners. Some of the arguments, e.g. the culture or heritage approach, will have little impact on young learners. But others may well convince them, if put forward both explicitly and implicitly. Table 2.2 gives a summary of the main justifications which can be used by science teachers.

Principles into practice

These principles may appear somewhat academic and divorced from the classroom. But in fact, as well as determining *why* we teach science, they can be used to guide *what* we teach, and *how* we teach it. They have a direct bearing on classroom practice. For example, if we pursue the citizenship argument then classroom activities should involve:

• examining newspaper and other media presentation of science in a critical way;
• the presentation and discussion of controversial issues i.e. issues, on which there is considerable debate and no clear-cut answer;
• some teaching and learning on the nature of science itself, the work of scientists, and the status of scientific evidence.

To neglect any of the above three strategies is to ignore the citizenship argument. Similarly, the culture or heritage argument demands that at least some science education should present the 'stories' of science, to show how science has changed and developed over time and how people have been involved. Stories might include: the history of nuclear energy; beliefs about evolution or the origin of the universe; changing views about the human body; immunisation or vaccination; the short (so far) story of BSE, and so on.

Third, if we are teaching science for its intrinsic value and interest, then we – and *future curriculum developers* – should include the 'Big Issues' of science rather than spending so long on the specific detail and the nitty gritty, certainly pre-16. When selecting topics we can only include so much: why not select (unashamedly) topics and issues which are exciting, interesting and motivating?

In the same way, the classroom teacher can deliberately select methods and activities which will capture interest and induce curiosity. A simple aid such as video can succeed here and will also show phenomena, events and entities which cannot be seen in the school lab. Multimedia, invaluable, for instance, in making 'the invisible, visible', and other forms of ICT can also help (that is if the science teacher can get hold of them).

Finally, the utilitarian arguments for science education demand that some practical work be done (in addition to some theory). Practical work can develop certain generic skills of value to all, which may transfer to other contexts. Similarly, work in science should be planned with the development of certain attitudes and dispositions in mind.

In summary then, the various justifications for teaching science can, and should, have practical implications for what is taught and how. An individual teacher's own lessons are guided by beliefs and principles, whether they are aware of them or not.

(An excellent discussion on guiding principles for science education is published in: *Beyond 2000: Science Education for the Future*. This is a 32-page report, edited by R. Millar and J. Osborne, based on a seminar series in 1998. It is obtainable from King's College, London SE1 8WA.)

Science teachers and the nature of science

Finally for this chapter we need to consider the teacher's own view of the nature of science. Our personal view of science and *what* science is has as great an impact on our teaching as our view of *why* science is important:

> As teachers we do not just act as the gateway to knowledge. We ourselves represent, embody, our curriculum. And, in our teaching, we convey not just our explicit knowledge, but also our position towards it, the personal ramifications and implications which it has for us.
>
> (Salmon 1988: 42)

There are many factors which affect the way that science teachers teach. Some are pressures, some constraints, while some will assist and enhance their teaching. Figure 2.3 gives a crude summary of some of the main factors involved:

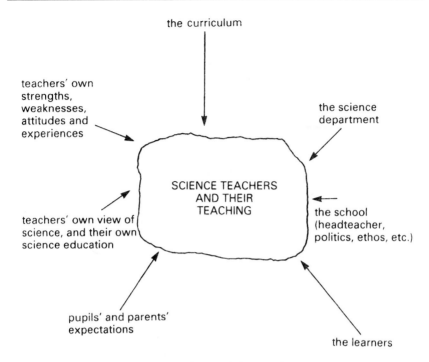

the curriculum

teachers' own
strengths,
weaknesses,
attitudes and
experiences

the science
department

SCIENCE TEACHERS
AND THEIR
TEACHING

teachers' own view of
science, and their own
science education

the school
(headteacher,
politics, ethos, etc.)

pupils' and parents'
expectations

the learners

Figure 2.3 Factors affecting science teachers and their teaching.

It is generally accepted that the teacher's own view of the nature of science is one of the important factors, although there is some debate as to the level of its importance (Lederman 1992). In this book we consider various notions of science: scientists' science, children's science, curriculum science, and of course teachers' science. These are just four of the different locations where different bodies of scientific knowledge reside (Gilbert *et al.* 1985). Imagine them as different repositories of science, all of which have importance for science education. Everybody forms their own personal construct of what science is. The activity of science teaching involves the interaction of these personal constructs. As Salmon (1988) puts it: 'Education is the systematic interface between personal construct systems.' This is an interesting definition and an important one for this book. It shows that successful teaching must achieve some shared meaning between the various parties involved, some sort of common ground between teachers' science, children's science and accepted scientific knowledge and process (see Figure 2.4 and Novak 1981).

A later chapter (4) looks at children's science and the well-known dictum of David Ausubel (1968): 'The most important single factor influencing learning is what the learner already knows. Ascertain this and teach him accordingly.' This chapter, however, is premised on the belief that what the teacher already knows is a factor affecting teaching. As Shuell puts it:

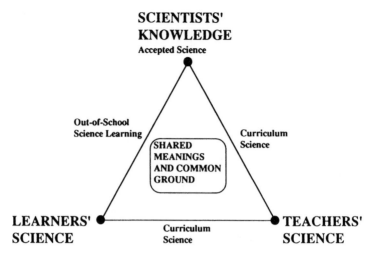

Figure 2.4 Common ground and shared meanings in science education.

> The conceptions and assumptions we hold about the nature of knowledge, the way knowledge is represented and the manner in which new knowledge is acquired determines what we study in science education, what we teach in science classrooms and the way in which the teaching of science is carried out.
>
> (Shuell 1987)

The teacher's own image or view of what science is does have implications for the way that they present and teach science in the classroom, both on content and process. With this in mind we present the activity in Appendix One. It is an activity which we (Nott and Wellington) have been using for some years with groups of experienced teachers and beginners. It is not meant to be a 'valid' or 'reliable' tool – it is more a way of getting teachers to think about science and scientific method. Using this activity in groups, in our experience, has never failed to provoke discussion. If you can find time to complete this activity (preferably with other consenting adults) before reading further it may help to clarify your own thinking.

Concluding remarks

It is often said that scientific knowledge is provisional, i.e. its ideas, laws and theories are subject to change. This is even more true of views on the nature of science. There is no general consensus on what science is, nor is there a commonly agreed view of what constitutes 'scientific method'. Many people argue that the way science is viewed and conceptualised varies from one discipline to another, for example, from life science to physical science (Lederman

1992). There is certainly a wide variation in view amongst the well-known philosophers of science from the past, ranging from Popper (1959) and Kuhn (1963) to Feyerabend (1975), with the latter arguing against the idea of there being any such thing as scientific method (see further reading). Other commentators on the nature of science such as Collins (1985) and Woolgar (1988) have focused on the way that scientists actually work. A single common message is that scientists do not have a rigid or fixed view of what science is, or of what constitutes scientific method.

In short, the message for teachers and curriculum planners is that there is no definitive view of what science and scientific method are, any more than science itself is fixed and absolute. It therefore makes no sense to accuse teachers of having an inadequate conception of science, nor to berate them for it (as has happened in the past: Lederman 1992). What can be expected of teachers, however, is that they do recognise in their teaching that science as a body of knowledge is provisional and that there is no single accepted view of scientific method. They should also emphasise that science and technology are not neutral or value-free activities. They are pursued within the context of a culture or society with its own economic and political pressures and constraints (Thorp 1991: 135).

This chapter has attempted to encourage readers to reflect on their own view of teaching and of science within those terms. Later in the book, Chapter 11 offers practical suggestions and guidelines for dealing with the nature of science in the classroom.

References and further reading

Professional development and mentoring

Bell, B. and Gilbert, J. (1996) *Teacher Development: A Model from Science Education*, London: The Falmer Press.

Bishop, K. and Denley, P. (1997) 'The fundamental importance of subject matter knowledge in the teaching of science', *School Science Review*, vol. 79, no. 286, pp. 65–71.

Brooks, V. and Sikes, P. (1997) *The Good Mentor Guide*, Buckingham: Open University Press.

Gilroy, D.P. (1993) 'Reflections on Schön: an epistemological critique and a practical alternative', in Gilroy, D.P. and Smith, M. (eds) *International Analyses of Teacher Education*, Oxford: Carfax Press pp. 125–42.

Schön, D.A. (1983) *How Professionals Think in Action*, London: Temple Smith.

Schön, D.A. (1987) *Educating the Reflective Practitioner: Toward a New Design for Teaching and Learning in the Professions*, San Francisco: Jossey-Bass.

Schön, D.A. (1988) Coaching Reflective Teaching, in Grimmett, P.P. and Erickson, G.L. (eds) *Reflection in Teacher Education*, New York: Teachers College Press.

Shulman, L. (1986) 'Those who understand: knowledge growth in teaching', *Educational Researcher*, vol. 15, no. 2, pp. 3–14.

Shulman, L. (1987) 'Knowledge and teaching: foundations of the new reforms', *Harvard Education Review*, vol. 57, no. 1, pp. 1–22.

Wilson, S., Shulman, L. and Richert, A. (1987) '150 different ways of knowing: representations of knowledge in teaching', in Calderhead, J. (ed.) *Exploring Teachers' Thinking*, London: Cassell.

Other useful books on mentoring include:

Allsop, T. and Benson, A. (eds) (1997) *Mentoring for Science Teaching*, Buckingham: Open University Press.
Arthur, J., Davison, J. and Moss, J. (1997) *Subject Mentoring in the Secondary School*, London: Routledge.
Furlong, J. and Maynard, T. (1995) *Mentoring Student Teachers*, London: Routledge.
Tomlinson, P. (1995) *Understanding Mentoring: Reflective Strategies for School-Based Teacher Preparation*, Buckingham: Open University Press.

What is science education for?

Millar, R. (1993) 'Science education and public understanding of science', in Hull, R. (ed.) *ASE Secondary Science Teachers' Handbook*, Hemel Hempstead: Simon & Schuster/ASE.
Millar, R. (1996) 'Towards a science curriculum for public understanding', *School Science Review*, vol. 77, no. 280, pp. 7–18.
Ratcliffe, M. (1998) 'The purposes of science education', in Ratcliffe, M. (ed.) *ASE Guide to Secondary Science Education*, Hatfield: ASE/Stanley Thornes, pp. 3–12.
Beyond 2000: Science Education for the Future (an excellent report resulting from a series of seminars funded by the Nuffield Foundation, available from: King's College, London SE1 8WA).

Teachers and the nature of science

Ausubel, D. (1968) *Educational Psychology: A Cognitive View*, New York: Holt, Rhinehart & Winston.
Bynum, W.F., Browne, E.J. and Porter, R. (1983) *Macmillan Dictionary of the History of Science*, London: Macmillan.
Collins, H. (1985) *Changing Order: Replication and Induction in Scientific Practice*, London: Sage.
Feyerabend, P.K. (1975) *Against Method*, London: New Left Books.
Gilbert, L., Watts, D. and Osborne, R. (1985) 'Eliciting students' views using an interview-about-instances technique', in West, L. and Pines, A. (eds), *Cognitive Structure and Conceptual Change*, New York: Academic Press, pp. 11–27.
Koulaidis, V. and Ogbom, J. (1989) 'Philosophy of science: an empirical study of teachers' views', *International Journal of Science Education*, vol. 11, no. 2, pp. 173–84 (shows that teachers vary in their views of science but that few are naive inductivists).
Kuhn, T.S. (1963) *The Structure of Scientific Revolutions*, Chicago: Chicago University Press.
Lakin, S. and Wellington, J.J. (1994) 'Who will teach the nature of science?', *International Journal of Science Education* (a study of teachers' views of science and the difficulties they face in teaching the nature of science).
Lederman, N. (1992) 'Students' and teachers' conceptions of the nature of science: a review of the research', *Journal of Research in Science Teaching*, vol. 29, no. 4, pp. 351–9.
Millar, R. (ed.) (1989) *Doing Science: Images of Science in Science Education*, Lewes: Falmer Press (a collection of articles on, broadly speaking, the relationship of science education to images and studies of the nature of science).

Novak, J.D. (1981) 'Effective science instruction: the achievement of shared meaning', *The Australian Science Teachers Journal*, vol. 27, no. 1, pp. 5–13.

Popper, K.R. (1959) *The Logic of Scientific Discovery*, London: Hutchinson.

Salmon, P. (1988) *Psychology for Teachers: an Alternative Approach*, London: Hutchinson.

Shuell, T. (1987) 'Cognitive psychology and conceptual change: implications for teaching science', *Science Education*, vol. 7 , no. 2, pp. 239–50.

Thorp, S. (ed.) (1991) *Race, Equality and Science Teaching*, Hatfield: Association for Science Education (ASE).

Wellington, J.J. (ed.) (1989) *Skills and Processes in Science Education: A Critical Analysis*, London: Routledge.

Woolgar, S. (1988) *Science: The Very Idea*, London: Tavistock Ltd.

Ziman, J. (1980) *Teaching and Learning about Science and Society*, Cambridge: Cambridge University Press.

Chapter 3

The science curriculum and science in the curriculum

The growth of the science curriculum: major shifts and recurrent debates

Science education, as part of the secondary school curriculum, has evolved over a period of more than a century. In that time there have been major shifts: at the start of the twentieth century it was a subject for a privileged minority, mostly male. In the twenty-first century, it would be unacceptable to suggest that science should be taught to only a tiny, male, 'higher ability' minority. Science is now seen as a subject for all pupils, all abilities, and both sexes. The slogan '*some* science for all' now seems to be undeniable. The questions of whether it should be 'the *same* science for all' or some science for some and more for others, are debatable however, and always have been.

Two excellent books, by Jenkins (1979) and Waring (1979) have traced the history of science education from the later nineteenth century to the eras of the 1970s and 1980s. A book of similar quality on the recent history of secondary science education has yet to be written. We cannot consider those histories in depth here. But they do show that certain debates have cropped up over and over again.

I   Who, and what, is science education for?

Should science education be aimed at a minority? Should a science curriculum for all be shaped and designed with this minority in mind? Is the aim of science education to train future scientists and to teach them science? . . . or is the aim to develop 'scientific literacy' and the public understanding of science for *all* citizens? Should the science curriculum aim to teach pupils *about* science and how it works? Should there be 'girl-friendly' science? Should both sexes receive the same diet? These questions have been, and will be, perennial. (The specific questions of who and what science education is for were explored in Chapter 2).

2 Breadth and balance

Similarly, how broad should science education be? Should it concentrate on only the three Big Sciences (physics, biology and chemistry) or should it bring in others such as geology, psychology and archaeology? Are the latter really 'science'? Where do we draw the line between a science and a non-science? What should be the balance between various components?

The term 'Balanced Science' was first introduced in the UK in 1979 (see Dunne 1998: 24), but since then it has become almost a slogan or a buzzword. It needs to be re-examined (see pp. 48–9).

3 Integration v. separation

This is one debate which seems to have gone away but in fact is still unresolved. Should each science be taught separately, or should the science curriculum (and science teachers) take a topic and teach it in an integrated way, bringing in all the relevant sciences?

In the UK in 1974, the Schools Council Integrated Science Project (SCISP) was a major initiative in trying to introduce an integrated approach to teaching science. A topic such as flight, for example, can be taught using a range of sciences: physics to explore the aerodynamics, biology to consider animals in flight, chemistry to consider fuel and its by-products, and so on. Even psychology might be brought in to consider the job of the pilot or the air-traffic controller. There are many other topics which could be tackled in an integrated way: growth, movement, the air, rocks and soil, the origins of life in the universe, buildings, and the environment.

For various reasons the integrated approach of the 1970s has never caught on. It may be due to the entrenched subject specialisms of teachers which may in turn be due to the structure of science degree courses in Higher Education, which are rarely integrated. It may be due to the examination boards or the way secondary education is timetabled and compartmentalised. Whatever the reason, the integrated approach of the 1970s gave way to the pleas for 'broad and balanced science' in the 1980s and, in the UK, the introduction of a statutory national curriculum with clear boundaries between the sciences.

Yet arguably the scientific issues and debates of the twenty-first century demand an integrated approach. We explore the ideas of breadth, balance, integration and separation later.

4 Process and content

A fourth recurring issue has been the extent to which science education should be about the skills and processes of science, as opposed to the facts, laws and theories of science, i.e. content. Again, we explore the process–content debate later.

Within the realm of content there has also been disagreement over whether *values* should come into science teaching or should we just present the 'facts'. In teaching recent scientific issues it has become increasingly difficult to draw a clear line between facts and values. Many facts have become value-laden (see Wellington 1986, on the nuclear debate). Similarly, values have become dependent on whose facts we choose to take account of, e.g. in considering BSE, GM foods or even the use of mobile phones. Science teachers may well say 'Let us teach the facts and leave the values to the Humanities staff' – but this approach has become increasingly untenable, even if it ever was justifiable.

5 The place of practical work and the role of ICT

Finally, one debate which is over a century old concerns the place and purpose of practical work. Ever since the days of H.E. Armstrong (see Jenkins 1979) the idea of children doing experiments for themselves and 'learning by discovery' has been a subject of debate. Can children discover science for themselves? Does exploratory or investigational practical work motivate children and help them to learn and understand science? Or will children discover the 'wrong science'? Is discovery learning realistic in a 50–minute science lesson when history shows that it took scientists decades to discover vaccination or develop a working telescope? Can the pupil really be a scientist? (see Driver 1983).

This debate will run and run. H.E. Armstrong's notion of discovery learning was rediscovered by the advent of 'Nuffield Science' in the 1960s and 1970s with its emphasis on practical work, children's own discoveries, and the motto 'I do and I understand'. It has been given a new lease of life by the recent emphasis on Investigation in Science (a statutory part of the UK national curriculum). But to what extent do children make discoveries in this kind of work? What happens if they discover the 'wrong answer'?

In a later chapter we examine the place and purpose of practical work. One related issue is the role of ICT. Many traditional 'experiments' can now be done using multimedia, using perhaps a CD-ROM or the Internet. Should practical work be done 'virtually', or will this take away the means to develop important skills? ICT is widely used by 'real scientists', but will its widespread use in school science, e.g. for data-logging or for simulations, create a gap in science education? Again, this is discussed in the large chapter on ICT later in the book.

In the next section we examine in detail the important *dimensions* of the science curriculum which have been debated since science education began.

Science as part of the curriculum

Vertical and horizontal strands: the weft and the warp

One of the platitudes which science (and other specialist subject) teachers are inclined to lose sight of is that their own subject is just one part of a whole curriculum at secondary level. To state the obvious, it is one of a number of subject 'pillars': alongside maths, English, technology, the humanities, arts, physical education, and religious education. These subject pillars tend to become compartmentalised at secondary level, by both teachers and pupils. For example, how many students learn to draw graphs in mathematics but cannot transfer this to science? One of the jobs of subject teachers then, including scientists, is to try to make links between the subject pillars.

In addition, the secondary curriculum has cross-curricular elements and dimensions running across it: the horizontal strands. Curriculum planners in many countries have tried to build these in so that the curriculum structure has both a 'weft and a warp'. In the UK, for example, the national curriculum and its many published documents laid down *five* cross-curricular themes: health education, careers education and guidance, citizenship, environmental education, and economic and industrial understanding (EIU).

These were supposed to form the 'horizontal' part of every pupil's curriculum from 11–16. In reality, they have usually been treated as a lower priority than the subject pillars, and in many cases have been largely ignored. The latter three, i.e. citizenship, environmental education and EIU have been especially neglected. The Ofsted (1998) review described them as: 'the poor relations of the curriculum in many schools; such schools need to consider whether, in the light of this neglect, they are fulfilling their curricular aims.' (Ofsted 1998: 118.)

Linking and relating science to other areas

Science can be linked to other 'subject pillars', such as technology, geography and history, and it is up to both individual teachers and school policies and practices to make this happen. Dunne (1998) suggests several practical ways of achieving this.

Science can also make its own contribution to cross-curricular themes and dimensions. Its potential in enriching health education and education for the environment is obvious. It can also play a major role in education for citizenship, especially if the science curriculum deals with current and past controversial issues and examines the way in which decisions are made and how scientific evidence is used.

Two very specific areas to which science can contribute are literacy and numeracy. Indeed, science is a unique subject in the curriculum because of its major contribution to both.

(a) Literacy

Crudely speaking, science education can be used to develop both reading and writing skills. Pupils' reading skills can be developed by using directed, structured activities (DARTs or directed-activities-related-to-text) in science. A range of texts can be used: textbooks, readers, stories, newspaper cuttings, magazines, CD-ROMs and written material taken from the Internet. Pupils in science lessons can be trained to extract the key information from such texts – an extremely difficult skill, requiring training and coaching.

As for writing, science education is an ideal forum for developing writing skills. Science writing is often seen as having its own style and genre: the clear, concise account which describes or explains, using scientific terms carefully and accurately. But writing in science can also involve creativity and imagination. In addition, pupils can learn to write in different styles, e.g. letters to an alien, or for different audiences e.g. articles for a newspaper. Given home or school access to ICT, such as CD-ROM or the Internet, they can also learn to 'bring in' images or text from elsewhere (and to acknowledge its source, of course!). All these aspects of reading and writing are considered in later chapters.

(b) Numeracy

Science is also in an ideal position to enhance pupils' numeracy. Science activities can be used to develop: the ability to estimate; a feeling for the size of numbers and 'big' and small quantities; an awareness of large distances, e.g. light-years and very small ones, e.g. the size of a microbe; the ideas of ratio and proportion; the ability to rearrange simple formulae such as $V=IR$; working out averages; using fractions and percentages; plotting graphs and understanding what they mean (including the difference between line graphs and bar charts); drawing curves or lines of best fit and knowing which to draw; understanding probability and risk.

All these activities in science lessons will contribute to general numeracy. Equally, of course, maths teaching will (or should) enhance a pupil's science education. Science teachers, however, need to be aware of some of the common *specific* difficulties which pupils have, e.g. using fractions; understanding ratio and proportion; estimating rough orders of magnitude; expressing quantities in standard form. They also need to recognise the common general difficulty of *transfer*, i.e. being able to carry across skills and ideas learnt in the maths dept. to the science lab at the other end of the building.

Examining the science curriculum more deeply: breadth, balance, process and content

Why reflect on the science curriculum?

There are two good reasons for taking time for further reflection on the nature of the science curriculum. First, teachers as professionals need to be far more than 'deliverers' of a science curriculum. They have an important role to play in shaping and interpreting science and in adapting the science curriculum for the future. It is not set in tablets of stone – that would make neither economic nor educational sense in a rapidly changing society based on science and technology.

Secondly, any national curriculum in any country is laid down as a 'minimum entitlement' rather than a straitjacket or a set of immovable boundaries (although for many teachers it may feel like this). To use the metaphor adopted by the Association for Science Education (ASE), the national curriculum is a 'skeleton' which needs the flesh of the real world and the 'life force' of the teacher to bring it alive. Within its framework, teachers have flexibility in the way they present science, for example, as essentially about processes and methods or, in contrast, as a body of accumulated knowledge. They can also decide whether they present the various sciences as an integrated whole or as separate disciplines.

Dimensions and aims in the science curriculum

How many people reading this have experienced a broad and balanced education, let alone a balanced science education? Few, I would imagine. Many will have pursued an education biased towards the sciences perhaps from the age of 14 or earlier, and certainly from the age of 16 onwards. Within their science education, many will have followed a course geared either to the life sciences or to the physical sciences, with the choice of route depending on such fortuitous factors as the school, the teaching staff or their own gender. Some will have followed a science course that included little or no practical work. Many will have gone through the system to graduate in a science without having studied earth science, cosmology, astronomy or ecology, let alone the nature and history of science.

So we need to recognise that many of those responsible for providing a broad and balanced science education to pupils have not had the benefit of such a curriculum themselves. Teachers need to be aware of their own background and the views and beliefs about science which they hold themselves – this is the basis of the activity which is shown in Appendix Two. This activity invites you to consider your own position on two issues: first, the question of whether the science curriculum should be seen as separated out into discrete sciences, or the study of science should be seen as an integrated whole; secondly, the question of whether the science curriculum should focus largely on the processes and methods of science rather than on the content or body of knowledge which science through the years has accumulated. The activity therefore focuses on the two poles, integration versus separation, and process versus content.

There are, however, other dimensions to breadth and balance that need to be remembered, principally that of the affective aspect of science education as opposed to the cognitive aspect. The affective element includes the pupil's attitudes and disposition towards science: interest, excitement, enthusiasm, motivation, eagerness to learn and openness to new learning. These are important dimensions of any science curriculum which are neglected at our peril (Claxton 1989). The notion of different elements or 'domains' of educational aims goes back to Bloom's (1956) taxonomy of educational objectives which is still valuable in considering a balanced science curriculum. A summary of these three elements is given in Table 3.1.

Table 3.1 Groups of aims in science education

Cognitive	Psychomotor	Affective
Factual knowledge	Manipulative skill	Interest Enthusiasm
Understanding	Manual dexterity	Motivation Involvement
Application	Hand-to-eye coordination	Eagerness to learn
Synthesis		Awareness and openness
Evaluation		

Striking a balance?

The question which is still relevant for science education is: how should the various parts of science come together to form some sort of coherent whole, i.e. a broad and balanced science curriculum? Balance and integration are not synonymous. There are insufficient grounds for a truly integrated science or science curriculum, i.e. there is no unifying principle involving the concepts, content or processes of science which can bring about integration. We are thus faced with a mixture rather than a compound in devising a balanced science course. What should this mixture contain?

My own suggestion, which is presented as an Aunt Sally, is that it should include the following:

* a study of the content and concepts of the sciences, giving a balanced coverage of the main sciences and some mention of the less commonly covered sciences;
* consideration of the practices and processes of science, i.e. scientific methods and procedures (whilst remembering that there is no clear consensus on a single scientific method);
* study of the links between science, technology and society;
* consideration of the history and nature of science.

It does seem desirable that science education should be presented as a balanced, coherent and concurrent mixture of these parts, i.e. various sciences taught alongside their methods, their applications, their impact on society, with some consideration of their nature and limits. Is this expecting too much? It is certainly a goal that can be achieved within the framework of any national curriculum.

As for the process versus content debate, it cannot be doubted that the traditional, content-led approach to the science curriculum with an over-emphasis on factual recall, inert ideas, irrelevant laws and theories and difficult abstractions has been long overdue for change. But a swing or backlash towards an exclusive emphasis on processes and skills is equally undesirable, philo-

Table 3.2 Balanced science education

Science education can be seen in terms of three categories of knowledge that people who have received a science education should possess:

Knowledge that	Knowledge how (to)	Knowledge why
Facts, 'happenings', phenomena, experiences	Skills, processes, abilities	Explanations, models, analogies, frameworks, theories

sophically problematic and probably as likely to fail its students as a content-led approach. Particularly dangerous is the belief that processes could and should be taught in isolation from content (Wellington 1989).

There are various ways of conceiving balance, none of which is definitive but all of which can be valuable aids to thinking about the goal of a balanced science curriculum as an entitlement for all pupils. A final framework for considering balance in both science lessons and schemes of work is offered in Table 3.2. It presents three kinds of knowledge (Ryle 1949) as being important in science education: knowledge *that*, i.e. traditional factual recall and the experience of events and phenomena in science; knowledge *how*, i.e. processes and skills; and knowledge *why*, i.e. a knowledge of explanations, laws, frameworks and theories. Science teachers and curriculum planners could usefully employ these three categories in considering their teaching, science courses and curricula for the future.

A 'balanced' science education will not focus on *one* of these three categories at the expense of the others.

The changing face of the post-16 curriculum

One of the most hotly debated areas of the curriculum, since curriculum debates began, has been the post-16 phase. This has evolved, and some would say been passed from pillar to post, for decades. In the UK, for example, the debate has largely been about A-levels, GNVQs and NVQs – what are they, who are they for, and where did they come from? Similar debates about academic versus vocational qualifications (and which are 'worth' the most) have occurred elsewhere in the world, not least in North America and Australasia.

In the UK, the 1980s saw a growing drive to produce a better match between education and training and actual job requirements – this is part of the change often referred to as the 'new vocationalism'. This drive involved employers in stating their requirements (as far as they could) and in helping to develop new qualifications. In the UK the National Council for Vocational Qualifications (NCVQ) was set up in 1986 to monitor existing awarding bodies in the vocational area and to sort out the complicated mixture of qualifications then available. The NCVQ set about developing a new approach to vocational education and training based on the key ideas of 'outcomes' and 'competencies', both of which (in theory) could be assessed and measured (Jessup 1995).

This led to a system of National Vocational Qualifications (NVQs) which are directly related to certain jobs and can be acquired at any level from 1 to 5. Level 3 is said to be 'equivalent to' Advanced Levels, while the higher levels 4 and 5 are deemed to be Higher Education. Then, in order to 'bridge the gap' between the directly vocational and job-related NVQs and the academic, non-vocational A-levels another new qualification was brought in: the GNVQ.

GNVQs and GNVQ Science

The General National Vocational Qualification (GNVQ) was first announced in the Government White Paper *Education and Training in the 21st Century* published in May 1991. The Government intended that GNVQs, together with NVQs, would replace other vocational qualifications and become the main national provision for vocational education and training. They would be available at foundation, intermediate and advanced levels.

Although GNVQs are primarily aimed at the 16–19 age group, they are available to adults and, credit towards them may also be gained by the 14–16 age group. One of the main objectives of GNVQs is to provide a genuine alternative to A-level qualifications for the increasing number of students staying on in full time education beyond the age of 16. In particular, the GNVQ at Advanced Level is designed to be of comparable standard to A-levels (first called, in 1992, the 'vocational A-Level').

GNVQs were designed to provide a broad-based vocational education. In addition to acquiring the basic skills and a body of knowledge underpinning a vocational area, all students have to achieve a range of core skills (now called key skills). This combination of vocational attainment plus core or key skills provides a foundation from which students can progress either to further and higher education or into employment and further training. The position of GNVQs in the 'qualifications framework' is shown in Figure 3.1.

Core skills (now 'key skills')

The NCVQ proposed the idea that while developing 'occupational competencies' students should also develop fundamental, core skills. These were identified as:

- problem solving
- communication
- personal skills
- numeracy
- information technology
- competence in a modern foreign language

The key skills for GNVQs are now only communication, IT and application of number.

National qualification framework

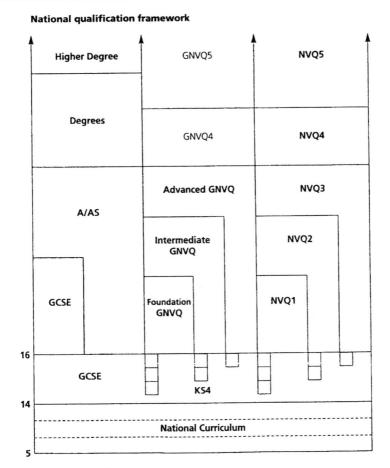

Figure 3.1 Qualifications framework.

GNVQ specifications for science

GNVQ specifications have been modelled closely on the NVQ format. Although three awarding bodies (RSA, BTEC and City and Guilds) accredit GNVQ Science, RSA was responsible for setting up the advisory and working groups which devised the mandatory units for GNVQ Science.

(A) INTERMEDIATE GNVQ SCIENCE

For intermediate GNVQ in science students study:

* certain *mandatory* vocational units, which all students take
* *optional* vocational units
* *key skills* units, which all students take

They also take two optional units. These give the opportunity to study a subject in more detail, or to look at something completely new. For example, they can specialise in sports science, health and fitness, or forensic science.

(B) ADVANCED GNVQ SCIENCE

At this level there are eight *mandatory* units. Students then take an additional four optional units and the three core skills at level 3 to make an Advanced GNVQ which is equivalent to *two* A-levels. To make a complete 'weekly timetable' students may take additional GNVQ Science units *or* units from other GNVQ programmes *or* an A/AS level *or* extra GCSEs.

GNVQs have not been without their critics. They have been accused of being of lower status and poorer quality than A-levels; they have also suffered from a lack of 'parity of esteem', meaning in practice that certain schools have not touched them and those pupils choosing them have had (on average) lower grades at GCSE level. However, A-levels themselves have not been without their critics.

Some criticisms of A-level

Over recent years many teachers and educators have challenged the appropri-ateness of Advanced Level examinations for the changed population staying in full-time education post-16. Some of these criticisms will now be examined but it should be remembered that A-levels themselves have changed over the years.

(a) Narrowness

The narrowness of the A-level curriculum has been recognised for at least twenty five years and a number of government initiatives to broaden the cur-riculum have failed to secure change. According to Pring (1995) this narrowness can be of *content, learning styles* and *relevance*. Narrowness of *content* arises because science students rarely continue to take a foreign language and arts students rarely continue with science or mathematics studies. The narrow-ness of *teaching style* is related to the nature of the content and volume of materials to be taught which leads teachers to adopt traditional teaching styles (and student learning styles) which may not necessarily be the most effective or beneficial for the students. This has been exacerbated by the wider range of teaching and learning styles encouraged by GCSE. Narrowness of *relevance* relates to the tight prescription of content which precludes students from spending time on those issues that are especially meaningful to them. In science, for example, this may be a concentration on theory when the students are more interested in the human and moral implications of what they are learning.

(b) Wastage

By and large, students who take A-levels are probably the top 25 per cent of the year group. One concern, therefore, is the relatively high failure rate associated with these courses. In the past, some 30 per cent of those who started A-levels either left without completing the course or failed to achieve the minimum pass grade in one subject. This represents a considerable wastage of potential.

(c) Links to GCSE

Changes to the curriculum in the compulsory phase of education (largely brought about in the UK by the introduction of the national curriculum) and the moves towards a balanced science course occupying 20 per cent of curriculum time (as opposed to students being able to follow three separate sciences in, perhaps, 30 per cent of curriculum time) have resulted in students not having covered some of the content that has traditionally been assumed on entry to A-level. In practice, students may have a broader picture of science and possess different, valuable skills but this still places added pressure on both teachers and students (see Winn 1998).

(d) Continuity

With over 60 per cent of the school population in the UK now remaining in full-time education beyond the compulsory school leaving age, the break at age 16 in the curriculum and examination courses framework becomes less relevant and this has resulted in some pressure to reconsider the whole of the curriculum from 14 to 18.

(e) The 'gold' standard

A-levels have, in the past, been labelled the 'gold standard' or the 'jewel in the crown'. The use of a cliché such as the 'gold standard' immediately sets up a barrier. Not surprisingly, set against the academic background of A-levels, GNVQ courses may be found wanting. In fact, what needs to happen is for courses and qualifications to be judged against their own aims and values, against the nature of students taking the courses and the learning they achieve. This is why the hope of creating *parity of esteem* of vocational qualifications with A-levels by calling the former qualification a 'vocational A-level' when it is quite obviously a different creature was almost certainly bound to fail.

Changes at A-level

These criticisms ignore the fact that A-levels have themselves changed. The content load has, in many cases, been reduced. Key skills (IT, numeracy and communication) are being introduced for A-level students. 'Broadening' is being encouraged through the A/S level (see below). The mode of delivery has shifted from terminal examination to a modular approach followed by module tests. Over a period the teacher has had a greater involvement in the assessment of practical skills rather than externally set practical examinations. Elements of choice have been introduced (especially through modular schemes), project work has been facilitated and work experience included in some syllabuses. Completely new syllabuses, all of which were required to include a nationally agreed subject core, were introduced for first examination in June 1996 and a wide variety of Advanced Level syllabuses became available (Knutton 1994: 120).

Probably the most significant change over previous A-level syllabuses was the introduction of modular courses. Modular courses were advocated because they have certain advantages over traditional courses. Parkinson (1994: 45–6) identified these advantages:

- they are more student-centred than the traditional courses, with students choosing modules (if the school can provide the staffing);
- they give more choice (a wider range of modules);
- they provide short-term goals and regular feedback;
- the modules may bridge the academic-vocational divide;
- students can build up credits over a period of years – useful for part-time students;
- upper and lower sixth can be taught together.

Parkinson also identified certain disadvantages which include:

- students will take module tests which assume an A-level standard after just six months with no allowance for their lack of maturity;
- modules may not have the same degree of difficulty and the tests may not be equally demanding;
- it is not clear that the modular A-level will be equally regarded by HE and employers (most UK first degree courses are now modularised).

A modular approach may also encourage a fragmentary, 'bitty' approach to knowledge of a subject, as opposed to a holistic approach viewing a subject (e.g. physics) in its entirety.

Advanced Supplementary (AS) Levels

Advanced Supplementary examinations were introduced in the late 1980s as one way of encouraging the broadening of the curriculum post-16. These examination courses were defined as half the content of an A-level course but at the same academic level. Originally a wide range of both contrasting and complementary subjects was envisaged. These courses have enormous potential for introducing breadth and flexibility into the curriculum but, so far, the response from schools and colleges has been lukewarm for a variety of reasons. A major danger is the possibility of AS-levels being used as a half-way house towards A-levels with the students facing examinations at 16, 17 and 18 years. Another problem for schools is organisational – unless the sixth form is very large it is unlikely that viable AS groupings will be generated (unless they can be taught at the same time as the A-level students).

Causes for concern in post-16 science

Despite the length and heat of the debate about the post-16 curriculum and the huge efforts to offer alternatives to students, there are still a number of concerns over current provision, many of which apply internationally:

(a) Numbers and conflicting policies

Over a period of three decades the numbers of students post-16 taking science and mathematics has been a cause for concern – especially to Higher Education Admissions Tutors. In practice, the percentage of the total *age* cohort taking these subjects has remained fairly static at between 5 per cent and 6 per cent. But as the numbers remaining in full-time education post-16 have risen steeply, the proportion of those staying on and studying science and mathematics has dropped. In the meantime, subjects like business studies have seen a massive growth.

There has also been a direct contradiction between the rhetoric of politicians and their policy. The politicians' rhetoric is that a strong economy depends on a good supply of young people with skills, knowledge and understanding in science and technology. However, research by Fitzgibbon (1996) suggested that the policy of enforcing national league tables for school exam results has discouraged schools from allowing students to follow maths and science A-level courses, fearing that they might fail. As a consequence, the numbers of students going on to Higher Education in these areas is decreasing. This vicious circle, and the contradiction between rhetoric and policy, is obvious but extremely damaging for the future of science.

(b) Quality and breadth of teaching

The style and quality of teaching post-16 has often been criticised. The 1998 Ofsted review states quite simply: 'Post-16, the teaching of science subjects compares unfavourably with that of most other subjects' (Ofsted 1998: 133). They comment on 'spoon-feeding' and, not allowing students to 'think for themselves'.

As for breadth, many schools have turned to the International Baccalaureate (IB) to overcome the narrowness of A-level. The IB is an international qualification with candidates in 95 countries. Students can take six subjects from different areas of the curriculum (e.g. mixing arts and sciences).

(c) Parity of esteem

NVQs and GNVQs (and similar qualifications in other countries) are still looked down upon, often quite unjustifiably. This lack of esteem occurs in the eyes of teachers, students, parents and even employers.

(d) Coherence and cohesion

There is still very little coherence in post-16 pathways. 'Crossing the track' between academic and vocational options, or mixing the two, is still very difficult in practice. There are still too many differences in forms of assessment, syllabus styles, 'culture' and methods of learning and teaching in the different pathways. The move to introduce core or key skills to all post-16 courses may help but the academic–vocational divide is still a large gap to bridge (see Hodkinson and Mathinson 1994).

Perhaps the only way to achieve coherence is to 'start from scratch' and create a single, unified framework for all post-16 qualifications. At present, the post-16 picture with its wide range of qualifications ranging from NVQ to the Baccalaureate does remain something of a quagmire. It is little wonder that employers claim to be mystified by it and that *some* universities (explicitly or implicitly) favour applicants with so-called traditional qualifications.

Conclusion

The future of post-16 science education looks murky and uncertain. However, what can be said with certainty is that:

(a) Post-16 science courses in the future will need to meet a diverse range of needs, they will need to be flexible (perhaps modular), and will need to cater for lifelong learning.
(b) Unless the vicious circle of fewer students taking science post-16 and in Higher Education, resulting in fewer graduates able or willing to teach science, is broken, then the long-term future of science education and science itself is uncertain.

References and further reading

The evolution of the science curriculum

Dunne, D. (1998) 'The place of science in the curriculum', in Ratcliffe, M. (ed.) 1998, pp. 23–32.
Driver, R. (1983) *The Pupil as Scientist*, Milton Keynes: Open University Press.

Jenkins, E. (1979) *From Armstrong to Nuffield*, London: John Murray.
Waring, M. (1979) *Social Pressures and Curriculum Innovation*, London: Methuen.
Wellington, J. (1986) *The Nuclear Issue*, Oxford: Basil Blackwell.

Examining the science curriculum more deeply

Bloom, B.S. (1956) *Taxonomy of Educational Objectives*, Cambridge, Mass.: Harvard University Press.
Claxton, G. (1989) 'Cognition doesn't matter if you're scared, depressed or bored', in Adey, P. (ed.) *Adolescent Development and School Science*, Lewes: Falmer Press.
Claxton, G. (1991) *Educating the Inquiring Mind: The Challenge for School Science*, London: Harvester Wheatsheaf.
Jenkins, E. (1989) 'Processes in science education: an historical perspective', in Wellington, J.J. (ed.) *Skills and Processes in Science Education: A Critical Analysis*, London: Routledge.
Millar, R. (1989) 'What is scientific method and can it be taught?', in Wellington, J.J. (ed.) *Skills and Processes in Science Education: a Critical Analysis*, London: Routledge.
Ryle, G. (1949) *The Concept of Mind*, London: Hutchinson.
Screen, P. (1986a) *Warwick Process Science*, Southampton: Ashford Press.
Screen, P. (1986b) 'The Warwick Process Science Project', *School Science Review*, vol. 68 no. 242, pp. 12–16.
Smail, B. (1993) 'Science for girls and for boys', in Hull, R. (ed.) *ASE Secondary Science Teachers' Handbook*, Hemel Hempstead: Simon & Schuster.
Wellington, J.J. (ed.) (1989) *Skills and Processes in Science Education: A Critical Analysis*, London: Routledge.

(For an interesting discussion on what constitutes a balanced science course see: Kirkham, J., Balanced science: equilibrium between context, process and content, in Wellington, J.J. (ed.) 1989.)

The post-16 curriculum

Fitzgibbon, C.T. (1996) 'Official indicator systems in the UK: examinations and inspections', *International Journal of Educational Research*, vol. 25, pp. 239–47.
Gadd, K. (1994) 'GNVQ Science – quality in learning', *Education in Chemistry*, vol. 31, no. 5, September 1995, pp. 133–4.
Hodkinson, P. and Mathinson, K. (1994) 'A bridge too far? The problems facing GNVQ', *The Curriculum Journal*, vol. 5, no. 3, pp. 323–36.
Jessup, G. (1995) 'Outcome based qualifications and the implications for learning', in Burke (ed.) *Outcomes, Learning and the Curriculum*, London: Falmer Press.
Knutton, S. (1994) 'What's on offer – the A-level syllabuses for 1996', *Education in Chemistry*, vol. 31, no. 5, pp. 120–21.
Parkinson, J. (1994) *The Effective Teaching of Secondary Science*, Harlow: Longman.
Pring, R. (1995) *Closing the Gap: Liberal Education and Vocational Preparation*, London: Hodder and Stoughton.
Winn, P. (1998) 'From GCSE to A-level: what do students think?', *Education in Chemistry*, May 1998, p. 65.
Wolf, A. (1991) 'Assessing core skills: wisdom or wild goose chase?', *Cambridge Journal of Education*, vol. 21, pp. 189–201.
Yeomans, D. (1998) 'Constructing vocational education: from TVEI to GNVQ', *Journal of Education and Work*, vol. 11, no. 2, pp. 127–49.

Young, M. (1993) 'A curriculum for the 21st century? Towards a new basis for overcoming academic/vocational divisions', *British Journal of Educational Studies*, vol. 41, no. 3, pp. 203–22.

The entire issue of *Physics Education*, vol. 31, no. 4, July 1995, was devoted to GNVQ Science.

Key skills and their place in science

Key skills have been growing in importance for a number of years, in the UK and in other parts of the world. They shifted from being a core feature of 'vocational' courses such as NVQ and GNVQ to becoming a central part of all post-16 courses. More recently they are becoming an explicit element of all subjects in secondary and primary education. With the focus largely on communication, working with others, the use of ICT and the application of number the science curriculum has been an 'ideal home' for their development. In fact, science classrooms (primary and secondary) provide as good a context as any subject for the opportunity to nurture them.

The April 1999 issue of *Education in Science* provides an excellent starting point for further reading in this area, with five short articles on key skills at different phases.

Practical approaches to science teaching

Chapter 4

Learning in science

Jon Scaife

Student teacher to chemistry class:	You won't be able to do question one because you haven't done ionisation energy.
Class teacher to student teacher:	They should be able to do it.
Student teacher to class teacher:	Have they done ionisation energy?
Class teacher to class:	You did it with me. Before Christmas.
Student 1: and after further discussion . . .	*You* might have done it. We haven't!
Student 2:	*What* is it we're supposed to have done?

(From a school in Yorkshire, England)

The thing that struck me about this exchange was that nobody could agree about learning. Everyone was uncertain about it. This was an odd state of affairs, because lessons are supposed to be for learning. If not, then what is the point of education? It would be odd if some people produced a newspaper but could not agree what was in it. And you would be surprised if a car maker could not tell you the car's specifications (It's blue, no it's green, with a few doors . . . er . . . we're not sure whether it's got an engine.)

Introduction

The trouble with learning is that it isn't a 'thing' in the way that a newspaper or car is. That makes it elusive to observe and even to think about – and perhaps that is why teaching often has a higher profile than learning in education. To illustrate, picture a science class you've been in fairly recently. Think of the teaching: what was taught, how well it was taught, who taught it, was it taught scientifically appropriately? Now think of the learning and check the same four questions, substituting learned for taught. Hard? Virtually impossible unless you're a mind-reader because there's absolutely no guarantee that what was taught is what was learned. In fact there's a lot of research evidence that suggests the two are often distant relatives.

In this chapter the main aims are to summarise some of the longer-standing perspectives and also some recent ideas about learning (some people call these 'theories') and to look at teaching in the light of these ideas. In the course of this it will be useful to settle on some working definitions for words like learning, knowledge, understanding and so on, because they are overworked in everyday language and confusions easily arise. A glossary is included at the end of the chapter. Science teachers are used to this problem, with words like power, chemical, animal and so on, which have everyday usage but which need more precise definitions to be used scientifically.

Why theories?

For quite a while 'theory' has been an unpopular word to use in talking about education (Adey 1995b). But there are two good reasons for science teachers not to fear the T-word. The first is that science itself is full of theories. It is a massive achievement in human theorising; more than that it is an amazingly productive synthesis of thinking and doing. Science is 'living' evidence that theories and practice aren't opposites, they are jigsaw pieces that more or less fit together. The second reason for science teachers to be comfortable with theory in education is that they have written quite a bit of it themselves. As we will see there are several 'big names' who have been both science teachers or scientists and also thinkers about learning.

Why though are some teachers sceptical, even hostile towards educational research? Perhaps this is because so little 'official' research is carried out by teachers themselves. The trouble with teaching is that contrary to some public opinion, it takes a lot of time. After teaching, assessing and doing everything else the job entails, most teachers have neither the time nor the energy to do any in-depth checking or other researching into the effects of their work, the nature of their job, the curriculum or anything else. Surveys, comparisons and evaluations are very difficult for teachers to carry out at the same time as holding down a full timetable. The problem with this, as Spinoza pointed out over three hundred years ago, is that those who ignore history are condemned forever to repeat it. If teaching is to develop and change in a changing world, there must be a place for reflection and research.

> Some educators and researchers in education have come to the conclusion that, as a foundation for their activities, they must develop some theoretical ideas as to how children build up their picture of the world they experience. They believe that unless they have a model of the student's concepts and conceptual operations, there is no effective way of teaching.
>
> (Glasersfeld 1991: 21)

What can theories offer to teachers?

The first thing is that if a theory is any good it should at least add something to common sense. It might do so by extending, reinforcing or even conflicting with common sense. Its perspective may be sharper or its conclusions firmer. It may spotlight differences that to the common-sense view are invisible. The theoretical ideas in this chapter have things to say about children's learning. The topics include the following: How do people learn? Do students know any science before they are taught it? How can teachers find out what students have learned? How does mental maturity influence thinking? Can mental maturing be accelerated? Do students know what they're doing in science lessons? Is there more than one kind of learning? Do students learn from practical work? From discussion? From teachers' questions? Can we learn how to learn?

This chapter is based on the idea that if more could be learnt about how people learn, then pupils and teachers would both benefit. The chapter sets out to give a brief introduction to some theories of learning, to some ideas that children have in science and to some possible approaches for teachers. Suggestions for further reading are given at the end.

What's the problem?

Most science teachers are well qualified in science and have completed school science courses with considerable success. Does this show that science teaching and learning are on sound footings?

Consider these views:

> Never . . . has there been a time when the public at large, or even its highly educated segment, could be considered literate in science.
>
> (Shamos 1995)

> The average citizen's knowledge of science is far less today than at any other time since science became a part of the school curriculum . . . science educators have not been successful in transcending school science literacy to adult science literacy.
>
> (Kyle 1995)

> Unfortunately we must face the bitter truth that most students in schools all over the world do not understand. In other words, given situations in which they must apply their 'school knowledge', they do not know what to do.
>
> (Gardner 1993a)

Imagine all the children born in, for example, Britain in 1970. Figure 4.1 illustrates what I think has happened to their average level of science knowledge over thirty-odd years. It improved during schooling and peaked at school leaving age, at GCSE grade F or equivalent. Since then it has declined steadily. If you doubt this, select a few adults more or less at random and ask them some science from key stage three of the national curriculum. It costs a fortune to educate the nation in science as ineffectually as this! There is plenty of scope to make science teaching more effective in terms of peoples' long-term learning.

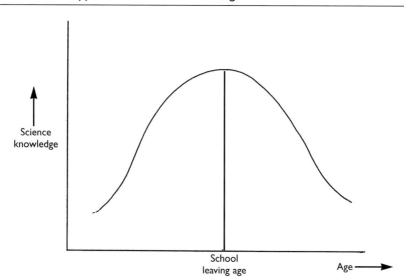

Figure 4.1 Variation of mean science knowledge with age.

Why learning: why not focus on teaching?

The most common concern shared by student teachers in the early stages of their qualification courses is survival in the classroom. 'Will they (children) listen to me? Will they do what I tell them? What if they don't?' If you are in the grips of this stage, take heart, it usually wears off quite early in the first teaching placement. The second stage in the development of new teachers focuses strongly on the acts of teaching: 'Am I doing it right? Am I covering the curriculum? Is the class properly controlled?' This is the stage where the curriculum, and teaching performance, take over from survival as the main concerns.

In the third developmental stage the teacher is concerned with the effects of teaching on students' learning: 'What are the students learning? What do I want them to learn? How can I enhance their learning?' Isn't this the main point of teaching? The first two stages of teacher development are means to an end – and learning is the 'end'. The more we know about learning the better we can teach. This even has 'official' support: included in the British Department for Education 'Standards for the Award of Qualified Teacher Status' (DfEE 1998) is a statement that new teachers are required to:

- understand how pupils' learning is affected by their development;
- know pupils' most common misconceptions in science;
- plan teaching to achieve progression in pupils' learning;
- assess how well learning objectives have been achieved and use this to improve teaching;
- keep up to date with research and developments in pedagogy and science education.

How do people learn?

I Some data

Let's start right here. Can you think of something that you're reasonably, or even very, good at – anything at all, not just school work. How did you get that way? How come your learning in that field has been successful? What would you pick out as the key factors that have contributed to your successful learning? You might be able to come up with responses to these questions in a matter of seconds. Do your responses have anything to say about teaching? In other words, can anything be learned about effective teaching from your own successful learning?

If you respond to these questions you're actually carrying out research into learning. Don't get carried away though, because data obtained from 'introspection' is bound to be personal or 'subjective'. Much more research would be needed before generalisations were justifiable. But self-reflection is a good start.

2 Learning and mental development: Piaget

As people grow they develop intellectually as well as physically. Their powers of reasoning and their capacity to experience ranges of emotions increase. As they grow they are able to learn new ideas. What kinds of tasks and problems can children solve at different ages? This question was studied in detail by Jean Piaget.[1] He drew inferences about the cognitive processes employed by individual children as they attempted to solve various kinds of problems. The result of this experimental work, together with Piaget's view of intelligence as an adaptively favourable characteristic in natural selection, led him to propose a theory of children's cognitive development. The impact of Piaget's ideas on teaching in Britain has been very considerable.

According to Piaget, children make meaning for themselves: they learn through actively constructing knowledge. A new experience might be *assimilated* by a child into her or his current cognitive structure. The experience might, however, be in conflict with the child's current cognitive structure, possibly resulting in the structure changing or *accommodating* to the new information. Piaget saw these processes of assimilation and accommodation as helping to bring about 'equilibrium' between the child's cognitive structure and the environment.

Piaget believed that although cognitive development in children is a continuous process, it does not take place smoothly, at a steady rate. He identified three principal *stages* of development, which occur in a definite order, as illustrated in simplified form in Figure 4.2. Children of school age have normally reached either the concrete operational stage or the formal operational stage.

Concrete operational thinking involves processes such as classifying, sorting and ordering objects. The child has developed ideas of conservation and reversibility; when a ball of Plasticine is moulded into a new shape and then rolled back into a ball, the child may know that the amount and weight of

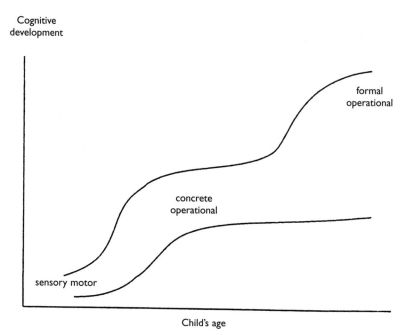

Figure 4.2 Piagetian stages of development.

Plasticine remain unchanged through the cycle. Driver (1983: 55) illustrates the type of inferential logical problem that might be solved at this cognitive stage: if water in beaker A is hotter than water in beaker B, and water in beaker B is hotter than water in beaker C, which beaker has the coldest water in it?

Formal operational thinking is associated with the use of hypothetical models for the purpose of explaining things. It is characteristic of situations involving several variables and also of the use of the mathematical notions of ratio and proportion.

The significance of these cognitive stages of development for science teachers, then, is that some forms of learning cannot be achieved until children reach the formal operational stage. Piaget's experimental work led him to believe that formal operational thinking can take place in 12-year-olds but subsequent research (Shayer *et al.* 1976; Lawson and Renner 1978) indicates that most children develop formal thinking much later than this and some do not develop it at all.

It has been argued that familiarity with the idea of stages of cognitive development will allow teachers to devise approaches to the science curriculum with greater insight (Shayer and Adey 1981). A science scheme, 'Thinking Science', which has been designed with explicit reference to Piaget's model, will be described later in this chapter.

Piaget was educated as a biologist and his view of knowledge as adaptively useful to an individual clearly draws on his science background. The idea of knowing as adapting has been extended by Glasersfeld; this is explored in the following section. But this is not the only direction in which the connection between biology and thinking has developed. Indeed, it has been predicted that, just as the twentieth century has witnessed an 'explosion' in physics, the twenty-first century will see an equivalent process in neurobiology and the study of the mind/brain. For further reading in this field see, e.g., Edelman (1992), a neurobiologist, and Dennett (1991) and Searle (1997), both philosophers.

3   Learning as knowledge construction: constructivism

A major scientific debate took place during the late nineteenth and early twentieth centuries. The question was: Is space full of aether? Aether was an attractive idea because it gave a sense of absoluteness to space and it helped to overcome difficult puzzles such as how light travelled through space from the sun to the Earth. A famous experiment by Michelson and Morley in 1887 was designed to show the effect of the Earth moving through the aether. No effect was found. Within twenty years Einstein proposed that we cannot detect *absolute* physical properties of space; the only properties we can detect are *relative* ones. People's views of the physical universe depend on their relative circumstances (such as whether they are moving relative to each other). The aether is a property of absolute space; Einstein's ideas imply that we cannot know if aether, or absolute space, exists.

There are some similarities between the evolution of these ideas in physics and those in some fields of psychology and philosophy. For a long time, a dominant cultural view in the West has been that there is a universe 'out there' and that scientists are gradually uncovering fragments of truth about it. This perspective is sometimes called 'inductive realism' (see, e.g., Selley 1989 and other chapters in this volume). At the same time, the dominant model of science teaching has been that teachers draw their pitchers from the wells of truth and pour knowledge from them into the empty vessels which are their pupils' minds. Another name for this model of teaching is the *tabula rasa* or blank slate approach; (it used to be commonplace in undergraduate lectures). The inductive realist view has been seriously challenged by numerous writers for many years. So far, in this field there is no equivalent of the Michelson–Morley aether experiment but this has not stopped people from questioning the relevance of the idea of an *absolute* universe: 'I have never said (nor would I ever say) that there is *no* ontic world, but I keep saying that we cannot *know* it.' (Glasersfeld 1991: 17).

In the view of Glasersfeld and others who describe themselves as 'constructivists', people do not acquire knowledge about an independent reality; rather they *construct* knowledge to fit what they experience: 'the world we come to know [is] assembled out of elements of our very own experience'. (Glasersfeld 1991: 19). Glasersfeld's version of constructivism, known as 'radical constructivism', is based on the following premises:

1   Constructivism is about knowing (Glasersfeld 1991: 17).
2   Knowing is a state of adaptation of an individual to the individual's environment (Glasersfeld 1989: 125; 1991: 16). ['Environment' is intended here to include social, cultural and physical aspects and also the self.]
3   The individual's state of adaptation, and knowledge, are dynamic and ever-changing.
4   New knowledge is learned through the construction of new states of adaptation of the individual to the environment (Glasersfeld 1989: 128).
5   New knowledge is constructed by the knower from the interaction of experiences and current knowledge, beliefs and emotional states.
6   Knowledge is not something that is 'out there', in the environment. Nor is it something that is passed about in immutable form.
7   We can have no certain knowledge of an absolute, objective reality. This includes scientific knowledge.

Radical constructivism has both strong supporters (myself included) and vigorous critics. Its opponents have accused it of implying that:

- all learning is discovery learning
- no-one can be taught anything
- learning is an individual, not a social, process
- knowledge can only be constructed through the experience of the senses
- my knowledge is the equal of your knowledge in terms of truth and merit
- there is no absolute objective reality

Constructivism is a contemporary view of knowing, distinct from the traditions of realism and rationalism. As with any serious challenge to tradition, it has prompted a range of reactions from curiosity and excitement to anxiety and hostility. Despite this variety, constructivism has undoubtedly established a place in science education: 'The view that knowledge cannot be transmitted but must be constructed by the mental activity of learners underpins contemporary perspectives on science education' (Driver *et al.* 1994).

To sample the views of both supporters and critics of constructivism, see the journal *Science and Education*; the whole of volume 6, numbers 1 and 2, (January 1997) is devoted to the topic.

4 Vygotsky and Bruner: Learning with a little help from friends

No man is an Island, entire of it self; every man is a piece of the Continent, a part of the main.

(John Donne, c.1571–1631, *Devotions*)

If John Donne were writing today, I imagine that he would include women and children too. Up to now, intellectual development and knowledge construction have been considered from the point of view of the individual. But we are a social species, the more so by virtue of our possession of language. Is this significant? Do *interpersonal* processes influence how and what we learn? The biologist Humberto Maturana (1991: 30) certainly thinks that they do: 'Science is a human activity. Therefore, whatever we scientists do as we do science has validity and meaning, as any other human activity does, only in the context of human coexistence in which it arises.' Central to this coexistence is language. For Maturana, we exist in language, experience takes place in language and we know what we know through its constitution in language.

Maturana may be regarded by some as holding a radical view but the underlying point, that knowledge is constructed by individuals through interpersonal processes, is now shared by many people. Jerome Bruner (1964) stressed the importance of language in cognitive development nearly thirty years earlier. Around this time, the work of L.S. Vygotsky began to appear in the West, having been suppressed for two decades in Russia. Vygotsky (1978) believed that, 'children undergo quite profound changes in their understanding by engaging in joint activity and conversation with other people'. This view is shared by Edwards and Mercer (1987), who regard knowledge and thought as 'fundamentally cultural, deriving their distinctive properties from the nature of social activity, language, discourse and other cultural forms'. The implication is that *meaning* is constructed not only through processes operating on individuals – such as the stimulation of senses or the mediation of prior knowledge – but also through processes of social communication.[2]

Vygotsky worked extensively with people with learning difficulties. He used to test their capabilities by asking them to attempt various tasks. Similar practices continue today: a familiar case is the obtaining of data about students' 'reading ages'. This measure compares a child's reading with the average reading capabilities of each year group. Imagine carrying out a large number of such measures, each assessing the child's performance at different tasks, in different cognitive domains. The result would be a 'profile' of the child. Now suppose that a teacher sat with the child, offering well-judged prompts as he/she attempted the tasks. The result would be another profile, with generally higher values in the measured domains than when the child worked alone. Vygotsky described the relationship between the two profiles, using an expression which translates from Russian as 'zone of proximal development'. Some authors have shortened this to ZPD or 'zee pee dee'. One account of this (Vygotsky, 1978: 86) is that a child has a personal ZPD that represents 'the distance between the actual developmental level as determined by independent problem solving, and the level of potential development as determined through problem solving under adult guidance or in collaboration with more capable peers'. Interpreted in this pragmatic way, the ZPD is an *extra* amount of constructing that can be done by the child, and its 'size' depends on:

- the child's current level of development
- the child's current mental constructions
- the discourse between the child and her or his environment

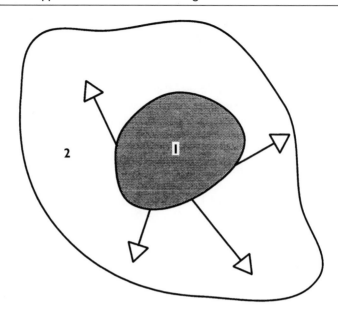

Figure 4.3 'Pragmatist' model of a ZPD.

Region 1 is a zone which represents the child's current development. Region 2 is the child's ZPD, representing potential development in the near future. The arrows in Figure 4.3 represent learning, leading towards new development. Since a central issue in teaching is the promotion and guidance of learning, the effectiveness of teaching could be judged according to how it assists (or otherwise) the construction and direction of these arrows.

The adult's action in guiding the child's learning has been likened by Bruner (1985: 25) to the construction of scaffolding: 'the tutor in effect performs the critical function of 'scaffolding' the learning task to make it possible for the child . . . to internalize external knowledge.' A word of caution is appropriate here, because the word 'scaffolding' can conjure up a variety of images. One image which is sometimes implied in discussion of Bruner's scaffolding idea is that of a temporary structural support; a 'buttress' would be a more accurate term for this. The purpose of scaffolding in the building trade is to support the process of construction, not to support the structure itself. Bruner's choice of word suggests a process, but who does the building – the child or the adult?

Newman and Holzman (1993) are fiercely critical of 'pragmatic' interpretations of the ZPD. They argue (page 88) that 'the ZPD is not a zone at all' but rather that it is (page 147) 'a reorganising of environmental scenes to create new meaning and a learning that leads to development'. This is a much broader notion than the functional object described above: e.g. (page 112): 'Speaking (verbalizing, using a language) is, perhaps, the single human performance that best exemplifies . . . the form and substance of the life space of everyday human performance, the ZPD.' According to these authors the school by no means necessarily contributes constructively to development through learning:

> Traditional schools are not ZPDs; they teach children and adults alike to devalue and even destroy ZPDs. In the typical classroom children are taught to view the major activities in the ZPD – working together, imitating that produces something other than mere repetition, collectively changing the total determining environment into something that is not predetermined, reshaping the existing tools of language and play into new meanings and discovery – as illegitimate.
>
> (Newman and Holzman 1993: 195)

Vygotsky's view is that learning *leads* development in the ZPD. When teaching, guidance or collaboration moves ahead of development it 'impels or wakens a whole series of functions that are in a stage of maturation lying in the zone of proximal development' (Vygotsky, quoted in Newman and Holzman, page 60). This contrasts sharply with the idea that learning can take place until it reaches limits imposed by the current level of development, a view associated with Piaget.

The ZPD represents current *potential* learning, leading to new development (Vygotsky referred to it as containing 'buds' of development). In a systemic view it is not a characteristic of the child alone but rather it is an aspect of the large, complex *system* consisting of the child and her or his environment. 'Environment' is used here in the most general sense, including the child's peers, parents, teachers and school, the physical environment and also the social context, its history and the history of the child. Whether the child's potential learning is actually realised depends on the operation of the system as a whole.

5 Ausubel: rote/meaningful and reception/discovery learning

The educational psychologist David Ausubel made a helpful distinction between two extreme types of learning. What he labelled as 'rote learning' is sometimes referred to as learning parrot fashion. Occasionally a mental catalyst (a mnemonic) is used to help rote learning, such as 'Richard of York gave battle in vain' for the colours of the visible spectrum (which inevitably prompts children to ask about indigo!). Meaningful learning contrasts with this because it results in knowledge that is not superficial or arbitrary but is well connected with other knowledge.

> [M]eaningful learning takes place if the learning task can be related in non-arbitrary, substantive (non-verbatim) fashion to what the learner already knows . . . Rote learning, on the other hand, occurs if the learning task consists of purely arbitrary associations . . . if the learner lacks the relevant prior knowledge necessary for making the learning task potentially

meaningful, and also (regardless of how much potential meaning the task has) if the learner adopts a set merely to internalize it in an arbitrary, verbatim fashion (that is, as an arbitrary series of words).

(Ausubel et al. 1968:27)

Ausubel's distinction between rote and meaningful learning is complex. Learning can, for example, be both meaningful and rote, depending on context. In school, children sometimes learn to use technical language in skilful, socially meaningful ways, without having any technical understanding of the words. John Holt described this as 'right-answerism': it gets teachers off pupils' backs. In a study of 16-year olds who had been taught about 'the living cell', Dreyfuss and Jungwirth found that pupils had invented a variety of explanations for the scientific phenomena in question, irrespective of the technical plausibility of the explanations:

> [S]uch pupil explanations of 'abstract' biological phenomena are usually never discussed by the teachers . . . Pupils then adopt them because of their efficacy, not in the solving of scientific problems, but in satisfying the teachers.

(Dreyfuss and Jungwirth 1989: 51)

There are traps for the unsuspecting teacher here. I fell into one when my daughter announced that her class was 'doing buildings next term' and could I tell her something about them? Over the next few days we had stories and drawings of bridges, walls, portal frames, triangles and arches. Finally I suggested we finish off with doors, windows and lintels. I drew a brick wall with a hole in for a window. We agreed that the window probably couldn't hold up the weight of the bricks above it. I drew another wall with a window hole and a space above for a lintel. 'What shall we do to hold the bricks up?' I asked. 'Use a lintel!' was the confident answer. I was in the process of congratulating myself about my teaching when came the question 'Dad . . . what's a lintel?'

Another distinction drawn by Ausubel concerns the situations in which people learn. One extreme is 'reception learning', where people are completely passive in a social sense, that is , they just 'sit there'. Ausubel contrasted this with 'discovery learning' where in order to learn anything of substance, the person has to do something. Both of these learning situations have been sharply criticised. After a period in the 1960s and 1970s when discovery learning was fashionable in science education, it has gone out of vogue. The trouble was that it clashed with the curriculum: students didn't always discover what they were supposed to. There is little educational support for reception learning but it is thought to have an economic advantage: mass lecturing, or computer-based alternatives to lecturing save on teachers' pay.

6 Memory: Gagné et al.

Robert Gagné (I pronounce his name 'Gan yay') developed a model of how human memory functions, with a corresponding model of how 'bits' of know-

Table 4.1 Seven types of memory element

Element	Brief definition	Example
String	A sequence of words or symbols recalled as a whole in an invariate form	'To every action there is equal and opposite reaction'
Proposition	A description of a property of a concept or of the relation between concepts	The yeast plant is unicellular
Image	A mental representation of a sensation	The shape of a thistle funnel; the smell of chlorine
Episode	Memory of an event one took part in or witnessed	An accident in the laboratory; the setting up of a microscope
Intellectual skill	The capacity to perform a whole class of mental tasks	Balancing chemical equations
Motor skill	The capacity to perform a whole class of physical tasks	Pouring a liquid to a mark
Cognitive strategy	A general skill involved in controlling thinking	Perceiving alternative interpretations; determining goals; judging likelihood of success

Source: White 1988.

ledge get remembered. Memory is essential: without it there can be no learning. If we can theorise about how we remember, some useful implications for teaching may arise. Gagné (1997) and later, Gunstone, White and others suggested that we remember knowledge in the form of various types of memory elements. White's (1988) version is in Table 4.1:

In his richly informative book *Learning Science*, White explores this model and its implications for teaching. White and Gunstone (1992) developed this approach further.

7 Engage and connect

If I want to learn something, I focus my attention on it. Attention seems to me to be necessary for learning. (The question of just how much attention in needed is interesting. When asleep we learn how to cope with the edge of the bed so as not to fall out; this suggests a minimum level of attention for learning. If we were drunk, however, this level of attention may not be feasible!)

Why don't students pay attention to teachers all the time? I think the answer is because it is unnatural. Curiosity is a human characteristic. We inherit a roving attention, which is adept at scanning the environment. Particular things capture our attention naturally: movement, change in environment, unusual or surprising things, attractive and interesting things, and so on. The teacher is part of the student's environment and the teacher's actions compete with many other things, external and internal to the student, for the student's attention and engagement. It sometimes surprises me how much attention some teachers manage to get given the competition!

Attention may not be enough. People obviously pay attention when driving or riding a bike but they can rarely provide much detail about a completed journey. If, say, you knew you were going to be asked how many traffic lights you stopped at or whether there was a post box on a particular corner, you would focus your attention on that particular issue. You would be 'engaging' with the issue. In the cognitive domain (which includes much of school science) for anything more than superficial learning to occur, engagement is necessary.

It was observed earlier in this chapter that learning is widely regarded as a process of constructing. New knowledge is sometimes said to be constructed by synthesising current experiences and current knowledge. I don't think this is quite right, since it looks like mixing apples and pears. I prefer to think of the new knowledge as emerging from thinking about current experiences and about current knowledge, with the thinking itself influenced by current knowledge. I include conscious and non-conscious thoughts in this. If this all seems rather abstract, hold on to the central point: learning arises from making constructions between the present and the past. We learn all the time. We're always making meaning of the present in terms of what we know – is it familiar, or is it novel? It is in our biology to do this.

8 The affective domain

Mental activity is sometimes described in terms of knowledge, feelings and emotions. The first of these is the 'cognitive domain' and the other two constitute the 'affective domain'. Educational research and classroom teaching have both tended to focus attention on cognition. But there are those who argue that the affective domain cannot be ignored. 'Affect', a person's emotional and intentional state, is a gatekeeper to cognition. A familiar example is motivation – a person's will or intention to act or think.

We can explore this now. You're reading this text: do you sense any influences, acting on you right now, competing with each other to determine what your mind dwells on next? I am aware of several current influences: I want to finish this chapter, I am thinking rationally about what I'm writing and I would like another mug of tea! Are children's thoughts in the classroom all that different? In the vividly titled paper, 'Cognition doesn't matter if you're scared, depressed or bored', Guy Claxton (1989) describes a set of pupil 'stances' which determine not only the 'amount' of learning that takes place but also the direction or domain in which it takes place. Claxton's labels are deliberately evocative: swot, thinker, boffin, socialite, dreamer, rebel and sinker. This classification is not based on any empirical data; nonetheless the stances have some 'chalk-face' appeal and they lend support to the argument that 'attitude' and 'motivation' are key elements in determining learning.

The idea that people have different intelligences in different fields such as maths, art, personal interaction, sport and so on has been around for several years (e.g. Gardner 1993b). Schools have focused on cognitive intelligence, however, rather than other fields. As the view has grown that the affect strongly influences cognition, there have been calls for greater attention to be given to emotional intelligence, motivation and student self-image. There is 'an incontrovertible link between how pupils perceive themselves as learners and their subsequent capacity to achieve' (Broadfoot 1998). In one study described by Salmon (1995), some children were asked to attempt some school-type tasks. After doing some of the tasks the children were asked to pretend that they were 'boffins', or high flyers. The standard they achieved while pretending was markedly higher! A strong influence on students' self-image is the expectations that the teacher holds for them. This conclusion is supported in many studies, one of which led to it becoming known as the 'Pygmalion effect'.

9 Is that it?

No, for two reasons: (i) this chapter contains my selection of significant theoretical views on learning and other people may have made other selections or may view mine differently; (ii) this is a rapidly developing field and new ideas are currently emerging. As Edelman puts it:

> We are at the beginning of a neuroscientific revolution. At its end, we shall know how the mind works, what governs our nature, and how we know the world. Indeed, what is now going on in neuroscience may be looked at as a prelude to the largest possible scientific revolution, one with inevitable and important social consequences.
>
> (Edelman 1992)

Children's ideas in science

One of the main themes of this chapter so far is that a person's current knowledge and ideas strongly influence what they will learn. When applied to science teaching, this prompts the following questions: do children have any ideas in science and if so, what are they like?

As shown in Figure 4.4, in an investigation of their understanding of the word *plant*, children were asked: Would you say any of these pictures are of plants? (Osborne and Freyberg 1985: 6).

This response from a 9-year-old is not atypical: 'Grass is a plant; a seed is a plant – well it'll grow into a plant. Definitely not a carrot – it's a vegetable. And not an oak tree; it's a small tree then it's a big tree, not a plant.' A response like this indicates that the child has definite ideas about the scientific topic (classi-

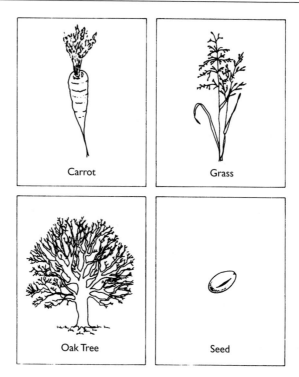

Figure 4.4 'Would you say that this is a plant?'
Source: Osborne and Freyberg 1985.

fication, in this case) and further, that these ideas are not the same as the scientific community's views.

Another study reported by Osborne and Freyberg used cards like those shown in Figure 4.5 to investigate children's views about light. Concerning card (a) students were asked: 'Does the candle make light? What happens to the light?' Where it was relevant the children were then asked: 'How far does the light from the candle go?'

Following the last question, four students said: 'One metre at the most'; 'About one foot'; 'Just stays there and lights up'; 'Stays there.' Two of these responses came from 10-year-olds and two from 15-year-olds. The 15-year-olds had studied light as a science topic and they could define terms like refraction and reflection reasonably well.

Commonality of alternative ideas

In the course of a major survey in England, Northern Ireland and Wales[3] the Assessment of Performance Unit asked 15-year-olds of all attainment backgrounds the following question (see Figure 4.6): 'When the plunger of this

Figure 4.5 'Does the candle make light?'
Source: Osborne and Freyberg 1985.

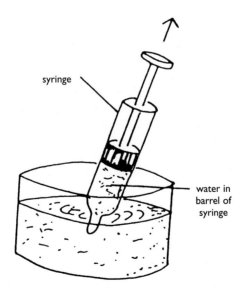

Figure 4.6 Diagnostic question: syringe.
Source: Holding *et al.* 1990.

syringe is pulled up, water goes into the barrel of the syringe. What makes the water go into the syringe? Explain as fully as you can.'

Here is a sample of students' written responses (including original spellings, emphases, etc.), reported in Holding *et al.* (1990: 42):

- The water goes up into the syringe because of two reasons: (1) atmospheric pressure pushing down on the water; (2) *the suction* and less atmospheric pressure inside the syringe.
- The sucktion of the handle and the vaccum caused makes the water travel up the syringe.
- Air pressure on the surface of the water forces the liquid in to the barrel of the syringe.
- As the syringe is drawn up it creates a vacume thus somthing has to fill the vaccume. The watter is therefore sucked in.

Again, these responses show different views from those held in the scientific community but this time there is evidence of a clear, coherent alternative idea, namely that *suction* is an active causative agency.

Commonality between some of the alternative views held by students about science has been revealed regularly in research carried out by the Children's Learning in Science (CLIS) team at Leeds University (see, e.g., Brook *et al.* 1984). The team found, for example, that:

- many children use 'heat' and 'temperature' synonymously;
- the sensation of coldness is due to transfer of 'cold' towards the body;
- particles swell: this explains pressure change and expansion;
- the word 'mixture' is often used for 'compound';
- 'food' for plants is anything taken in from the outside, e.g. water, minerals, air.

Some of these more commonly occurring ideas will be familiar to teachers. But sometimes the ideas seem so disconnected from the teacher's that their origins appear to be a complete mystery: 'They focus on things I would never dream of looking at!' said an experienced teacher about children's practical work.

Useful summaries of research into children's ideas can be found in Driver *et al.*, (1985, 1994) and Osborne and Freyberg (1985). The journal *School Science Review* is another good source.

Student teachers' ideas in science

In the national curriculum of England and Wales, science is a very broad subject. It contains strands of astronomy, biology, chemistry, earth science and physics. In contrast with this the typical degrees held by science teachers and student teachers are narrow. I have yet to meet a student teacher who has been justifiably confident in all strands of the key stage 3 science curriculum (for most

11–14 year olds). Many experienced science teachers have gaps in their curriculum knowledge. Knowing about the gaps is half the battle. From 1999 newly qualified science teachers in Britain are required by the Department for Education to have found and filled their gaps at key stage 3 during their teaching courses. Responsibility for this falls in large measure on the student teachers themselves, because of the short time spent in university or college and because of the teaching commitments of staff in schools.

One way of identifying gaps that has been used successfully by student teachers is to use the diagnostic questions described in the previous section. These were devised for researching children's ideas but they are also handy for probing adults' understanding of science at this level. Here are some for you to try.

1   See Figure 4.7.
2   A ball is thrown up into the air. As it travels up, what do you think happens to: its speed? Its acceleration? The force on it?
3   When water boils in a pan or kettle, big bubbles appear. What do you think is in the bubbles? (a) air; (b) nothing; (c) water vapour; (d) a mixture of hydrogen and oxygen gases?

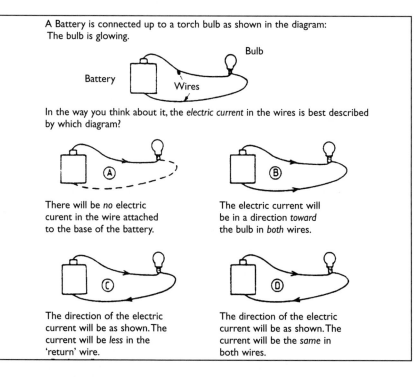

Figure 4.7 Diagnostic question about electric current.
Source: Osborne and Freyberg 1985.

I gave student teachers a set of diagnostic physics questions and asked them to rate their confidence in their responses. These were the results:

- the most problematic topic was mechanics;
- the topic in which they were least confident was current electricity;
- the average of the men's and women's scores were similar;
- the men rated their knowledge much higher than did the women; the men tended to be over-confident and the women under-confident.

Before tackling the diagnostic questions the student teachers had self-assessed their knowledge by going through the national curriculum. Compared with the self-assessment, the diagnostic survey was far more informative and useful in highlighting the gaps that the students needed to fill.

Children's perceptions in science lessons

In a short, informative paper Ross Tasker (1981) reported the findings of a series of classroom observations of 11–14-year-old children in typical science lessons. The aim of the study was to learn about children's perceptions and interpretations of practical work. Tasker found that there was often a large mismatch between teachers' and children's views about what was taking place.

- Teachers saw connections between lessons but students saw them as stand-alone events.
- Students tended not to connect the work they were doing with other science they had met. Teachers, on the other hand, referred to such connections as if they were self-evident.
- Students often have completely different ideas from the teacher about the purpose of a lesson or an activity.
- Two common purposes from the students' viewpoint are 'to follow the instructions' and 'to get the right answer'. When asked why they are following instructions, students are likely to reply 'because he/she told us to'.
- Teachers may wrongly assume that students understand experimental procedures and have appropriate skills, such as how to use a balance. Tasker noted that this particular mismatch was liable to lead to off-task and possibly disruptive behaviour.
- Teachers may wrongly assume a level of conceptual knowledge of science in students.
- Students see things differently from teachers. Something that the teacher regards as trivial may be regarded as highly significant by the students and vice versa. (One instance from my own teaching arose with the use of digital ammeters. I wanted to show the same current on either side of a bulb and I duly got readings such as 0.123A and 0.124A. Some students saw the difference and concluded that current is indeed used up in the bulb! I have used analogue meters ever since.)

Teaching: what learning about learning teaches about teaching

Anything that is known about learning has potential implications for teaching. That is the subject of this section. The basic question is this: how can knowledge about learning help make teaching more effective? In this section I will stick with the belief that learning involves constructing connections and I will adopt a broadly constructivist view. Glasersfeld points out the benefits of this:

> The most widespread effect has been achieved by the very simple construc-tivist principle that consists in taking whatever the student produces as a manifestation of something that *makes sense* to the student. This not only improves the general climate of instruction but also opens the way for the teacher to arrive at an understanding of the student.
>
> (Glasersfeld 1991:24)

Driver and Bell (1985), working in the context of the school science curric-ulum, identified a set of key points which they referred to as a *constructivist view of learning*. These points are:

- Learning outcomes depend not only on the learning environment but also on the prior knowledge, attitudes and goals of the learner.
- Learning involves construction of knowledge through experience with the physical environment and through social interactions.
- Constructing links with prior knowledge is an active process involving the generation, checking and restructuring of ideas and hypotheses.
- Learning science is not simply a matter of adding to and extending existing concepts, but may involve their radical reorganisation.
- Meanings, once constructed, can be accepted or rejected. The construction of meaning does not always lead to belief.
- Learning is not passive. Individuals are purposive beings who set their own goals and control their own learning.
- Students frequently bring similar ideas, about natural phenomena, to the classroom. Some constructed meanings are shared by many students.

For a short, readable discussion of this constructivist view of learning see Scott (1987).

Active construction, active learning and activity

The previous section put forward the view that people actively construct new knowledge of their own, rather than being passive recipients of someone else's knowledge. This apparently simple idea could have very significant implications for teaching (and also for parenting and for some of the ways in which we try to persuade people to change their views). How is the notion of active construction related to 'active learning'?

If the job of a science teacher were simply to *transmit* knowledge to a class, then the teacher might rate the following lesson characteristics highly:

- quiet, attentive class
- a lot of work 'got through' in each lesson
- efficient coverage of the syllabus
- students able to demonstrate knowledge in written tests

Such a teacher would tend to operate in 'transmission mode' and would cast her or his students into the role of 'passive learners'. Clive Carré (1981) lists several reasons why a teacher might choose this mode of teaching:

- time: if teacher talks and students listen the curriculum appears to be covered much more quickly;
- tradition: transmission mode was often 'good enough' for the teacher so it is good enough for the students;
- student pressure: many students indicate that they prefer the teacher to do the work – and in particular, the thinking;
- security: transmission mode allows the teacher to keep tight hold of the reins and feel secure in what is going on in the lessons;
- status: transmission mode allows the teacher to maintain the role of 'expert'.

Contrast the 'passive learning' environment with what Bentley and Watts (1989) described as a necessary set of requirements for 'active learning':

- a non-threatening learning environment
- pupil involvement in the organisation of the learning process
- opportunities for learners to take decisions about the content of their own learning
- direct skill teaching
- continuous assessment and evaluation
- relevance and vocationalism

Contrasted above are two types of learning *environments*. I do not believe that these environments create two types of learning *processes*, one active and one passive, because I think that learning is essentially an active process. But different environments can and, I believe, inevitably do result in the construction of different kinds of new knowledge. An appropriately designed learning environment can *focus* learning; it can help to concentrate the energy of knowledge construction towards a particular domain of thought and experience. In an inadequately designed learning environment, children still have intellectual energy and they still construct new ideas, but the focus is uncertain – it *could* be the carbon cycle but it could equally be determined by any of a whole spectrum of personal needs of each individual child.

Neither of the environments described above can be guaranteed to bring about meaningful science learning, because this depends on more than the environment. As to which is the better designed, each will have its supporters. In much the same way, *activity* is not, in itself, any guarantee of meaningful science learning. Students may be on their feet in a laboratory, handling scientific apparatus, talking and listening to each other, writing observations and so on but this guarantees very little about the nature of the learning that is taking place, as Tasker (1981) observed. Activity may be necessary for some forms of knowledge construction but it is by no means sufficient. In particular, as is pointed out by Driver and elsewhere in this volume, science practical activity is rarely an end in itself:

> Many . . . practical lessons end abruptly when the prescribed task is complete and little, if any time is given to the interpretation of the results obtained, although this is just as important as the activity itself. Pupils need time to think around and consolidate the new ideas presented to them. After all, they may have developed their own ideas as a result of many years of experience. It is unlikely that they will easily adopt new ways of thinking as a result of one or two science lessons . . . perhaps the time has come to help children make more sense of those practical experiences. What is being suggested is not a return to a more didactic teaching, but an extension of the range of types of activities in science classes.
>
> (Driver 1983: 83)

In one respect, the currently established practical approach to school science in Britain stands out for having legitimised learning through social interaction, since pupils almost always carry out experimental work in small groups and it is generally accepted that they will talk to each other in the process. Whether this talk results in meaningful learning in science depends greatly on the design of the practical task and its context in the lesson. Practical tasks which are designed on a recipe basis, or with the principal aim of simply occupying the class, are likely to result at best in rote learning – and if that is what is wanted then there are surely better ways of promoting it.

Would you agree that there is more than one way to cook a potato? One way may suit one person and another may suit another. Some may like chips today and mash tomorrow. Forgive the obvious – but it's rather similar in teaching. The approaches in this section are not in competition or opposition, any more than chips are in opposition to mash. They are alternative teaching approaches, all based on understandings about learning. Of course, if teachers were teaching two or three students at a time, it would be possible to 'tune' the approaches to suit the needs of the people concerned. But in school-sized classes this isn't feasible. The solution in school is to provide a 'balanced menu', in other words to mix and vary the teaching approaches.

I Cognitive conflict

This is a teaching strategy that links well with Piaget's ideas. The psychological background is that if somebody experiences a surprise or a novelty, they may try to make sense of it in terms of what they know already. That would be known as 'assimilation'. But if they cannot manage this, they may amend their knowledge to make new sense of the novelty. In this process of change, known as 'accommodation', they are learning something.

Here is an illustration: some children connect an electric bell to a battery. They can hear it ringing loudly and see that the arm of the bell is moving. The teacher then produces a second, similar bell inside a glass jar. Everyone can see that the bell is connected to a battery and that its arm is moving like the first bell, but it can only just be heard. Why is this? (First cognitive conflict.) Pupils might assimilate the experience by suggesting that the glass is stopping the sound or that the arm is not hitting the sounder. The teacher, who has earlier pumped air from the jar, opens a valve to let air back in and the bell can now be heard clearly (second cognitive conflict). This is harder to assimilate! The intention is that pupils will accommodate a new idea, in this case that air can carry sound.

Scott *et al.* (1991) list several varieties of teaching approaches that use cognitive conflict. Cognitive conflict is a good strategy but it is not infallible. Some students presented with a surprise may just want to switch off. The teacher's skill is then to keep them engaged. Some students may have their ideas shaken but not stirred enough for them to make an instant switch to a new conceptual belief. They may need time to digest and reflect on what they have experienced. They may need further evidence to persuade them to adopt a new belief. Other students, especially those used to struggling with science, may feel threatened by the uncertainty of cognitive conflict. This may cause them to entrench, to cling firmly to a position, not because of its scientific plausibility but because it is there, something to hold on to. Clearly this calls for a degree of sensitivity and 'mind-reading' from the teacher. Despite these possible difficulties, well-managed cognitive conflict can be a highly effective teaching strategy in terms of promoting changes in students' concepts and beliefs.

2 Chunking

How many 'bits' of information can you hold simultaneously in your short-term memory? Here's a test: in a moment, look at the first letter in this line of text, and the first of the line below (or above) and the first of the line below that. Then look away. Can you remember the three letters? Easy! Try it again with more. What is your short-term memory capacity?

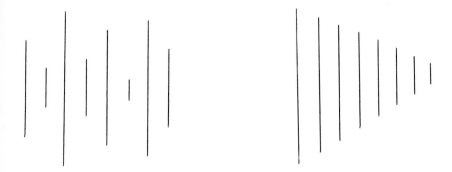

Figure 4.8 Matchstick patterns.

In a study which is famous for the simplicity of its conclusion , Miller (1956) found that most people can cope with roughly seven bits at once. Above that, errors creep in. So how do we recognise complex things, with many more than seven bits? The answer is that we 'chunk'. We learn how to make mental economies. Consider the two patterns in Figure 4.8.

The patterns are drawn from exactly the same elements, eight lines of different lengths. Why is the second pattern so much easier to recall? It's because we only need a few bits of information to conceptualise it. We chunk information about it into a few bits.

There are very many connected ideas in science. Teachers find it much easier than children to take overviews of topics. That is because teachers have learned to use bigger chunks. But when it comes to teaching, the skill is to find learner-sized chunks. This can be tricky: make the chunks too small and there are too many of them to join together; make them too big and errors creep in. Figure 4.9 illustrates how the teacher may think in big chunks but needs to rethink in smaller chunks for the students.

Teachers do not normally set out to teach students to chunk, either directly, or implicitly through presenting materials and ideas with gradually increasing complexity. As White (1988) notes there is much potential here for teaching to improve learning.

3 Diagnosing students' ideas

It is widely believed that learning is strongly influenced by what the learner already knows. When teachers first encounter this idea they are understandably bothered about coping with up to thirty different learners each with their own starting points. This would be impossible to deal with if all of the children had strikingly different ideas. Fortunately for class teaching however, there are often just a few commonly occurring alternatives amongst children's ideas. Some

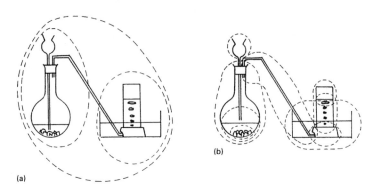

Figure 4.9 Hypothetical chunking of gas generation apparatus by (a) a teacher and (b) a
    student.
Source: White 1988.

examples were discussed earlier in this chapter. Research into children's pre-
teaching or 'prior' ideas has provided a platform on which science teaching can
build. It has shown that it is worthwhile for teachers to diagnose children's prior
ideas and that the results of the diagnosis are manageable: they can be used by
the teacher. A teacher summed this up neatly to me like this: 'I take my starting
point from the kids.'

There are at least three other good reasons for diagnosing students' knowledge:

1   to evaluate learning after teaching. This gives the teacher feedback on the
    effectiveness of her/his teaching;
2   to be able to map progression in the students' ideas;
3   to check for retention: in other words, to check whether new knowledge
    has been retained weeks or even months after the teaching.

Some practical ways of diagnosing students' ideas are illustrated in following
sections.

4 'Development of ideas' approach

Children have alternative ideas from the science community; all of the teaching
approaches in this chapter acknowledge that. In the development of ideas
approach (DoI), the aim is to teach children about the scientific ideas without
requiring them to reject their own. In this sense DoI contrasts with the use of
cognitive conflict. One version of DoI described by Brown and Clement (1989)
contains four stages. First the students' ideas are elicited, using a 'target
question'. Suppose for example that the teacher is trying to convince students
that there is a downward force on a ball which has been thrown in the air, even
when it stops at its highest point. (Students often find it hard to accept that a

stationary object can be accelerating.) The second stage is to find an analogous situation which is more plausible to the learners. This is called the 'anchor'. In the example, the teacher might ask a student to hold the ball near to where it reached its highest point and ask: 'do you need to use any force to keep the ball there?' If the students are unable to connect the anchor with the target, the teacher uses intermediate or 'bridging' analogies to help them. 'What if you take the force away by letting go?' 'We could keep the ball stationary at its top point by attaching a string to it and tying it to the ceiling. Does the string hold the ball up?' and so on. The teacher is working towards the fourth stage, which is to get the students to compare the anchor or bridging cases with the target.

Another version of DoI is to provide a concrete example before students meet a related but more abstract problem. Stavy (1991) gives the example of students observing evaporation of iodine and then attempting to understand the evaporation of acetone. The key is that iodine is visible after evaporation. This is the 'concrete' experience that helps students to cope with the additional abstraction caused by the acetone vapour's invisibility. The concrete case acts as a bridge from students' prior knowledge to their knowledge of the abstract case.

A more radical version of DoI has been described by Niedderer (1987). As far as science concepts and language are concerned, students often seem to inhabit two worlds: an everyday world and a world of science lessons (Solomon 1987). In the everyday world they (and the rest of us) talk about 'using energy', 'keeping the cold out', a football 'having a curl on it', the sun 'going down', ' not behaving like an animal' and so on. Solomon argued that children learn the appropriate words and propositions in science classes (e.g. 'energy cannot be created or destroyed') but these do not replace everyday ideas. Instead, they linger temporarily alongside and eventually fade away. Niedderer's aims are to encourage students to see the scientific view, to acknowledge differences between this and everyday views and to understand where both views came from. This final aim is strikingly distinct from traditional science teaching. However, since the traditional approach has failed in terms of public scientific literacy, it may be time to try something radically different.

5 Learning to learn: 'metacognition'

Compared with other animals, human beings are not only expert learners, we are also capable of metacognition. In evolutionary terms, metacognition is like having a cognitive turbo charger. We are born into a culture and we immediately learn from and within it. Culture directs us to take enormous short cuts. We don't bother learning how to use a flint tool because it's more useful to learn how to use the Internet. And it is easier to do that if someone guides us to take further short cuts. Learning like this is not arbitrary, it is tuned to help us get along successfully in our world. We don't have to think much about this ('shall I learn flint-sharpening today?') because we have some inherent knowledge about what is useful to learn. (For a current neurobiological perspective on this see

Edelman's discussion of 'value categories': Edelman 1992 Chapters 9 and 11.) Is it possible to go further than this inherent capacity for metacognition? It certainly is: we can not only learn to learn better, we can be taught to do so. White (1988) argues strongly that if students were taught to use appropriate 'cognitive strategies', their learning would accelerate apace. He states though (page 99), that 'revolutionary changes should occur in the organisation of schools, in curricula and in teaching methods' in order to achieve this, but that 'if it should prevail it will bring about the [most] major change to occur in the practice of teaching since the 19th century'. How can these cognitive strategies be taught? White makes several practical suggestions:

- *Student-generated questions.* The act of asking questions requires engagement and creative thought, two core cognitive strategies.
- *Purpose.* Tasker's study illustrated how students may embark on activities in an unthinking, recipe-following fashion. White argues that students should be taught to ask: 'What is this all about? What does it relate to? What am I supposed to do?'
- *Planning.* Some strategies for solving problems in science are better than others. Can students be taught how to plan problem-solving strategies?
- *Paraphrasing.* It is well known that you find out how well you know something when you try to teach it. Teaching involves rephrasing sets of ideas. Students can be taught how to do this: how to paraphrase a scientific argument or the solution to a problem. In my view this is a particularly valuable cognitive strategy to teach.

6 Questioning

Questioning is one of the most widely used teaching devices. It can take many forms. Even very young children quickly learn to decode peculiar-sounding teacher enquiries such as: 'Are you a packed lunch?' A general way of classifying teachers' questions is this: open, closed, pseudo. Pseudo-questions are not questions in an everyday sense. In these examples: 'Shall we start?' and 'John! What do you think you're doing?' either everyone knows that the teacher already knows the answer, or no answer is required. Some pseudo-questions are actually instructions: 'Question 1. Use the table to complete a graph of length against time.'

Questions that ask simply for the recall of information rarely evoke deep thinking. On the other hand, questions looking for explanation especially in the students' own words can prompt 'higher level thinking'. Compare these: '1. Does the sun set in the east or the west?' '2. Why does the sun appear to set in the west?' And: '1. Which drink cooled fastest?' '2. How did you decide which drink cooled fastest?' In each case question 1 simply asks for a statement whereas question 2 is looking for a connected thread of ideas. Connections are the hallmark of deeper thinking.

In research involving observation of 35 science lessons, a colleague and I classified the teachers' questions as follows:

Table 4.2 Classification of question types and corresponding mental operations

	No.	Description of questions	Types of mental operations	Examples of questions
LOWER-LEVEL THINKING	1	Recalling facts/events or remembering and repeating definitions from previous lessons. Included are questions that usually begin with *what, when, where*.	Recalling episodes	'Do you remember what we did two weeks ago?'
	2	*Describing* the elements of an experiment situation, *identifying* variables and providing simple relationships.	Judging	'How do these tubes vary?' 'Which bulb is the brightest?'
HIGHER-LEVEL THINKING	3	Questions that basically begin with '*how*'. Description of the procedure and the establishment of fair testing through a controlled experiment.	Justifying judgements (justification of procedures)	'How did you test whether the length of a tube affects the pitch of the note?' 'How did you establish a relationship between . . .?'
	4	Questions seeking *proof/evidence*.	Justifying judgements (justification of judgements)	'Does this prove that width makes a difference?' 'What evidence have you got for that?'
	5	Recognising the *pattern* in a dataset or describing the *trend* of a graph. (This category refers only to visual representations of data.)	Judging	'Can you see a pattern in the runs of heads?'
	6	Questions beginning with '*why*', seeking a reason behind the procedure followed.	Justifying judgements (justification of arguments or explanations)	'Why is this a wise decision?' 'Why is this fair?'
	7	'*What-if*' questions.	Hypothesising	'What would be the problem if . . .?' 'If I already have two heads in a row, then what is the chance of getting another head on the third throw?'
	8	Giving *predictions*.	Hypothesising	'Having in mind the previous results, could you tell me how far the next roller ball would go?'
	9	Getting to *conclusions*.	Reframing	'What is the whole point of sampling?' 'What did we learn about the fair test today?'

Source: Koufetta-Menicou and Scaife 2000.

The table indicates that low-level thinking is prompted by requests to recall, describe or identify. If we want students to think beyond the superficial, our questions should ask them to justify, explain, hypothesise, predict, reframe or sum up.

Whether a question is closed or open depends on the expected response. If the question presupposes an either/or option or a small range of possibilities it is closed: 'Is lithium a metal?' and 'Can you tell us the name of a halogen?' Open questions can have a wider range of possible responses: 'What do you think might happen if I put the sodium into the water bath?' and 'Where do you think plants get their food from?' All three of these general types of questions have their uses and, as is often the case in teaching, a mixture is probably a sound approach.

Study of children's reactions to questions reveals a surprising difference between open and closed questions (Waterman 1998). If children are asked questions that they can't make sense of, or they think are silly, they will tend to respond if the questions are closed but not if they are open. In the former case the child is not able to connect with the teacher's intended meaning, but produces a response that may hide the depth of misunderstanding from the teacher. In the latter case the teacher will not be so misled.

Mini strategies using questioning

The ideas below have come from observations of teaching in which questioning appeared helpful to students' learning. They come from too many teachers and student teachers to acknowledge!

- *Pausing.* A 13-year-old said to me: 'If you want to answer in our class you've got to be quick.' Nothing obviously wrong with that is there? Then she went on: 'The trouble is it's the same few boys who shoot their hands up first and the teacher always lets them answer.' White (1988) comments on how widespread this is in teaching. We fret about gaps in discussion, perhaps out of a concern not to lose momentum. But short pauses, (typically one second) are unhelpful. They encourage superficial impulsive thinking; they deny access to the discussion to students who prefer to think before speaking; and they may broadly suit boys more than girls. When the pause is longer, say 4 or 5 seconds, the message to the class is 'everyone think about this'.

- *Bouncing.* The 13-year-old above added a final comment: 'And then [the teacher] assumes the rest of the class have got it.' There are several ways round this problem. One fruitful way is to take a student's answer and 'bounce' it around the class: 'Do you agree with Jane's idea, Carl? Who else agrees? Vinod, what do you think? Why don't you think Jane is right, Sandra?' As these examples indicate, bouncing often leads to further development of ideas.

- *Wrong answers.* I don't believe that it is educationally sound for teachers always to correct wrong answers. Most answers mean that the student has given some attention and perhaps some deep thought to the question. Teachers can turn wrong answers into learning experiences: Teacher: 'Which do you think is denser, the water or the ice?' Student: 'The ice.' Teacher: 'Who agrees?' Teacher (to someone who agrees): 'What's you're reasoning?' Student: 'Because ice is a solid and molecules pack closer together in solids.' Teacher (to someone who disagrees): 'Why do you think the water is denser?' Student: 'Because the ice is floating on it.' In the first exchange the initial (wrong) answer has been used by the teacher to diagnose a misconception (that ice molecules are closer packed than liquid water molecules). The teacher's questioning has also led to a challenge to the faulty view from a peer. The challenge will be strengthened when the teacher's own views are introduced. The emphasis in this exchange was on learning; judgements about rightness and wrongness were used to support learning through thinking.

- *Third-party ideas.* An alternative to asking questions of a class directly is to ask them to judge other people's ideas. They may be more willing to do this than to risk putting forward their own ideas. This can be especially fruitful when the teacher picks topics from the list of common science misconceptions (see earlier in this chapter). Teacher: 'Some people think that there's no gravity on the moon because there's no air. What do you think of this?' 'Andie says green plants would die without light and water. Brett says they need food as well. Chelsea says they make their own food. Dean thinks they have to have air but he's not sure. Who do you agree with?' Questions like these would suit whole class or group work.

- *Diagnostic questioning.* The aim in using diagnostic questions is to obtain as clear a picture as possible of the students' ideas about a topic. (Reasons for diagnosing were discussed earlier.) The trouble is that students often assume that questions are being used to grade them and that they have to try to get the right answers. We don't want this in diagnostic teaching – we want the students' beliefs about science, not their beliefs about what we want. First, the students need to know that a diagnostic survey is not a test and their scores will not be identified. Second, the questions need wording in ways that elicit students' beliefs and don't stress the importance of being right. The question in Figure 4.7 is a good example. Contrast that with the following: 'Draw a circuit diagram of a bulb lit by a battery and use arrows to show the current flow.' This may be adequate for testing students but it certainly is not suitable for diagnosing their ideas. A useful strategy in making up diagnostic questions is to include words like 'you' and 'your'. This helps to communicate the intention of finding out about the students' own beliefs.

- *Turning telling into asking: Socratic questioning.* Two and a half millennia ago, according to Plato, the Greek philosopher Socrates demonstrated to his companion Meno that an uneducated slave boy could construct a solution to a quite difficult geometric problem. The point Socrates made to Meno was that the boy had accomplished the solution without being told anything. He was guided on the way only by Socrates' questions. Teaching using well-judged leading questions is sometimes known as Socratic questioning. Is this more effective than 'transmission teaching' in which the teacher lectures and tells things to the students? Some people argue that it is more effective because the students have to engage more deeply than in lectures in order to be able to answer the questions. And the answers to the questions are 'owned' by the students which may mean that they are highly plausible to them. Because ideas in science are strongly linked by causal connections there is much scope for Socratic questioning in the subject.

- *Curiosity.* I would like to conclude this survey of questioning in science teaching with a single simple notion that can act as a guide. If questioning is fuelled by curiosity about students' learning then it is highly likely to enhance learning.

7 PEOR: predict, explain, observe, react

Asking students to make predictions can be highly effective in promoting learning. This is especially so in science, where predictions linked to practical activities can be confirmed or confounded by the outcome. In the 'PEOR' cycle, students are first asked to make a prediction. This encourages engagement, interest and curiosity. It is important to follow predictions with questions asking for explanations. This discourages guessing and promotes higher-level thinking. Students next observe the activity and then they are asked for their reactions. There is plenty of scope in PEOR cycles for teacher-managed peer discussion, adding further stimulus to engagement and learning.

8 Knowledge retention

As infants, we learn a few words and then our vocabularies go on growing through to old age. We learn to crawl, then walk, then swim, and then perhaps ride a bike. By the time we might learn to drive a car we have acquired and retained much knowledge about moving. Such knowledge has proved stable; once learnt it tends not to be lost. Is this also the case with learning in formal science?

Consider the following account of Vanessa, an 11-year-old whose science lessons had included a topic on electric current. Vanessa was interviewed some months after the topic had been taught. She was asked to connect up a bulb to a battery, which she achieved quickly and correctly. She was then presented with the question shown in Figure 4.7, which she had previously encountered during the teaching of the topic.

Vanessa:	At first I thought it was Model B, because I didn't realise that if it was B the battery would go flat very soon. So now I think Model C is best . . . quite a bit of current comes into the bulb, and some of it wasted up. It can't take it all at once so some of it takes it back.
Interviewer:	Did you do things with meters? [*Experimentally test which model is valid.*]
Vanessa:	Yeah, we found that Model D worked with the meters. But I don't understand D. I know it works but I don't understand how it works.
Interviewer:	Did your teacher discuss it?
Vanessa:	Yes, and I kind of knew how that went . . . it made sense a little bit . . . but afterwards I thought of some other ideas . . . How did that work? . . . What happened? and, How did he explain . . .? I got muddled up. If you are not using any power in the bulb how is it going on? But I understand C.

(Osborne and Freyberg 1985: 25 and 96–7)

Vanessa's description of her thinking is revealing. She remembered that Model D was the official answer and indeed at the time of teaching 'it made sense a little bit'. But despite this she has chosen Model C. This is not arbitrary; her reasoning is that some of the current is 'wasted up'. It is evident that she has compacted the notions of current and energy into something that has properties of both. The formally sound view that: 'If you are not using any power in the bulb how is it going on?' has been made equivalent to current getting used up. Perhaps the key to Vanessa's selection is in the last sentence. She was able to answer Model D during the teaching, knowing that this was the appropriate answer for the formal context of the science class. But her belief in C, stemming from her construction of an adequately consistent rationale for understanding it, has resulted in Model C being retained in the longer term.

This trend of regression towards intuitive or internally consistent knowledge is also evident in the following data (Osborne and Freyberg 1985: 122) from a group of fifteen 11-year-olds who were given the same question as Vanessa:

Table 4.3 Changes in the views of a group of 11-year-olds over time

	A (%)	B (%)	C (%)	D (%)
Before lessons	0	7	86	7
After lessons	0	0	14	86
One year later	0	13	40	47

Source: Osborne and Freyberg 1985.

9 Progression

One of the DfEE requirements for new teachers is that they should plan teaching to achieve progression in students' learning. This is easier to say than do. Most science departments rely on published courses to present curriculum material in an appropriate sequence and at a suitable depth. A common approach is the 'spiral curriculum' in which topics are periodically revisited during a child's schooling, each time at a higher level. This ensures that the curriculum is organised sensibly for teaching but it cannot guarantee anything about children's learning. Some forms of assessment are needed to check that students' knowledge is progressing at a reasonable rate and to check the match between the curriculum and the students' capabilities. Ordinary pen-and-paper end-of-topic tests give some indication, but of what? A colleague and I have argued that traditional assessment tends to reward factual recall and low-level thinking in science (Abdullah and Scaife 1997). A different approach to checking progression is to use student interviews before and after teaching a topic. Interviews can be time consuming and it would only be practical for a teacher to survey a sample of students in a class. Nevertheless interviews can provide rich and detailed information about students' knowledge and understanding. We used semi-structured interviews, designed to keep students talking about the science topic but leaving them otherwise unconstrained. Interviews were taped and the responses were analysed using a framework derived from White and Gunstone (1992). Students' propositions (assertions and factual statements), episodes (usually autobiographical) and images were listed. They were then evaluated in terms of: 1. The total number of propositions, episodes and images; 2. Their precision or correspondence with scientific ideas appropriate for the age group; 3. Their self-consistency. We called these measures extent (E), precision (P) and consistency (C). A student's E score appeared to us to be a good indicator of the breadth of her/his knowledge whereas the quality of that knowledge, in other words the student's understanding of the topic, was indicated by a combination of the P and C scores.

Data was obtained for samples of students before and after topics were taught. This yielded indications of progression, not only in factual knowledge but also in understanding. Four distinct types of progression emerged from the various groups of students: 1. All three scores increased; 2. P and C increased but E decreased; 3. E increased but P and C decreased; 4. E and P increased but C decreased (Abdullah 1997). Students who showed progression of types 1 and 2 had improved their understanding, though over a narrower knowledge base in type 2. Those showing type 3 have learned some new scientific vocabulary but, in Piaget's terms, they have not accommodated the new experiences and they are 'disequilibrated', or confused. The students in this group need time to consolidate their new experiences and ideas. Those in group 4 are inconsistent. They have more scientifically precise ideas than before teaching but they are also holding on to other inconsistent views.

Armed with detailed knowledge such as this about the students' progression the teacher is in a good position to judge what to do next. Clearly it is unlikely that a single whole-class approach will suit all the students.

10 The 'Heineken effect'

You may have been wondering when ICT was going to appear in this chapter. In a way it already has, because it can be used just like any other resource to enhance teaching in the various ways described above. But ICT has some distinct characteristics of its own. It is well suited to self-managed learning, such as project and investigative work, although students probably benefit from 'scaffolding' – Bruner's term describing light-handed directing – without which there may be a risk that they will tour superficially through software. Another general advantage is that ICT is 'cool' at least in comparison to most science equipment. It may motivate students, some of whom would not otherwise be interested in science. Opportunities for peer teaching are likely to arise. Some students are more competent than their teachers at ICT and this has the potential to be very good for self-esteem (given support from the teacher).

As well as these broad learning opportunities, ICT offers some specific advantages. Current technology has the capability to sense, process and display data so quickly that it appears to human senses to be instant. Helen Brasell (1987) investigated the effect of differing delay times in the display of feedback to students who were experimenting with a motion sensor. The sensor recorded how far away the students were and the data were displayed graphically for the students to see. They were given instructions that required them to connect physical and graphical frames of reference. Brasell found longer-lasting, deeper learning when the delay times were short (below 25 seconds). The actual delay time in normal use is virtually zero; this was an impossibility prior to the arrival of ICT in science teaching. In this sense, ICT has opened up a new possibility for learning: it has reached parts of the mind that older technologies could not reach!

11 CASE: thinking skills

Does children's cognitive development take place at an inexorable rate, uninfluenced by external factors, or can it be speeded up? Some people believe that not only learning, but also rate of cognitive development, is dependent on the child's social and physical environment. Included in the child's environment, of course, is the school and the influence of teaching.

The Cognitive Acceleration through Science Education (CASE) project has grown from research which compared the stages of cognitive development typically found in secondary-aged children with the cognitive demands of various attainment standards in science courses, including the national science curriculum. The research examined, among other things, the extent to which science curricula matched students' current capabilities. Materials from the project have been published as a teaching package known as 'Thinking Science' (Adey 1995a). This package has been designed explicitly to encourage 'the development of thinking from concrete to formal operational' – in other words, it is based on the view that children's cognitive development *can* be accelerated through appropriate teaching. One reason for wanting to do this, according to the author, is because students will be unable to achieve standards equivalent to GCSE grade D or above unless they can use formal operational thinking. The themes of the activities in the package are: control of variables, proportionality, probability, compensation and equilibrium, combinations, correlation, classification, formal models and compound variables (see also Adey 1987a). As can be gathered from this list, the emphasis is on relatively 'content-free' processes. The authors describe this approach in teaching as 'intervention', as opposed to instruction.

The CASE materials were trialled with 11- and 12-year-old pupils in several schools by dedicating approximately one science session per fortnight to the project, for a period of two years. This amounted to approximately a quarter of the science curriculum time. Pupils from project and control classes were followed up age 16, to investigate the nature of any effects arising from the intervention. At the end of the two-year intervention programme, there were no significant differences between the two groups, which at least indicated that the programme had not disadvantaged the project group through disruption to their science courses! After this, however, the project students began to out-perform the control students, gradually drawing ahead up to and including their GCSE year. More intriguing still was a 'far-transfer' effect reported by the CASE team. There was evidence of the project students' attainment advancing more rapidly than that of the control students not only in science but also in mathematics and in English.

Some people are sceptical about any claims of long-term and far-transfer effects. On the other hand, the point has been made elsewhere that if the potential payoff is big enough, even the highly improbable would be worth exploring! This argument seems to have been persuasive, since increasing numbers of school science departments have adopted 'Thinking Science' alongside their key stage 3 science courses. Observations of 'CASE lessons' in action have suggested that it is a challenging and demanding scheme of work, both for students and for teachers. There are indications, however, that there is a potential payback, not only in terms of improved student attainment but also in increased interest in learning in both students and teachers. For a detailed description of the CASE project and associated research see Adey (1987b) and Adey and Shayer (1994).

12 The CLIS project

The Children's Learning in Science Project based at Leeds University has been responsible for much valuable research into children's ideas in science. The project built on these findings to devise teaching approaches that are broadly compatible with a constructivist viewpoint (see earlier in this chapter). The example that follows makes use of several teaching approaches outlined above, including diagnosing students' prior ideas, the PEOR teaching cycle and cognitive conflict.

Conservation of mass

Three year 8 classes had been working on the topic of dissolving. They had explored whether salt and sugar are still there when they dissolve. Most students had come to the view that salt and sugar *are* still there, even though they cannot be seen. The next topic, conservation of mass, was introduced with a worksheet (Figure 4.10) which asks for students' views about whether dissolving affects mass.

Of 66 students, 27 held the scientific view (B), while 34 expected the side with dissolved sugar to be lighter. Now aware of these views, the teachers devised an activity to help move students' ideas from their current positions towards the scientific view. (Rosalind Driver likens this to someone phoning you for directions; you would probably say first: 'Where are you now?') The activity used the 'Balance' worksheet (Figure 4.11) to take pupils through a 'PEOR cycle' (see page 92).

Groups of students discussed and recorded their predictions and then watched the four demonstrations. After this they wrote down and attempted to explain what they had seen. These events were recorded by CLIS researchers. Here are short extracts from pupils' discussion during one of the pre-publication trials. The demonstration involved the addition of red ink to the water and the discussion took place before pupils saw the outcome of the mixing:

S1:   No, it won't balance.
S2:   I think it will.
S3:   It will balance because, er . . .
S1:   It won't.
S4:   Maybe because it's a liquid.
S3:   So? It'll still be the same amount of liquid, won't it?
S4:   No, because the level will go *up* on that one there.
S3:   Yeah, I know, but you don't add owt!

These pupils are evidently engaged with the scientific issue. The comments show perception and thought, and they are challenging to each other's views. The key question, though, is this: can the PEOR cycle result in learning in science? In order to test this, the students were asked, after the demonstrations, to reconsider the 'Liz and Bob' worksheet (Figure 4.10). If they wanted to change their view they were asked to explain why. One student who did change wrote: 'The four experiments we did it came to same because it is the same amount of sugar and it got dissloved it is the same.' And that means norfing has been substracted or

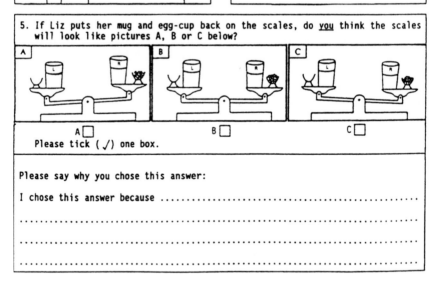

Figure 4.10 'Pre-teaching task used to elicit understanding of mass of dissolved substance'.
Source: Holding et al. 1990.

BALANCE

For each experiment:
PREDICT - what do you think will happen?
OBSERVE - what actually does happen?
EXPLAIN - why did that happen?

1. Glass stopper

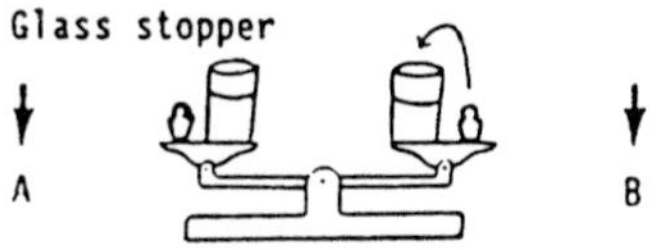

	Predict	Observe
A goes down		
B goes down		
Stays balanced		

Explain: ....

....

2. Rubber bung

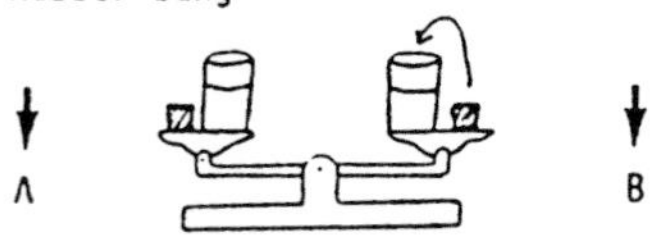

	Predict	Observe
A goes down		
B goes down		
Stays balanced		

Explain: ....

....

3. Chalk dust

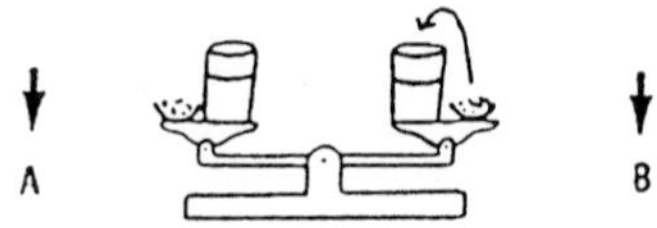

	Predict	Observe
A goes down		
B goes down		
Stays balanced		

Explain: ....

....

4. Red ink

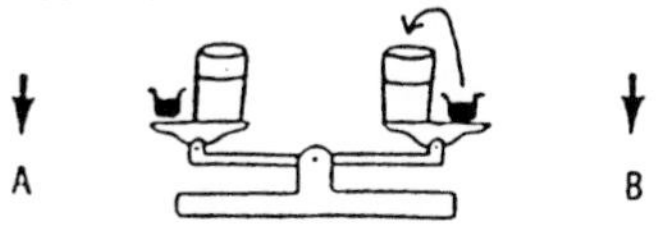

	Predict	Observe
A goes down		
B goes down		
Stays balanced		

Explain: ....

....

Figure 4.11 Intervention experiments.
Source: Holding *et al.* 1990.

added so it is the same.' After this stage, almost unanimous agreement was reached that when salt or sugar dissolved, there was no change in mass.

An anxiety sometimes expressed by teachers about the approach described above is that it is time consuming. Would it not be better for the teacher just to do a simple demonstration, showing that mass is conserved? If such a demonstration were a reliable and effective way of promoting desired learning then it would indeed be hard to justify the constructivist approach. On the other hand, observations which seem unequivocal to teachers may be interpreted quite differently by pupils. As Asoko *et al.* (1993) point out, 'pupils do not always "see" what they are intended to see, and even minute movements of the balance pointer may be taken as evidence that supports their view and refutes the science idea'. When people are deciding whether or not the meaning of an observation is significant, they base their judgement on prior knowledge. This prior knowledge is generally different for each of us and so it is no wonder if we reach different conclusions about the meanings of the observation.

13 A behavioural approach

A behavioural approach in teaching focuses on *training*. Behavioural theories emphasise the significance of *observable actions* rather than private consciousness. Behaviour is modified through a process known as conditioning, and change can be accelerated or inhibited by *reinforcement*.

Learning, in a behavioural context, is defined as an observed *response* to particular *stimuli*. This is the type of learning that is assessed in some British schools by tests such as 'SATs' (Standardised Assessment Tasks). The aim in behavioural teaching is therefore to identify and manage appropriate stimuli so as to bring about desired behaviour. Wheldall and Merrett (1989: 5) list what they call 'the five principles of Positive Teaching':

1   Teaching is concerned with the observable
2   Almost all classroom behaviour is learned
3   Learning involves change in behaviour
4   Behaviour changes as a result of its consequences
5   Behaviours are also influenced by classroom contexts

They argue that good teaching involves the maintenance of an appropriate environment for desired learning to take place, a sentiment strongly supported by Marland (1975), Rogers (1991) and others: 'We have been concerned with methods of encouraging pupils to behave in ways which will maximise their opportunities for learning appropriate academic skills and knowledge' (Wheldall and Merrett 1989: 18). Wheldall and Merrett describe how teachers can set about systematically categorising their pupils' behaviour as either desirable or undesirable. Potential stimuli and reinforcers for these behaviours can be identified and ultimately teachers' own behaviours can be modified so as to bring about desired changes in their pupils. A brief illustration, frequently found during initial teaching experience, is that of pupils repeatedly interrupting the teacher while he or she is carrying out a demonstration to the class. This is readily identifiable as undesirable behaviour! On closer observation it becomes apparent that whenever the teacher is interrupted in this way, he or she responds there and then to the pupil concerned. The teacher's response is acting as a reward to the pupil to continue to behave in the same way: the teacher is inadvertently 'reinforcing' the pupil's behaviour. As a result of this analysis, the teacher's action can be modified to prevent the reinforcement from taking place. Student teachers have found analysis such as this to be helpful because it offers a way forward, out of a difficult classroom problem. (I don't think that there is any single 'right' response in the situation described. Which of a range of alternative actions would be the most appropriate could only sensibly be judged in the teaching context).

John Holt (1964) warns strongly that if undue emphasis is placed on desired behavioural outcomes, students will find it worthwhile to learn responses simply to please, so as to get the teacher off their backs. However, a behavioural approach in teaching could complement many of the approaches described earlier. It may be attractive in circumstances in which the applicability of the 'cognitive' approaches seems limited. Safety procedures in laboratories, maintenance (as opposed to negotiation) of social rules for class discussion and training in the use of equipment are examples which might benefit from this approach.

Punishment, used as a tool for managing pupils' behaviour, can be wearing and stressful for teachers. It can become a routine response, which does little, ultimately, to bring about the change for which it is nominally employed – that of improving the quality of the learning environment. As an alternative to punishment Wheldall and Merrett's approach is likely to be less stressful, both to teachers and pupils, because it emphasises *positive reinforcement* of desired behaviour as a baseline teaching approach, rather than punishment of unwanted behaviour. Teachers who find themselves constantly repeating commands to pupils might, by reflecting on their actions in behavioural terms, be able to bring about significant improvements not only in their pupils' learning but also in the quality of their professional lives.

14 Planning for learning: an example

In this example the teacher is in the middle of a topic on current electricity with a mixed attainment class of 12-year-olds. We will take a detailed look at a lesson plan, focusing on the decisions the teacher has made to influence students' learning. The curriculum aims for the lesson are to promote learning about current flow, single-loop circuits, circuits with two branches, switches and the use of circuit diagrams. The teacher also wants to use the lesson to improve students' skills of logical thinking and their procedural skills in setting out and connecting circuits. In terms of class management the group is typical for children of this age.

Before the lesson the teacher will draw two large circuit diagrams on the board: one very simple and one containing branches and switches. He knows (from Piaget) that this abstract representation will be difficult for many of the students to grasp. To help their learning he needs to make as many links as possible with 'concrete' experiences. His plan is to start with a demonstration of a very simple circuit and to use questions and discussion to assess the collective ZPD (Vygotsky) of the class.

The electrical components are fairly small, which is problematic for demonstrating. He wants the students to be able to identify all of the components in the demonstration circuit and to see how they are joined together. He will then be able to 'bridge' between the concrete experience of seeing the circuit and the abstract circuit diagram. To make the demonstration more concrete the teacher has prepared some coloured cards, with the names of electrical components on them. He plans to lay the cards out on the demonstration table in exactly the same configuration as in the first diagram on the board. When he puts the components on the cards he will put the battery the same way round as in the diagram – he learned this idea originally from some students who were having difficulty sorting out the plus and minus connections between battery holders and meters. The teacher also noticed that because the battery holders were opaque it would not be obvious that batteries were inside them. To reduce students' guesswork he wrote 'BATTERY' in large letters on the sides of the holders. The other components (bulbs, switches, wires) were easy to identify.

When the teacher has laid the components on the cards he will check a sample of students by bouncing questions to see whether they are satisfied that the arrangement matches the layout of the diagram. He will then connect up the wires, pointing out practical matters on the way: 'To unplug, pull on the plug not the wire'; 'It doesn't matter what colour wires you use.' He has done enough electricity teaching to know that it is worth having some spares handy, especially bulbs. This will help give the students confidence in him. He has also requested a multi-meter with the equipment.

After connecting the simple circuit, he will give a concrete demonstration of the flow of current by tracing a path round the circuit with his finger. He will tell the students to use this method when they set up their own circuits later.

Next he plans to progress to the more complex circuit (Figure 4.12). However, he can't be sure in advance that the students will be ready to make this leap, so he will use questions and discussions to assess their new ZPD. If necessary he will set up an intermediate demonstration. He will use cards again and lay out the components until the students are satisfied that the arrangement matches the second diagram. The new circuit contains three switches so he has made up three coloured cards labelled ON and OFF on either side. This is because he wants the students to make deductions about the bulbs in terms of the switches and it will not be obvious from the switches themselves whether they are on or off. He is going to use a PEOR cycle with this circuit. For each on–off arrangement of the switches the students have to predict which bulbs

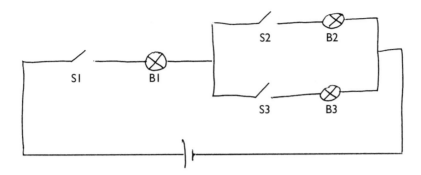

Figure 4.12 Circuit with two branches.

Table 4.4 Switch and bulb logic table

S1	S2	S3	B1	B2	B3
OFF	OFF	OFF			
OFF	OFF	ON			
OFF	ON	OFF			

will be on. The teacher plans to draw a logic table on the board, to be filled in by a volunteer during the PEOR discussion (Table 4.4). He then plans another PEOR cycle in which they have to predict which switches need to be on to obtain various arrangements of lit bulbs.

In the PEOR cycles he will use various types of questions and questioning: Socratic, looking for explanation, highlighting cognitive conflict, exploiting wrong answers, bouncing. All the time he will be trying to assess the students' ideas and judging how to respond.

Parts of this account involves formal planning such as preparing the cards and the blackboard. Other parts come from habits that the teacher has learned, like seeing through the students' eyes and continually checking their knowledge, using what he knows about learning.

A daft idea: which is the best?

We live in a culture which celebrates being 'best', especially when being best is said to accord with common wisdom or current values. Complex systems like human beings, however, do not readily lend themselves to such a simplified measure. It is one thing to try to answer: 'Which is the best size for the print in this book?' and quite another thing to address the question: 'Who is the world's best author?'

None of the approaches described above is claimed to be the best. It has not been an aim of this chapter to come to a judgement of a 'best buy', for that would have been an artificial and a misleading simplification. The approaches have been included because there is merit in each and each merits consideration. My guess is that there will be times when each is tremendously effective in promoting learning.

Glossary

This is not a list of dictionary definitions, it is an attempt to clarify the sense in which certain important words have been used in this chapter.

Ability   When used to describe a person as a whole this is a defunct and unhelpful notion. No such single word reliably predicts a person's future accomplishments. It may be useful though when used in specific contexts, e.g. 'Jo has musical ability'. Note that if we don't *show* ability, it doesn't mean that we have low (or even no) ability. The two are often confused. The claim for example, that 'Albert has little mathematical ability' is actually an admission that so far nobody has seen much mathematical ability in Albert. Something like that was said of Einstein.

Affective domain   Mental activity associated with feelings and emotions (sometimes also includes intentions).

Development   A result of changes that tend to occur over longer time-scales than in learning. Developmental changes tend to be more reliably permanent that changes resulting from learning. But learning and development are not clearly distinct: do birds learn to fly or develop to fly?

Knowledge   In this chapter I have taken knowledge to refer to something that a person has: I have knowledge by virtue of the way my neurons or neuronal groups interconnect. These connections depend on my entire life history. One of the things that influenced them was my education. Not everyone shares this view however, and this is one of the richly developing areas on the boundaries between education, psychology, philosophy, neuroscience, sociology and artificial intelligence. Further reading: Bickhard (1997), Churchland (1994), Dennett (1991), Edelman (1992), Harré (1986), Phillips (1997), Piaget (1972), Searle (1997), Vygotsky (1978).

Learning   The process by which changes occur in knowledge, skills, understanding, beliefs, values and attitudes.

Ontology, ontic   To do with the idea *being*, or of *what is*. A branch of metaphysics concerned with being in the abstract.

Pedagogy   The science, art and craft of teaching.

Teaching   Lecturing, instructing or telling ('transmission teaching'); also modelling, questioning, diagnosing, facilitating, coaching and more.

Understanding   A person's current understanding is their current capacity to apply knowledge and skills appropriately in various contexts. Understanding is not separate from knowledge and skills; to comment on someone's understanding is to comment on the quality, and particularly the connectedness, of their knowledge and skills.

Notes

1   For a short summary of Piaget's theory of intellectual development see Donaldson (1978). Donaldson argues that children's thinking may be less constrained by stages of development than was proposed by Piaget. She suggests that a crucial factor is the set of interpersonal contexts in which children's thinking develops.
2   *Common Knowledge* by Edwards and Mercer (1987) contains detailed instances in which classroom discussion is analysed in terms of the *common meaning* made of it by teacher and pupils.
3   Large samples of children have been surveyed by the Assessment of Performance Unit (APU) to investigate, among other things, the knowledge and understanding that children had in science. Summary reports, describing main findings and implications for teaching, are available from the Association for Science Education, College Lane, Hatfield, Herts AL10 9AA.
4   Rosalind Driver's paper (Driver 1989) takes a broad-based and pragmatic look at the implementation of a constructivist teaching scheme. She adds flesh to the bones described above, in the section on teaching models.
5   The generative learning approach to teaching described in Osborne and Freyberg (1985: 109) is based on Wittrock's 'generative' model of learning. There is much in common between this and the constructivist model of learning described by Driver and Bell (1985) and summarised above. For a summary of the generative learning model see Osborne and Freyberg (1985: 83).

References and further reading

Abdullah, A.T.S. (1997) 'Learning science in primary school: An investigation of children's knowledge and understanding of science concepts', unpublished Ph.D. thesis, University of Sheffield.

Abdullah, A.T.S. and Scaife, J.A. (1997) 'Using interviews to assess children's understanding of science concepts', *School Science Review*, June 1997, vol. 78, no. 285, pp. 79–84.

Adey, P. (1987a) 'Science develops logical thinking – doesn't it? Part 1. Abstract thinking and school science', *School Science Review*, June 1987, pp. 622–30.

Adey, P. (1987b) 'Science develops logical thinking – doesn't it? Part 2. The CASE for science', *School Science Review*, September 1987, pp. 17–27.

Adey, P. (1995a) *Thinking Science*, 1995 edn., Walton-on-Thames: Nelson.

Adey, P. (1995b) 'Barmy theories', *School Science Review*, March 1995, vol. 76, no. 276, pp. 95–100.

Adey, P. and Shayer, M. (1994) *Really Raising Standards*, London: Routledge.

Asoko, H., Leach, J., and Scott, P. (1993) 'Learning science', in R. Hull (ed.) *Association for Science Education Secondary Science Teachers' Handbook*, Hemel Hempstead: Simon and Shuster.

Ausubel, D.P. (1963) *The Psychology of Meaningful Verbal Learning*, New York: Grune and Stratton.

Bentley, D. and Watts, M. (1989) (eds) *Learning and Teaching in School Science: Practical Alternatives*, Milton Keynes: Open University Press.

Bickhard, M. H. (1997) 'Constructivism and relativisms: a shopper's guide', *Science and Education*, January 1997, vol. 6, nos. 1 and 2, pp. 29–42.

Brasell, H. (1987) 'The effect of real-time laboratory graphing on learning graphic representations of distance and velocity', *Journal of Research in Science Teaching*, 24(4), 385–95.

Broadfoot, P. (1998) 'Don't forget the confidence factor', *Times Educational Supplement*, 6 November, 1998, p. 25.

Brook, A., Briggs, H., Bell, B. and Driver, R. (1984) *Aspects of Secondary Students' Understanding of Heat: Summary Report*, Leeds: CLIS Project.

Brown, D.E. and Clement, J. (1989) 'Overcoming misconceptions by analogical reasoning: abstract transfer versus explanatory model construction', *Instructional Science*, no. 18, pp. 237–61.

Bruner, J. (1964) 'The course of cognitive growth', *American Psychologist*, no. 19, pp. 1–16.

Bruner, J. (1985) 'Vygotsky: a historical and conceptual perspective', in J. Wertsch (ed.) *Culture, Communication and Cognition: Vygotskian Perspectives*, Cambridge: Cambridge University Press.

Carré, C. (1981) *Language, Teaching and Learning: Science*, London: Ward Lock.

Champagne, A.B., Gunstone, R.F. and Klopfer, L.E. (1985) 'Effecting changes in cognitive structures among physics students', in West, L.H.T. and Pines, A.L. (eds) *Cognitive Structure and Conceptual Change*. Orlando, Florida: Academic Press.

Churchland, Paul M. (1994) *Matter and Consciousness* (revised edn.), London: Bradford Books.

Claxton, G. (1989) 'Cognition doesn't matter if you're scared, depressed or bored', in P. Adey (ed.) *Adolescent Development and School Science*, London: Falmer.

Dennett, D.C. (1991) *Consciousness Explained*, London: Penguin.

Department for Education and Employment (1998), 'Teaching: High status, high standards', Circular No. 4/98 (also available on the Internet via http://www.open.gov.uk/).

Donaldson, M. (1978) *Children's Minds*, reprinted 1985, London: Fontana.

Dreyfuss, A. and Jungwirth, E. (1989) 'The pupil and the living cell: a taxonomy of dysfunctional ideas about an abstract idea', *Journal of Biological Education*, 23, no. 1, 49–55.

Driver, R. (1983) *The Pupil as Scientist?*, Milton Keynes: Open University Press.

Driver, R. (1989) 'Changing conceptions', in P. Adey (ed.) *Adolescent Development and School Science*, London: Falmer.

Driver, R. and Bell, B. (1985) 'Students' thinking and the learning of science: a constructivist view', *School Science Review*, March 1986, pp. 443–56.

Driver, R., Guesne, E. and Tiberghien, A. (1985) *Children's Ideas in Science*, Milton Keynes: Open University Press.

Driver, R., Squires, A., Rushworth, P. and Wood-Robinson, V. (1994) *Making Sense of Secondary Science*, London: Routledge.

Edelman, G. (1992) *Bright air, brilliant fire: on the matter of the mind*, London: Penguin.

Edwards, D. and Mercer, N. (1987) *Common Knowledge*, reprinted 1993, London: Routledge.

Gagné, R.M. (1977) *The conditions of learning* (3rd edn.), London: Holt, Rinehart and Winston.

Gardner, H. (1993a) 'Lost youth', *The Guardian (Education)*, 12 October 1993, p. 6.

Gardner, H. (1993b) *Frames of Mind: The Theory of Multiple Intelligences* (2nd edn.), London: Falmer.

Glasersfeld, E. von (1989) 'Cognition, construction of knowledge and teaching' *Synthese*, no. 80, pp. 121–40.

Glasersfeld, E. von, (1991) 'Knowing without metaphysics: aspects of the radical constructivist position', in F. Steier (ed.) *Research and Reflexivity*, London: Sage.

Glasersfeld, E. von (1995) *Radical Constructivism*, London: Falmer.

Harré, R. (1986) 'An outline of the social constructionist viewpoint', in Harré, R. (ed.) *The Social Construction of Emotions*. Oxford: Blackwell.

Head, J. (1982) 'What can psychology contribute to science education?', *School Science Review*, June 1982, pp. 631–42.

Head, J. (1989) 'The affective constraints on learning science', in P. Adey (ed.) *Adolescent Development and School Science*, London: Falmer.

Holding, B., Johnston, K. and Scott, P. (1990) *Interactive Teaching in Science: Workshops for Training Courses*, Workshop 9: Diagnostic teaching in science classrooms, CLIS project, Hatfield: Association for Science Education.

Holt, J. (1964) *How Children Fail*, revised edn. 1990, London: Penguin.

Howe, A.C. (1996) 'Development of science concepts within a Vygotskian framework', *Science Education*, vol. 80, no. 1, pp. 35–51.

Koufetta-Menicou C. and Scaife, J.A. (2000) 'The types of questions asked by science teachers and their importance for science teaching', *School Science Review (in press)*.

Kyle, W.C. Jr. (1995) Editorial, *Journal of Research in Science Teaching*, no. 32, p. 9.

Lawson, A. and Renner, J. (1978) 'Relationships of science subject matter and developmental levels of learners', *Journal of Research in Science Teaching*, no. 15, pp. 465–78.

Marland, M. (1975) *The Craft of the Classroom*, London: Heinemann.

Maturana, H. (1991) 'Science and daily life: the ontology of scientific explanations', in F. Steier (ed.) *Research and Reflexivity*, London: Sage.

Millar, R. (1993) 'Science education and public understanding of science', in R. Hull (ed.) *Association for Science Education Secondary Science Teachers' Handbook*, Hemel Hempstead: Simon and Shuster.

Miller, G.A. (1956) 'The magical number seven, plus or minus two: some limits on our capacity for processing information', *Psychological Review*, 63, 81–97.

Needham, R. (1987) *Teaching Strategies for Developing Understanding in Science*, Leeds: CLIS Project.

Newman, F. and Holzman, L. (1993) *Lev Vygotsky: Revolutionary Scientist*, London: Routledge.

Niedderer, H. (1987) 'A teaching strategy based on students' alternative frameworks – theoretical conceptions and examples', in *Proceedings of the Second International Seminar. Misconceptions and Educational Strategies in Science and Mathematics 2*, pp. 360–7, Cornell University.

Osborne, R. and Freyberg, P. (1985) *Learning in Science*, Auckland: Heinemann.

Phillips, D.C. (1997) 'Coming to grips with radical social constructivism', *Science and Education*, January 1997, vol. 6, nos. 1 and 2, pp. 85–104.

Piaget, J. (1972) *The Principles of Genetic Epistemology*. London: Routledge and Kegan Paul.

Rogers, B. (1991) *You Know the Fair Rule*, Harlow: Longman.

Salmon, P. (1995) *Psychology in the Classroom*, London: Cassell.

Scott, P. (1987) *A Constructivist View of Learning and Teaching in Science*, Leeds: CLIS Project.

Scott, P.H., Asoko, H.M. and Driver, R.H. (1991) 'Teaching for conceptual change: a review of strategies', in Duit, R., Goldberg, F. and Niedderer, H. (eds) *Research in Physics Learning: Theoretical Issues and Empirical Studies*. Proceedings of an International Workshop. (Available on the Internet at: http://www.physics.ohio-state.edu/~jossem/ICPE/TOC.html)

Searle, J. (1997) *The Mystery of Consciousness*, London: Granta.

Selley, N.J. (1989) 'Philosophies of science and their relation to scientific processes and the science curriculum', in J.J.Wellington (ed.) *Skills and Processes in Science Education*, London: Routledge.

Shamos, M.H. (1995) *The Myth of Scientific Literacy*. New Brunswick, New Jersey: Rutgers University Press.

Shayer, M. and Adey, P. (1981) *Towards a Science of Science Teaching*, London: Heinemann.

Shayer, M., Kuchemann, D.E. and Wylam, H. (1976) 'The distribution of Piagetian stages of thinking in British middle and secondary school children', *British Journal of Educational Psychology*, no. 46, pp. 164–73.

Solomon, J. (1987) 'Social influences on the construction of pupils' understanding of science', *Studies in Science Education*, no. 14, pp. 63–82.

Solomon, J. (1989) 'Social influence or cognitive growth?', in P. Adey (ed.) *Adolescent Development and School Science*, London: Falmer.

Stavy, R. (1991) 'Using analogy to overcome misconceptions about conservation of matter', *Journal of Research in Science Teaching*, vol. 8, no. 4, pp. 305–13.

Tasker, R. (1981) 'Children's views and classroom experiences', *The Australian Science Teachers' Journal*, vol. 27, no. 3, pp. 33–7.

Vygotsky, L.S. (1978) *Mind in Society: The Development of Higher Psychological Processes*, London: Harvard University Press.

Waterman, A. (1998) Private communication, 19.11.1998, University of Sheffield Psychology Department.

Wheldall, K. and Merrett, F. (1989) *Positive Teaching in the Secondary School*, London: Paul Chapman Publishing.

White, R.T. (1988) *Learning Science*, Oxford: Blackwell.

White, R.T. and Gunstone, R. (1992) *Probing Understanding*, London: Falmer.

Chapter 5

Planning and managing learning in science

In a sense, the whole of this book is about planning and managing learning in science. This chapter, however, is aimed solely at offering practical ideas, frameworks and guidelines on preparing for and managing learning in science. They are presented for readers to consider, with a minimum of discussion: suggestions for further reading therefore are important and lengthy.

Planning and preparing

Schemes of work

The first task for many teachers is to prepare a scheme of work to cover perhaps from a half-term's to a year's work in science. This is usually a broad outline stating in brief what is to be taught lesson by lesson and often how it is to be taught, with perhaps additional notes on the resources needed. This is often a shared activity in a science department which achieves several aims:

- a shared, co-ordinated approach to the curriculum for a given year group
- a division and saving of labour amongst staff
- on a practical level, a guide which can help in the case of staff absence
- a record of the coverage of the curriculum (which should form the basis of the scheme)
- a record which can be used in liaison between schools, for example junior to secondary

What might a scheme of work for secondary science look like? My own view is that it should be clear and concise with the detail coming in the lesson plan. The starting point is to examine the relevant curriculum area and then to divide it into convenient themes, topics or areas of study. A possible format is shown in Table 5.1 below, but readers are encouraged to look around at other ideas and formats in order to develop their own, which they and the school they work in are happy with.

Table 5.1 Headings for a scheme of work

Area/theme of study (for example, the environment, energy, force, health and diet)

LESSON ONE (for example, Your surroundings, What is energy? Feeling forces, Eating for health, etc.)

Lesson aims:

Content/activity

Learning and teaching ideas, for example, demonstration, circus, role-play

Resources needed (special notes on safety)

Assessment plans and opportunities

Links to other parts of the curriculum

LESSON TWO . . . and so on.

Planning individual lessons

Planning each lesson within a scheme of work is the next stage – a somewhat enigmatic activity in that beginning teachers find it extremely time consuming and demanding whereas experienced teachers are able to give the impression that there is absolutely nothing to it. Appearances are misleading: lesson planning is a vitally important part of good teaching, not only in producing a well-structured, varied, carefully paced, well-timed and scientifically correct lesson but also in ensuring good management and control. Good lesson planning is the first step to good control and discipline. Pupils can see for themselves if a lesson has been carefully thought through, clearly structured and pitched at the right level – indeed, it is a good teaching ploy to outline the what, the why and the how of a lesson at the outset. Surely teachers should tell pupils what they are about to do, how, why and for how long?

There are almost as many schools of thought on lesson planning as there are schools. This section offers a fairly traditional view and format for lesson planning for readers to consider. In another chapter an alternative view is offered from a 'constructivist' perspective, in which the lesson begins with the pupils' own conceptions of a concept or topic and the lesson is based upon that foundation. This obviously demands much greater flexibility and spontaneity on the part of the teacher. The ideas offered below take a much more content- and teacher-led perspective.

From this perspective, a lesson plan should include at least the following ten elements:

1 Basic information. for example, the class, time, room, etc.
2 The aims of the lesson, i.e. what the pupils should know/be able to do/understand at the end of the lesson which they did not know/were not

able to do/did not understand when they walked in. These might be phrased in terms of cognitive aims, for example, recall, explain, understand, calculate, interpret, classify, etc.; or affective aims, for example, appreciate, enjoy, be aware of, gain a liking for, etc.; or 'doing' aims, for example, measure, observe, carry out, choose, etc.

3   The resources needed: What equipment will be needed? Which visual aids? How will it be organised and distributed in the room?

4   Safety notes – more on this later.

5   The overall structure for the lesson itself, for example, introduction, development, conclusion.

6   Detail (greater or lesser depending on preference) within that structure. Some people like to write virtually a script; others confine themselves to listing the questions they will ask; others use the briefest of notes.

7   Indication of timing, perhaps in a margin in the side.

8   Notes indicating what the teacher and the pupils are doing in any given part of the lesson, for example, 'teacher activity/pupil activity'. This can be valuable in ensuring the variety and pacing of a lesson.

9   Homework ideas (where needed).

10 Space for evaluation (to be done after the lesson): a short section is needed to consider the progress of the lesson, and whether it achieved its aims, to list points to remember for next time, how you would do it differently if you taught it again!

A possible format or proforma for constructing lessons is presented in Table 5.2. Readers may wish to use it and gradually adapt it for themselves – lesson planning is quite rightly an activity which will vary from one teacher and one school to another. What is unacceptable, in my view, is not to plan at all.

A very different approach to lesson planning will be taken by those who adopt a constructivist view of teaching and learning in science. This is explored fully in Chapter 4, but in brief the lesson will begin with the elicitation of children's ideas, for example, by getting children to explore their own conceptions and ideas (on, say, energy, force, pressure, the environment, health, fuels, growth, evolution) with each other and the teacher. This would form the starting point of the lesson.

Keeping a lesson file

One of the things that students on teaching practice are widely expected to do, and yet experienced teachers are strangely reluctant to be seen with, is a lesson file. In my view, it is a necessary part of professional teaching, even if seasoned teachers pretend that they don't have one or don't need one (in reality, they are either subtle or they have a filing cabinet instead of an arch folder). Lesson files

Table 5.2 A possible lesson plan format

A	*Basic information*

A   *Basic information*

Class..   Date and time ....

Number of pupils ....   Place ....

....

Memo, e.g. homework reminder

....

Topic

....

B   *Resources needed*
   [NB Safety points:]

C   *Aims and objectives*
   Skills? Knowledge? Attitudes?

D   *Lesson summary (main section)*

TIME	ACTIVITY	NOTES AND COMMENTS	AIMS
0–5 mins	Introduction/ appetiser	Space for notes	
5–10	Development	(further expansion on separate pages if necessary)	
	Summary or conclusion		
e.g. 50 mins	Trailer for next lesson		

E *Evaluation and reflection*
   How did it go? Did you achieve your aims? Feedback from pupils/other teachers?

can usefully contain at least the following:

- schemes of work for each year/class
- class lists and records, with essential information, for example on very special needs
- seating plans (if used)
- plans for individual lessons, and evaluations
- photographic records, for example, of posters produced. wall displays, practical work, problem-solving activities, etc.
- samples of pupils' work
- OHP transparencies
- worksheets, DARTS, etc.

Asking questions

One of the activities that teachers engage in whatever their view of learning or lesson planning is that of asking questions. Indeed there is probably no other context in life (except perhaps the Houses of Parliament) where so many questions are asked by so few of so many. One estimate is that teachers ask questions for one-third of their classroom time with a total on average of 30,000 questions per year. Some teachers ask sensible, useful probing questions of pupils spontaneously and naturally – I would suggest that these Socratic people are few and far between. Most of us need to plan and prepare our questioning even to the extent of writing them into the lesson plan. Time spent on this can avoid embarrassment and disruption in the classroom. A question such as 'Where can I find sea-water?' is likely to lead to either dumb disbelief that any adult could ask such a thing, or worse still loud shouts of 'Skegness', 'Blackpool', or 'Hastings', depending on the region. Teachers need to examine carefully four aspects of questioning:

1   *Why* they should ask questions at all?
2   *When* are the best times to ask them?
3   How should questions be posed and presented, i.e. what makes for a good questioning technique?
4   *What* types of question can teachers ask?

The four aspects are closely interrelated: for example, the time and reason for asking a question will determine the technique and tone used – this should be remembered as we take each aspect in turn. A large amount has been said and written about questioning (see further reading); what follows below is a brief, potted summary.

Why ask questions?

There are many good reasons for asking questions in a classroom, including the following:

- to gain and keep attention, i.e. as a means of control;
- to get pupils to think;
- to keep them active and attentive, i.e. to avoid spoon-feeding;
- to stimulate curiosity and interest;
- to test/confirm their knowledge or understanding;
- to identify/diagnose any problems in learning, recall or understanding;
- to lead a class step-by-step through a topic or an experiment, i.e. Socratic questioning, 'bringing things out';
- to elicit pupils' prior knowledge or conceptions, i. e. finding out where they are already;
- to go over/revise a topic, for example at the end of a lesson or at the start of a new one;

- to gain feedback on whether and what they have learnt, to evaluate the lesson, for example 'Have aims been achieved?'.

When to ask questions?

The reasons for asking questions are connected with the best times to ask them, for example:

1   at the start, during the introduction, for example, to give a link with the previous lesson, to revise and reinforce earlier learning, to elicit pupils' ideas;
2   during the development of the lesson, for example, using key questions to guide pupils' thinking or to formulate a problem, working out the right steps, procedures and sequence for a practical instead of simply giving instructions;
3   during class activity, for example to sort out problems in small groups or with individuals;
4   at the end of a class activity, for example, to pool results, to consider results, to work towards a conclusion;
5   at the end of a lesson, for example, to go over, revise, reinforce, evaluate, lead up to the next lesson.

What kind of questions can be asked?

There are two important ways of classifying questions. First, questions can be grouped according to whether they are open or closed.

Closed questions usually have one correct, often short answer – for example, 'What is the symbol used for sodium?' or 'What is the capital of England?'. The teacher usually wants pupils to give an answer which she or he already knows. If there is a particular correct answer which the teacher is seeking, such as trachea rather than windpipe, then closed questions often become a 'guess what's in my head?' exercise.

With open questions a variety of responses can be acceptable, such as 'Why did London become the capital of England?'. They often ask what the pupils are thinking, and there will be more than one correct answer – however, for many teachers, some answers are more correct than others! In other words, except perhaps in a genuine brainstorming session, few questions are genuinely totally open. Thus a question like 'What did you notice about the copper as we heated it?' may invite many responses whereas the teacher may be seeking only one.

Second, questions can also be grouped by the intellectual demand made by the question. It may require any of the following:

- Factual recall, for example, 'Which gas makes up 0.03 per cent of the air?' or 'Which ore does iron come from?'. This will obviously involve asking closed questions.

- Understanding and application of a formula, a rule, a law, a theory, etc., for example, 'If a person lifts a weight of 50 newtons from the ground onto a shelf two metres above it, how much work has she done?'. (These are generally closed questions.)
- Analysis and evaluation of, for example, a process, a material and its use, an energy source, or a set of data. Analysis may sometimes have one correct answer, for example, in analysing data from a table, but evaluation may invite several 'correct' responses, provided they are based on careful consideration and analysis, such as, 'What are the benefits and drawbacks of using nuclear fission to provide energy?'.
- Predicting and hypothesising, for example, 'What do you think will happen if . . .?'.
- Interpreting and explaining, for example, 'Why did the wire become hot?'.
- Inferring, for example, 'If we add more weights to this spring what will happen?' (cf. predicting).

These are just some of the ways of classifying questions; such a classification is not definitive and there is also much overlap between the categories. Often we cannot tell if we are predicting, hypothesising or inferring – the three go together. But a classification of this kind is useful for two reasons. First of all, in lesson planning and evaluation, teachers can prepare and examine their questions to see if they are asking a fair balance. Are all their questions of the closed, factual-recall kind? Do they ask pupils to speculate, predict and hypothesise? Do they give opportunities for weighing up pros and cons, analysing points of view and assessing benefits and drawbacks, i.e. evaluation? These are all essential features of the science national curriculum.

Thus a classification of questions asked (in both spoken and written form) is useful in lesson planning and in ensuring coverage of the curriculum. It is also vital in considering assessment of students' learning.

How should questions be prepared and delivered in a classroom?

The final aspect of questioning is the 'how?'. Table 5.3 offers a set of guidelines on preparing and phrasing questions, and on presenting them to a class.

Safety issues

Safety in the lab is not just an important issue – it is the issue which overrides all others. In other words, whatever good reasons (educational, motivational or any other) there are for doing an activity or a demonstration, IF IT IS UNSAFE OR UNHEALTHY IN ANY WAY THEN DO NOT DO IT! This is the simple and cardinal rule. Having said that, there are many activities that can be carried out safely in science, given the right precautions, management and conditions.

Table 5.3 Guidelines for questioning

Preparing and phrasing questions

- Prepare key questions in advance, using the categories above.
- Relate the questions to the aims of the lesson.
- Phrase the questions clearly and at the right language level.
- Avoid ambiguous wording.
- Beware of 'nonsense' questions, for example 'Why does a pig have four legs?'; general questions, for example 'Where can we find sea-water', and other questions that invite stupid answers, for example 'What do you all do at least once a day?'.
- Make sure that questions are carefully sequenced.

Presenting and delivering questions

- Position yourself and the class carefully – ensure that you can see and be seen.
- Insist on the use of hands rather than shouting out.
- Spread questions around the class – look for a balance, such as back and front, male and female.
- Use pupils' names in directing and responding to questions.
- Draw ideas out from the pupils – don't give too much too soon.
- If the classroom situation allows it, keep probing and prompting in order to extend pupils' thinking, for example 'What do you mean by that . . .?', 'And then what might happen . . .?', 'What makes you say that . . .?', and so on.

Accepting and dealing with responses

- Be ready to record responses on a board, OHP or flip chart. This is a form of reward as well as a useful record, for example, of predictions.
- Use body language, such as nods, hand gestures, smiles, to encourage pupils to respond.
- Praise responses even if the answer to a closed question is incorrect – don't condemn answers to open questions purely because they don't coincide with what's in your head.
- Give leads and hints if responses are not forthcoming, perhaps by rephrasing and redirecting the question.
- Don't embarrass or humiliate by waiting too long for a response.
- Don't allow others to ridicule a pupil for an incorrect answer to a closed question or a strange answer to an open one.
- Open questions, although educationally desirable, lead to responses which can be far harder to manage and control than closed ones, such as long monologues from pupils or totally unexpected or zany replies. Developing a good questioning technique that includes asking and responding to open questions takes time and reflection.

Precautions for teachers

In my view the biggest single hazard in the lab is that which comes in with the pupils – in short, their bags and coats. Few comprehensives have a cloakroom or locker room where pupils can leave their paraphernalia. This means that many carry it around with them all day. Thus teachers can expect pupils to carry into a lab any or even all of the following: overcoat, bag, sports kit, saxophone/

guitar/clarinet etc., cooked produce or cooking containers, hockey stick, boots
. . . you name it. These are the first hazards in the lab and every teacher will
need a strategy or set procedure for dealing with it before any active work can
begin. Different schools and departments will have different tactics but the
universal rule is that no practical work can begin safely until all unneeded
belongings are safely away from aisles, stools, benches and tables. Pupils
themselves will need to feel safe and secure with this arrangement.

There are a number of other hazards in the lab which teachers need to be
aware of and prepared for. They may be chemical, biological, electrical or
physical. Fortunately, the advent of the Health and Safety At Work Act in 1974
forced schools to examine safety in science labs in a much more systematic,
open and responsible way. One of its subsequent outcomes has been the
production of a large and valuable range of documents, leaflets and books on
safety in science from a number of sources. These are essential reading for
science teachers and are listed at the end of this chapter. No attempt is made to
summarise them here as there is no substitute for reading them in full.

Training pupils for safety

In addition to teacher precautions, pupils need to be given safety training,
sometimes as lessons in themselves and sometimes within certain practical
lessons. Students must have a clear set of lab rules and guidelines, both in their
books and on display – but this is not enough. They should also be trained at the
very least to:

- spot all potential hazards (chemical, biological, etc.);
- consider and if necessary revise the lab rules;
- heat substances safely;
- wear safety goggles whenever at all desirable, i.e. when heating liquids, observing flames, etc.;
- identify electrical dangers, for example that a person's electrical resistance
  drops from about 10,000 ohms with dry hands to around 300 ohms with wet
  hands;
- use a bunsen burner correctly;
- know all the hazard warning symbols (which they actually quite enjoy
  learning).

Fortunately there are a number of useful published materials on safety that can
be used with pupils.

Management and control

The subject that perhaps most concerns all beginning teachers, and that relates
to lesson planning, asking questions and safety, is the management and control
of pupils during the lesson. This topic is another on which a vast amount has

been said and written, some of which is useful and practical (see further reading), part of which is too vague to be of value, and an element of which is pure scaremongering. Let us therefore start by putting classroom management issues into perspective. An important report in 1989 (HMSO 1989) showed that, in its sample of over 2,000 teachers, the five behaviours most commonly reported as a difficulty, in the order shown below, were:

1   pupils talking out of turn
2   work avoidance or idleness
3   *pupils* hindering other pupils
4   pupils not being punctual
5   pupils making unnecessary, non-verbal noise

Take a careful look at these, the top five. They do not include swearing at the teacher, acts of vandalism or physical attack – all of the incidents which a gullible reader of the popular press would infer are common in schools. The Elton Report and other published studies show clearly that those 'newsworthy' types of behaviour may sell newspapers but are relatively rare in the real, non-tabloid world. Thus we start here from the premise that the most common management goals for the teacher are quite simply to organise and control pupil talk in the classroom, and to keep pupils to task.

As mentioned earlier, a large number of books have been written about classroom management, and although they can never be a substitute for experience and observation they can give teachers at all stages useful frameworks for analysing their own practice. Many of the books (listed at the end of the chapter) offer practical advice on class management: Robertson (1989), for example, gives a useful checklist for 'successful teaching'; McManus (1989) provides a summary of 'teaching skills for classroom management'; Marland (1975), in one of the most widely read books in initial training, offers a guide to all aspects of the classroom component of a teacher's job, as do Kyriacou's books (1986, 1991). It would be impossible to distil all the practical wisdom from the wide range of books in this area. However, I have offered below a checklist which might be valuable to teachers to consider before and after a lesson. These points are a summary of much of the agreed wisdom on planning, preparing, presenting and managing lessons. They are offered to readers in a clear and direct style, but please do look carefully and critically at them.

Planning

- Plan a varied, interesting lesson.
- Make sure the pupils are busy throughout, according to your lesson plan, i.e. give them plenty to *do*.
- Plan some time-fillers, such as a quiz, spelling test, word-search or crosswords.

- Plan a lesson that makes sense and has some sort of logical pattern, sequence, or structure to it. Make it clear to the pupils *what* you are trying to teach them, and *why!*

Preparation

- Try all experiments and demonstrations before the lesson.
- Prepare some blackboard work and/or OHP diagrams beforehand, if possible.
- Check all the apparatus *before and after* each lesson. Count it all out – count it all back in again.
- Ensure that ventilation and lighting are adequate.

Self-presentation

- Try to *look* confident and professional: don't slouch, mumble, look at your feet or stare out of the window.
- Speak clearly, at a sensible speed.
- Project yourself.
- 'Scan' the group and make eye contact. Don't talk just to the front row.
- Put some life into it, for example, move your lips, don't stand in one place like a statue, appear enthusiastic.
- Be aware of what's going on ('with it'); look for feedback, such as yawns, glazed looks.
- Do use gestures and body language as well as spoken language, especially in a large and busy lab. Develop your own 'sign language' which can be extremely valuable during practical work (see Figure 5.1 for examples of useful sign language).

Relationships

Good relationships are both a cause and an effect of good classroom management. Also, they do take time.

- Be pleasant but never friendly – it's totally false.
- Be firm but not 'stroppy'. Pupils hate teachers who shout and moan at them all the time.
- Occasionally show that you're human (this is probably safest outside the classroom, such as on the games field).
- Don't court popularity.
- Try to enjoy what you're doing, but don't smile too much (don't spend two minutes getting the class quiet, then tell them a joke).
- Start learning names immediately (by studying the class list in advance and using mnemonics, even silly ones; when handing out books; as pupils answer questions; using a seating plan, etc.).

"make it much
wider/larger"

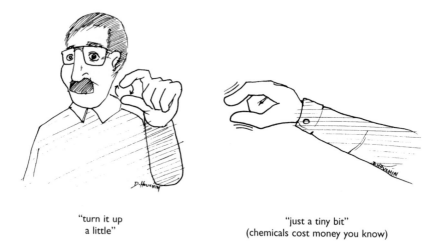

"turn it up
a little"

"just a tiny bit"
(chemicals cost money you know)

Figure 5.1 Gestures and sign language can be extremely valuable in management and control.
Source: Drawn by David Houchin.

- Use names as soon as you can (i.e., don't use 'You at the back', 'Yes, you').
- Use praise, both public and private.
- Respond positively to correct answers – don't just grunt or nod imperceptibly (for example, 'Very good' or 'Yes, well done').

Gaining attention

- Insist on silence when you are talking to the whole class – but don't overdo it (five minutes at a stretch?).
- Pick the right moment to address the class (for example, not while they're trooping out of or into the room).
- Give clear, positive starting signals to gain attention according to some sort of 'hierarchy' ranging from pleasant to curt. For example:

  Pleasant: non-verbal signals, such as standing waiting for quiet, or
  'Can I have your attention please?'
  'Will you all listen now?'
  'Be quiet everybody.'

  Curt: 'John – be quiet.' (i.e. focus on individuals)
  'Shut up.'

- Don't start the lesson until you have complete silence, even if you have to work through this range and repeat these signals.
- If spoken words won't shut the class up, try written words or a definite task; such as:

  'Copy these notes off the blackboard . . .'
  'Draw this diagram . . .'
  'Copy this OHP transparency' (a good way of gaining attention because (1) you switch it on and light appears and (2) you're facing the class.)

- Never, ever use 'Ssshh . . . ssshh . . .'. It's ambiguous and usually ignored anyway.

Keeping control

- Don't expect a class to follow the same activity (for example, note-taking) for an hour, or to listen to you endlessly. Variety is the spice of a lesson.
- Try to decide in *your own mind* what standards and norms you want to enforce – this is half the battle. (Commands are obeyed in direct proportion to how much you mean them.)
- Stick closely to the school norms whenever you can – it's easier.
- Be *determined* in enforcing these norms.
- There is no need to insist on silence during class or practical work but you can, for example, insist that pupils only talk to the person next to them.
- Be consistent and predictable over what you want and what you expect.

Starting and ending a lesson

- Stand near the door and look at each pupil as he or she comes into the room. (Don't, for example, write on the board, fiddle with apparatus, engage in deep conversation with a pupil or the lab technician, or sort out books as the class come in.)

- You may wish to make *brief* individual remarks as they enter, such as 'You're sitting on the front row today' or a similar witticism.
- Don't try to start a lesson *too quickly* (for example, don't explain Einstein's theory of relativity while they're still taking their coats off). Give them one to two minutes to settle down and get in the right frame of mind, with the occasional salutary remark from you (such as 'Put him down', 'Spit the chewing gum in the bin', etc.).
- On the other hand, don't start a lesson 10 minutes late.
- Try to sum up. and round off every lesson, then tell them what they're doing next time.
- Don't dismiss the class until they are all sitting in silence. Dismiss one row at a time.
- Stand by the door and watch each pupil as he or she leaves. Save long conversations, and reprimands, until others have gone.

If things go wrong . . .

- Avoid one-to-one confrontation. It's very difficult to win.
- Use other staff, for example, to send one or two (at most) miscreants to (extracting one or two pupils can save a lesson for the other 26).
- If you send a pupil out, send him or her to somebody specific, such as Head of Department, with a specific task to do.
- Don't make empty, 'unkeepable' threats, such as 10,000 lines, 90 minutes' detention.
- You can make small, keepable threats, such as 50 lines, 10 minutes' staying in.
- Don't be afraid to make pupils move seats.
- Don't get physical *in any way.*
- Raise your voice to the roof if necessary, but above all don't overdo it – it soon loses its impact.
- Seek advice. Talk over your lessons with staff and other students.
- Above all, don't take it personally.

Your worst class

If all the above fail:

- Try a totally different tactic, such as individualised learning instead of class teaching, lots of colourful worksheets, video, slides, OHP . . . anything!
- Find out how other teachers cope with them, if at all.
- Have a cup of tea, drink, walk or run before you carry out a post mortem (evaluation) on your lesson.

Every professional benefits from colleagues' help. Teachers are no exception.

Even if teachers do follow all the rules, tips, dos and don'ts, and handy hints dished out to them by everyone from their mentor in school, to parents, press and politicians, there will be lessons that do not go according to plan. It is worth returning briefly to the Elton Report to see what teachers in their sample did when dealing with difficult classes or individuals. The most common strategies and sanctions used were, in this order:

- reasoning with a pupil or pupils inside the room
- reasoning outside the room
- setting extra work of some kind
- detaining a pupil or pupils
- sending a pupil or pupils out of the room
- referring a pupil or pupils to another teacher
- sending a pupil or pupils to a more senior teacher

These are still likely to be the most common sanctions that teachers will continue to employ – it is unlikely that caning, hanging, drawing and quartering in return for deviant behaviour will make a comeback.

Feedback and marking

One of the clearest messages from studies of behaviour in classrooms is that although punishment has little effect in improving the behaviour of those punished (although it may have a deterrent effect on those who observe it), the use of praise can be extremely effective. Pupils like teachers who are well organised, interesting and humorous – there is also extensive evidence that they respond well to praise. Praise can be a tool for classroom control in encouraging pupils, keeping them to task, motivating them, and generally improving their self-esteem. Its value cannot be over-stated.

In general, the feedback that pupils receive from the teacher is vitally important. Humiliation and condemnation are not productive – praise and encouragement are. This is also true of marking pupils' written work. More will be said on pupils' writing and marking in Chapter 9 on language in science education, but it can be said briefly here that feedback on written work is as important as it is in the oral, classroom context. What guidelines can be offered on marking work? A short summary is given here which will be developed in the language chapter:

- Always mark pupils' work at frequent intervals, even if there is not time to mark it thoroughly, word by word, on every occasion. Some feedback, comment or praise is better than nothing. At least it shows pupils that the teacher cares and is keeping an eye on things.
- Use praise and encouragement as well as criticism. Find something positive to say about the work, however small. If appropriate, praise the work as you hand it back.

- The correction of spelling is a thorny and contentious issue. Spelling is important for at least three reasons: poor spelling inhibits the writer's fluency and distracts the reader from the content; the reader judges the content to be of lower quality, not least in a scientific context; spelling is seen in society as important, rightly or wrongly. For these reasons a teacher has a duty to consider a pupil's spelling when marking work in science and to use whatever strategy is best for that pupil in order to improve it. This is the nub of the issue. With pupils who make perhaps two spelling errors in a piece of work, correction of each is both practical and not too damning. With a pupil whose work is riddled with misspellings the situation requires tact. One strategy is to single out the more important errors and correct those tactfully but clearly. There may be persistent errors which a teacher can look for and attempt to remedy. Special help may be needed, for example through the use of IT. The process of correction and redrafting is far easier to handle and far less painful if a simple word processor is used, perhaps with a spell-checker. Presentation and self-esteem can be greatly enhanced by using a computer system to reveal the true extent of a pupil's writing. Teachers should not be misled into assuming that a poor speller, or a person with unsightly handwriting, is a poor writer.

There are many issues connected with marking and giving feedback to pupils that could be considered; the main message here, though, is that it should be based on reward, praise and encouragement rather than on negative criticism or condemnation.

Homework

The final job that falls to teachers at the end of the lesson is very often the setting of homework. Not only are teachers responsible for the learning and behaviour of pupils during school hours, they also extend their influence outside these hours by the tradition of homework! Like it or not, most secondary schools have a policy of setting and monitoring homework. It can be set for a variety of reasons:

- to finish work started in the lesson, such as finishing written work, writing up a practical;
- as a new piece of work relating to the lesson;
- as an assessment of the learning in a lesson, for example, a set of questions based on the lesson content;
- as an extension to the work in the lesson, for example, a worksheet of information, reading and questions;
- as an open, flexible piece of work that can be undertaken almost independently at home, such as a piece of mini-research, a project, an exploration. (This will obviously depend to a large extent on a pupil having access to resources at home or nearby.)

There may be other reasons and motives for setting homework. Ideally, a useful piece of homework should have the following features:

- It should be clear and manageable within a realistic time span.
- It should not make too many demands upon or assumptions about the home environment, for example, 'Look up the following words in *Encyclopaedia Britannica* . . .', 'Use the Internet to explore . . .'.
- It should be clearly connected to the lesson and the overall scheme of work.
- The purpose behind it should be clear to the pupil, i.e. why is this demand being placed upon them in their out-of-school time?

Homework can be valuable, and there might well be an outcry from certain quarters if the tradition of British homework disappeared. However, there are problems with it that have surfaced both in the everyday experience of teachers and in research studies of attitudes to it. The main, most common problems seem to be:

- pupils being unclear about what they had to do or how much, with no opportunity to seek clarification (this may arise from poor instructions in the lesson, not writing it down, not listening, not remembering, etc.);
- pupils not having the resources, such as secondary sources, or the equipment, such as a protractor or calculator, to carry out the work;
- pupils unable to obtain secondary sources, for example, from the public library (which may, like my own, be closed down);
- poor working conditions at home;
- badly written, unclear or poorly reproduced worksheets.

These are all problems that the teacher needs to be aware of, even if they are not all within the teacher's sphere of influence. Chapter 12 considers the important and connected issue of children's out-of-school learning in science.

References and further reading

Management and control

There is a wide range of books on classroom management and control. Here is a brief list showing a selection of those books with short notes on some. Although they cannot be a substitute for classroom practice and experience, they can help to provide a framework for analysing and reflecting upon them. There is nothing so practical as a good theory.

Cheesman, P. and Watts, P. (1985) *Positive Behaviour Management: A Manual for Teachers*, London: Croom Helm, pp. 80–4. (A discussion of the background to behaviour problems and ways of assessing them. Puts forward practical advice on intervention and a 'step-by-step' guide to positive behaviour management. The summary of suggestions for 'teacher behaviour' may be particularly useful.)

HMSO (1989) *Discipline in Schools: The Elton Report*, London: HMSO.

Kyriacou, C. (1986) *Effective Teaching in Schools*, Oxford: Blackwell.

Kyriacou, C. (1991) *Essential Teaching Skills*, Oxford: Blackwell.

McManus, M. (1989) *Troublesome Behaviour in the Classroom – A Teacher's Survival Guide*, London: Routledge. (A detailed account of troublesome behaviour, its causes and remedies; draws extensively on research findings, but also has many practical activities to try. Useful for students and experienced teachers alike.)

Marland, M. (1975) *The Craft of the Classroom*, Oxford: Heinemann. (Reprinted many times, this book is a short, well-organised and very practical classic covering all aspects of the new teacher's job; valuable if a little dated.)

Neill, S. (1991) *Classroom Non-verbal Communication*, London: Routledge. (Illustrates, with text and numerous drawings, the use of body language, facial expression and posture in the classroom. Very practical discussion and advice, based on recent research, offering suggestions for teachers on conveying enthusiasm, gaining attention, using space and interpreting pupils' body language.)

Neill, S. and Caswell, C. (1993) *Body Language for Competent Teachers*, London: Routledge.

Robertson, J. (1989) (2nd edn.) *Effective Classroom Control – Understanding Teacher–Pupil Relationships*, London: Hodder & Stoughton (short but detailed, with much good advice on teacher–pupil relationships; over half of the book is devoted to analysing and dealing with unwanted behaviour in the classroom.)

Rogers, C. (1983) *Freedom to Learn*, Ohio: Merrill. (A compendium of Rogers' research on person-centred learning, how to manage it and set it up so that pupils' curiosity and enthusiasm are not stifled. A stimulating and challenging book.)

Smith, C. and Laslett, R. (1993) (2nd edn.) *Effective Classroom Management*, London: Routledge.

Thorp, S. (ed.) (1991) *Race, Equality and Science Teaching*, Hatfield: ASE. (Has several useful activities involving looking at schemes of work, page 57, 'Looking at my classroom', pages 15–17 and reflecting on 'Groupings in the classroom', page 51.)

Planning

Baxter, M. (1998) 'Planning for teaching and learning', in Ratcliffe, M. (ed.) *ASE Guide to Secondary Education*, pp. 127–37.

Questioning

Brown, G.A. (1975) *Microteaching*, London: Methuen. (This book has been around for some time but has many useful points.)

Brown, G.A. (1984) 'Questioning', in Wragg, E.C. (ed.), *Classroom Teaching Skills*, London: Croom Helm.

Carr, D. (1998) 'The art of asking questions in the teaching of science', *School Science Review*, vol. 79, no. 289, pp. 47–50.

Kerry, T. (1982) *Effective Questioning*, London: Macmillan Education.

Sands, M. and Hull, R. (1985) *Teaching Science: A Teaching Skills Workbook*, London: Macmillan Education. (A useful collection of practical ideas on not only questioning but management, control, marking and safety.)

Wellington, J.J. (1998) 'Dialogues in the science classroom', in Ratcliffe, M. (ed.), pp. 146–58.

Safety

ASE (1988) *Topics in Safety*, Hatfield: ASE.

ASE (1996) *Safeguards in the School Laboratory*, (10th edn.), Hatfield: ASE (brief, comprehensive and up to date).

ASE (1996) *Safety Reprints*, Hatfield: ASE (a collection of articles and notes on safety).

ASE (1999) *Safe and Exciting Science* (a pack of training activities).

Burrows, P. (1998) 'Safety in science education', in Ratcliffe, M. (ed.), pp. 183–91.

DES (1984) *Safety in Science Laboratories*, DES Safety Series 2 (3rd edn.), London: HMSO. (The DfEE, formerly DES, produce a range of free 'Memoranda' on a range of safety topics such as laser use, radiation and AIDS obtainable from: The Publications Unit, Honeypot Lane, Stanmore, Middlesex HA7 1AZ.)

Everett, D. and Jenkins, E. (1990) *A Safety Handbook for Science Teachers*, London: John Murray (5th edn.). (Covers the whole field of safety in science teaching and contains a comprehensive list, over 600 items, of all major hazards.)

HMSO (1985) *Microbiology: An HMI Guide for Schools and Non-advanced Further Education*, London: HMSO.

Assessment

See the references in Chapter 1 (especially to Paul Black's work) and:

Gipps, C.V. (1995) *Beyond Testing: Towards a Theory of Educational Assessment*, London: Falmer Press.

Gipps, C.V. and Murphy, P. (1994) *A Fair Test? Assessment Achievement and Equity*, Milton Keynes: Open University Press.

Gipps, C.V. and Stobart, G. (1993) *Assessment: A Teacher's Guide to the Issues*, London: Hodder and Stoughton.

Hayes, P. (1998) 'Assessment in the classroom', in Ratcliffe, M. (ed.) *ASE Guide to Secondary Education*, pp. 138–45.

Sutton, R. (1992) *Assessment: A Framework for Teachers*, London: Routledge.

Chapter 6

Meeting special needs in science

No pupils, least of all those with learning difficulties, should be denied the opportunity of some sort of 'scientific experience'. This statement applies to all pupils with special educational needs (SEN), whether the difficulty they have in learning is general or specific, severe or less severe. Indeed, we should remember that we *all* experience difficulty of some kind or another in learning, whether it is due to tiredness, saturation or simply that it 'won't go in'. All pupils should receive a broad and balanced curriculum, relevant to their individual needs. How this might be achieved is the subject of this chapter.

What makes individuals different?

> . . . special needs can best be met when a general concern for individual differences is uppermost in teachers' thinking.
>
> (Postlethwaite 1993: 21)

Everyone is different. This is a tautology, but it is worth emphasising before spelling out the differences that science teachers need to be aware of. The differences that matter can be divided and summed up as follows.

Educational differences

Children bring different preconceptions (alternative frameworks), different abilities, knowledge, understanding and skills into science education. There is extensive evidence that children have a wide range of preconceptions on notions such as force, pressure, heat, energy, plant nutrition, animal, burning and indeed most of the concepts that are the concern of the secondary science curriculum. The important point for teachers is that these 'alternative conceptions' (so-called in that they differ from the accepted view of normal science) have served children in their life outside of the science classroom and are strongly held on to.

Children also have a huge variety of past experiences from home, parents, cubs or brownies, holidays, visits, etc. which leads to a wide and rich range of scientific experience, knowledge and understanding in any classroom of 20–plus people.

As for abilities, the Assessment of Performance Unit (APU, 1989) studies of secondary pupils showed that pupils varied enormously in their ability to:

- observe
- interpret observations
- interpret information
- plan investigations, including controlling variables

The APU studies revealed many other important differences, of course (see APU 1988 and 1989).

Perhaps the most important difference, however, is the huge range of linguistic ability that pupils bring to the science room. Science teaching takes place almost exclusively through the medium of language, both written and spoken (see Chapter 9). Hence teachers need to recognise the pupils' differences:

- in writing ability (for example, in reporting practical work, taking notes, or written assessment)
- in speaking and listening ability (for example, when answering oral questions or reporting by speech; in group or class discussion)
- in reading ability (for example, in reading instructions for a practical or an account in a textbook or worksheet)
- in organisational ability (for example, in sequencing tasks or instructions, even in organising their own time)

Psychological differences

It is a statement of the obvious to any practising teacher that pupils exhibit psychological differences. However, it can be helpful to divide them up according to three general categories:

1 General intelligence: There are dangers, however, in taking too much account of IQ scores, as Postlethwaite warns: '. . . an unfavourable score on an IQ test may alert us to the need to deal with a pupil in a different way, but it is not a trap which condemns that pupil to poor levels of performance' (Postlethwaite 1993: 31).
2 Motivation, personality and attitude.
3 Self-image and self-esteem: how many pupils shrug and say 'Well, I'm just no good at science'? This seems to be more common in the science area than in other subjects, and more true of girls than of boys. Past experience of failure in science will further lower self-esteem.

Learning difficulties and learning styles

Different people have different learning styles – some are 'holists' (looking for overviews and connections amongst different parts); some are: 'serialists', preferring to take an element at a time (Pask 1975). Pask argued that people learn most effectively if they are taught in a style that matches their preferred mode of learning – not an easy task for the teacher when actually teaching, but the difference should be borne in mind when arranging learning activities. From another perspective, it seems that some prefer to learn by moving from concrete specific examples to the abstract and the general; others prefer to start from the abstract and the general before meeting concrete examples. Both strategies are necessary for learning the powerful abstractions that make science important.

Similarly, some learners will experience difficulty of one or more kinds in learning science. Various types of difficulty will be encountered which cannot be discussed fully here, but they may include difficulties in: remembering, e.g. figures, abstractions, science knowledge; classifying; gathering information systematically; generalising from one situation to another; sustaining concentration. Postlethwaite (1993) gives a useful discussion of these difficulties and sensibly points out that they apply to most people at some time or another!

Physical differences

Examples include physically challenged pupils, for example pupils in wheelchairs and pupils with specific impairments such as visual or aural. There will be a wide range of physical difference between pupils in any secondary class. Perhaps the important point for science teachers is that practical work will need special attention, for example whilst giving instructions or in providing special resources/apparatus.

Social differences

Shyness, ability to listen to others, respect for fellow learners, willingness, enthusiasm, social skill, ability to work in a group, leadership quality – these are all important 'social differences' between pupils. They do relate to the four types of difference already listed, but there is not always a clear one-to-one connection (for example, 'not contributing to class discussion' may be attributable to a number of causes including shyness or introversion, lack of confidence, low self-esteem, or lack of knowledge).

Socio-economic differences

These include social class, family background, etc. This clearly relates to the final two points below.

Cultural differences

Different values, religious views, moral standpoints, attitudes to education, differing educational goals and aspirations – these are all factors that will affect science teaching and learning, not least in the treatment of controversial issues such as evolution, the origin of the universe, contraception and sex education.

Gender differences

Pupils' attitudes to the sciences appear to be gender-related (Postlethwaite 1993), and hence gender affects choices they might make at crucial stages in schooling. There has been some evidence (APU 1988) that boys are more competent than girls in some areas, such as using apparatus, and that girls better than boys in others, such as making and interpreting observations, but these generalisations are wide open to debate.

   All the differences listed above are interrelated, for example prior experiences and socio-economic background, but it can be useful to separate them out and summarise them in order to be aware of them and to attempt to address them.

Responding to differences

How can teachers respond to all these individual differences, characteristics and prior experiences which students of all ages and abilities bring to the class or lecture room? First, it needs to be recognised that every group is a mixed ability group. Teachers who are heard to make comments like: 'I don't hold with this mixed-ability teaching' ignore the truism that every group of every age presents different abilities, potential, experience and motivation. The only variable is the range of those differences in a given group.

   The second factor for both teachers and learners is to decide how controllable and how pervasive these individual differences are (Postlethwaite 1993: 44–5). In plain terms, the learner and the teacher can pose these two questions:

* Which differences affect *all* aspects of a pupil's work, whatever the context? In contrast, which differences affect only some aspects of work, in some contexts?
* Which of the differences can be controlled, altered and influenced, i.e. which factors can teachers and learners themselves actually do something about?

Within these two questions there are two other questions:

1   Internal or external? If the difference can be controlled, altered or influenced is it something *internal* to the learner, for example the effort they put in? Or is it something *external*, such as economic status? Is the problem that of the child or a problem of the context and background?

2   Stable/permanent or unstable/temporary? Is the difference something which is constant, unchanging or permanent, or is it short term or temporary, such as a broken leg?

These are all questions that can be asked of individuals, often in connection with their success or failure at certain tasks or activities. The basic questions are summed up in Figure 6.1 as a kind of continuum.

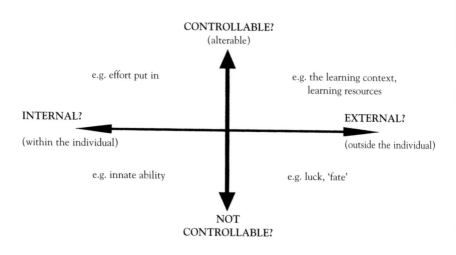

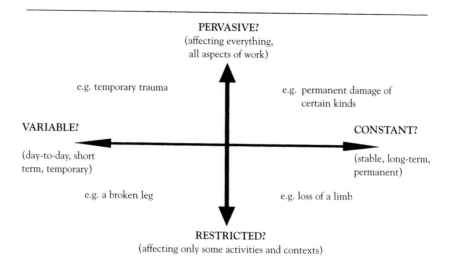

Figure 6.1 Why do people succeed or fail? Questions to ask of individuals' differences and attributes.

We often do this with ourselves when we consider our own successes and failures and the reasons for them. Is your sheer brilliance due to pure innate ability (internal, stable, not controllable), or is it a result of your drive, motivation and dogged hard work at crucial times (internal, controllable and unstable)? If, like me, you are totally incapable of writing poetry, is it your English teacher's fault because she killed it stone dead for you as a teenager (external, stable and uncontrollable), or is it your own lack of creativity and insight (stable, internal and possibly pervasive)?

Postlethwaite (1993: 35) explains that 'advantaged pupils' often attribute their own success to internal, stable and pervasive factors such as 'high ability' and those who often fail may attribute that failure to 'low ability' – 'I'm just thick' (internal, stable). They therefore expect to fail again, leading to a downward spiral of self-esteem. Thus the attributions that pupils make of themselves and those that teachers make of them are vitally important in deciding on future action.

It seems to me that an understanding of these attributions is vitally important in the science and the ICT areas. How many adults (few children) simply shrug and say 'I just can't use a computer'? How many children claim that they are 'just no good at science' without looking in detail at the reasons for saying that? It is hoped that the framework for analysing differences and causes in Figure 6.1 can be useful both for teachers and for pupils in considering action. It could also be a valuable tool in personal and social education, as well as in science.

Entitlement, access and differentiation

These are three terms which became buzzwords in the 1990s. The first, entitlement, captures the principle that all pupils, whatever their special needs, are entitled to have appropriate access to the science curriculum. The crucial words here are 'appropriate access', which is of course central to any good teaching. How can teachers ensure that access to their curriculum entitlement is appropriate for pupils with special educational needs?

There are different possibilities. One is segregation, i.e. separating some pupils from others, either in a different class or even a different school. This can allow what has been termed 'remedial help' for a special group. Another is to provide support, such as a 'support teacher' with one or a few pupils in a whole class.

One of the answers to coping with individual differences is to plan for differentiation. This term is widely used but rarely defined. The term is not new but is more topical than ever because of the levels, assessment and progression built into the formal curriculum. Differentiation can be of two kinds:

- by task or activity, i.e. by providing different tasks to meet the individual differences and needs of a group;
- by outcome, i.e. by allowing different results or outcomes from activities or tasks.

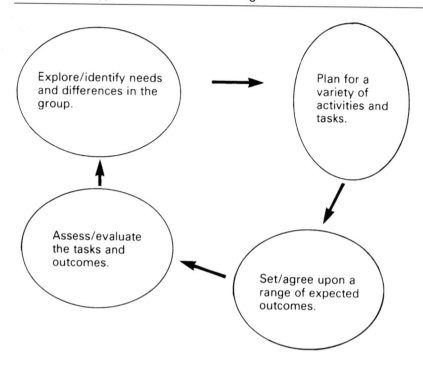

Figure 6.2 A strategy for differentiation.

The former, by task, suggests that certain activities – such as on a worksheet or in a practical session – should be made special and different for some pupils in order to cater for all needs. The latter implies that different outcomes, such as submitted work, can be planned for and accepted for (say) assessment. Thus differentiation involves first identifying needs, then planning a variety of activities or tasks to meet those needs, then agreeing and setting a range of outcomes from the activities which can be evaluated or assessed (Figure 6.2).

The NCC Curriculum Guidance 10 (NCC 1992b) gave a number of suggestions to teachers on planning for differentiation. The guidance suggested two main principles that are indisputable and indeed apply to any lesson planning:

1   Teachers should define their objectives, taking into account knowledge, understanding and skills, i.e. in a given lesson what do they hope to achieve in terms of those three areas and what knowledge, experiences and skills will pupils leave the room with that they did not have when they entered?
2   Teachers should plan activities appropriate to the class, to groups within it, and to individuals. (This is easier said than done, of course.)

Practical suggestions are given for achieving this key feature of successful teaching: appropriateness. Table 6.1 gives a summary of guidelines on planning, pacing and communicating.

Table 6.1 Planning and teaching for differentiation: basic guidelines

Planning and preparing

- Provide a range of activities which ensure the participation and involvement of all pupils (differentiated by task); and/or
- Provide similar work for the whole group but allow different outcomes for different individuals (differentiation by outcome).
- Plan for the possibility of pupils' work being recorded in different ways to suit their capabilities, such as using computers or video or audio tape.
- Plan for and make effective use of classroom helpers, support teachers and lab technicians where possible.
- Organise some work to be done in small groups so that pupils can demonstrate to each other what they can do.

Pacing

- Use a clearly defined, step-by-step approach that promotes a gradual development of skills, knowledge and understanding, i.e. break the lesson down into a series of small, achievable steps.
- Ensure that the pace of the lesson takes account of the differing work rates of individual pupils.
- Allow sufficient repetition to consolidate skills, knowledge and understanding.

Communicating

- Communicate in a range of different ways, i.e. speech, writing, pictures and diagrams, to give all pupils the opportunity to learn in a way which best suits them.
- Adapt communications for particular special educational needs, such as enlarged print, clear uncluttered illustrations, worksheets on audio tape.
- Use a consistent presentation for written material and a format for practical work which will avoid anxiety and encourage confidence and participation.
- Break down class worksheets into clearly itemised small steps.
- Use jargon-free, simple, unambiguous language; start from the pupils' own language and introduce words as needed.
- Explain new words to pupils so that they understand them and can then use them; display words in regular use so that they can be copied accurately.

Source: First adapted from NCC Curriculum Guidance 10 (NCC 1992b).

One of the problems, of course, is to put these guidelines into practice in the classroom. Differentiation by task is in many ways more of a challenge in the secondary school than in the primary. Primary teachers are experienced in organising and managing a classroom where a number of different tasks (practical, oral and written) are going on at the same time. In contrast, the norm for the secondary classroom is a group of children engaged in roughly the same activity, such as a practical task, following a worksheet or taking notes from an OHP or blackboard. The challenge for the secondary teacher is to introduce differentiated tasks that do not create resentment, jealousy, distraction or obvious streaming within the classroom.

The next section gives further explanation and some more examples of approaches for coping with a wide range of differences.

Some practical possibilities for the classroom

Working with 'support teachers' in comprehensive schools

A number of schools can now benefit from the work of a teacher on the staff who may be commonly called the 'SEN teacher', the 'support teacher' or the 'special needs co-ordinator'. None of these terms does justice to the potential role of a fellow professional who can work collaboratively with a science teacher in achieving the differentiation and access discussed above (Dyson 1991; King 1989). Such teachers must first be regarded by the science teacher as more than just an extra resource in the room, or a non-teaching assistant. They should be seen as someone who can be a consultant and collaborator at all stages of providing access to the mainstream science curriculum:

- in planning and preparing lessons, i.e. in producing lesson plans and schemes of work for individual teachers and for the science department; in preparing materials, such as worksheets or DARTs, or resources, such as equipment or activities for class practicals;
- in achieving differentiation both of task and outcome, for example, in building differentiation into curriculum planning;
- in teaching the lesson itself and supervising classwork;
- in post-lesson or post-scheme-of-work evaluation;
- in joint assessment and recording of pupils' progress in both written and practical work.

This collaboration is necessary whether the 'support' teacher gives in-class support or withdraws pupils, such as unusually able or timid pupils, for special work. Whatever the strategy, the co-operation/collaboration needs to be handled sensitively. The support teacher will often not be a science specialist and may often hold his or her science background in low esteem. Moreover, collaboration in the class will not work if the teaching style and environment is a purely didactic one, dominated by the 'scientist', the 'real teacher'. Collaborative teaching will work best in a resource-based, individualised-learning approach in the classroom. But this in turn presents problems; problems of reading, for example of worksheets or instruction cards, and of writing, for example responses or write-ups, are often the most important source of learning difficulties in the lab. Collaborative teaching will need to find ways of making this approach work – suggestions are offered in the next section.

Reducing language barriers

Difficulties with language in some form or another are almost certainly the most common problem for learners and teachers in the mainstream, comprehensive school science curriculum (see Chapter 9 on language). Most of the suggestions below are therefore connected with practical ways of trying to overcome language barriers in science learning.

1 Giving instructions

So many teachers are guilty of the 'I've told you so now you know' approach. This is not acceptable for learners with a variety of special needs (not least those with hearing impairment) and is poor practice anyway. Instructions should be given using a variety of visual or aural support materials, including:

- drawings, diagrams and pictures as support for the spoken word;
- written instructions on a workcard/worksheet, the blackboard or an OHP;
- for certain practicals, an example set up on the front bench that can be referred to;
- in some cases, especially for those with specific needs, instructions in the form of audio tape can be an extra help;
- for some practicals, prepared pictures with words of different stages in an experiment can be given and pupils asked to sequence them correctly and perhaps label them (obviously the sequence will need to be checked before starting).

Table 6.2 gives a list of possible teaching strategies for aiding comprehension by pupils, produced with the help of a communication therapist with an interest in helping the dyslexic student. However, they apply equally well to all science teaching situations.

Table 6.2 Possible teaching tactics to aid comprehension

1	Try to give explicit information and instructions in short manageable chunks.
2	Try to give a 'mental' set for the lesson by outlining what the whole lesson is about. Review the lesson at the end. This allows the child to tune in and pull everything together as a whole.
3	Structure your lessons around a number of 'main ideas' and put these (and a list of key words) on a handout.
4	Help structure the student's listening by giving questions at the beginning.
5	Encourage students to read the questions before reading a passage so they are aware of what points are important to mention and of what they should take special note.
6	Discuss subject-specific vocabulary and give a written list so the child does not have to spend time thinking about these spellings but can concentrate on the content of the lesson (these can be selected from the Word Bank).
7	Use illustrations/diagrams wherever possible, rather than just talking.

2 Worksheets

A separate chapter gives guidelines on producing written material for pupils. These apply to any group of mixed ability. With specific needs extra provision may have to be made, for example:

- Visually impaired children may need a Braille version of text and special aids for diagrams. An audio-tape version of the sheet will be a useful aid for both visually impaired and poor readers. Support may often be available to the science teacher in preparing these.
- Poor readers may need additional symbols and visual prompts to complete a task, such as filling in missing words. A symbol (for example, from the Rebus system) or simple diagram next to the blank may be a sufficient prod.

3 Variety in submitted work

As discussed earlier, differentiation by outcome implies that a range of submitted work will be accepted for, say, assessment. As well as hand-written work, teachers can consider more emphasis on diagrams and pictures; work printed from a computer that has been checked and corrected; audio-tape accounts or descriptions, such as of a process or an experiment; photographic records, such as of a practical or a product; video of, say, a group project on a topic or issue, or of an investigation.

4 Support with writing and spelling

Spelling is an issue that seems to generate more hot air than most. Spelling in science needs to be attended to and corrected but not in such a way that pupils are totally discouraged from attempting writing for fear of making spelling mistakes – a page of writing covered in red ink will not encourage. Certain guidelines can be followed by teachers and pupils in gradually improving spelling in science:

- If a large number of errors are made, teachers can select those which pupils are most likely to correct and learn successfully.
- Such errors can be identified with a 'Sp' in the margin and underlined. The pupil should then look along the line, find the error, and then either use a dictionary, ask a reliable friend or ask the teacher so that it can be corrected.
- Other errors can be identified with a 'Sp', and the correct spelling written in the margin or at the end, such as specialist terms in science. These can be added to a student's 'Science Wordbank' (see Table 6.3, below). The whole of the correct word can then be written above the mistake; teachers should avoid altering the word.

The main idea is to get pupils to try to find their own errors, to learn from their mistakes, and to correct misspellings themselves – not have the teacher do it for them.

5 Wordlists and wordbanks

A list of 'important', commonly used words in science could be produced and displayed in large lettering on the lab wall. These could be of great help to those who have difficulty in 'finding words' as well as those who need help with spelling. The word list could include common items of apparatus used in practicals, such as bunsen burner, flasks of different kinds; important labelling words, such as parts of a device, parts of the human body; words for important concepts and processes, such as photosynthesis, electrolysis, evolution; difficult nomenclature, such as for chemicals; the common units, for example joule, newton, metre, etc. These key words could be referred to whenever pupils are doing a written task. For home use they could be written in a 'Science Wordbank' at the end of the pupil's book. For some lessons with especially new and difficult language, a sheet could be given out at the start with a clear list of all the words. terms, etc. which will be used during the course of the lesson.

Table 6.3 shows an example of a wordbank with a collection of about 300 words. This is a list that I have formed from examining the science curriculum and a sample of recent science textbooks and from talking and listening to pupils and teachers. In my estimation, this rather daunting list contains most of the words and terms pupils will encounter in their linguistic journey to science examinations at 16.

6 Using ICT (for task and outcome)

Using computers for writing can be of enormous benefit not only to reluctant writers and poor spellers, but also to good writers whose handwriting is unreadable. The use of a word-processor can completely change attitudes to writing, correcting, redrafting and presenting written work (see Chapter 10). Laptops and portables can be versatile and valuable tools for all pupils in the science lab.

The use of computers in data-logging (again, see Chapter 10) can also be of great help to all pupils, including those with special needs. Learners who are slow and untidy at recording and presenting data can be helped by a simple-to-use system (such as First Sense), which collects data, for example on light levels or temperature, records it and presents it graphically. Although these skills still need to be developed manually, the occasional use of data-logging systems can show the way, relieve the drudgery sometimes and also raise self-esteem for many pupils.

7 Using laminated cards to help and enrich reading

Science textbooks have certainly improved in the last decade, thanks partly to the research which showed that the language level of most common texts was far too high. But a page of text on science can still be a daunting prospect to many pupils. One practical strategy for making reading more active, more

Table 6.3 A science wordbank for KS3 and KS4

A
absorption
acceleration
accommodation
accurate
acid
adolescence
aerobic
alcohol
alimentary canal
alkali
alkane
alkene
allele
alloy
alpha
alternating
aluminium
ammeter
ammonia
amplitude
animal
anode
antibiotic
aorta
artery
asexual
atmosphere
atom
audible

B
bacteria
barometer
base
battery
beta
biceps
bile
biodegradable
biomass
biosphere
Brownian motion

C
camera
capillary
carbohydrate
carbon
carbon dioxide

carbonate
cardiac
carnivore
cartilage
catalyst
cathode
cell
cellular
Celsius
charge
chemical
chlorine
chlorophyll
chloroplasts
cholesterol
chromatography
chromosome
circuit
clone
coil
combustion
compound
compression
concave
conclusion
condensation
conduction
conductor
conservation
constant
contraction
control
convection
convex
corrosion
covalent
crystal
crystallisation
current
cytoplasm

D
decompose
decrease
density
diabetes
diaphragm
diffraction
diffusion
digestion

dilute
diode
dispersion
dissolve
distillation

E
echo
ecosystem
effervescence
efficiency
electrolysis
electrolyte
electromagnet
electron
electrostatic
element
embryo
emulsion
endothermic
energy
environment
enzyme
equation
equlibrium
erosion
evaporation
evidence
evolution
excretion
exothemic
expansion
extinction

F
fermentation
fertilisation
fertiliser
field
filter
filtration
fission
flammable
foetus
food chain
food web
formula
fossil
frequency
fraction

fuel
fuse

G
galaxy
gamete
gamma ray
gas
generator
genes
genetics
germination
glucose
gravity

H
habitat
haemoglobin
half-life
halogen
herbivore
homeostasis
hormone
hydrocarbon
hydrogen
hygiene

I
igneous
immunisation
increase
indicator
induction
inertia
inference
infra-red
insulation
insulin
invertebrate
ion
ionic lattice
ionosphere
isotope

J
joule

K
kelvin
kidney

Table 6.3 (continued)

kilogram	nucleus		synapse
kinetic	nutrient	**R**	synthesis
	nutrition	radiation	
L		radioactive	**T**
larva	**O**	reaction	tectonics
ligament	observation	reactivity	temperature
liquid	oesophagus	reduction	tendon
longitudinal	ohm	reflection	terminal
loudness	omnivore	refraction	thermistor
luminous	ore	renewable	thermometer
lung	organism	reproduction	thorax
lymph	osmosis	repulsion	thyroid
	ovary	resistance	tissue
M	oxidation	resistor	tract
magma	oxide	resonance	transfer
magnesium	oxygen	respiration	transformer
magnetic	ozone	result	transpiration
mass		retina	transverse
measurement	**P**	reversible	triceps
meiosis	parallel		tropism
membrane	parasite	**S**	troposphere
menstruation	particle	saliva	
metabolism	penicillin	salt	**U**
metallic	periodic table	satellite	ultrasound
metamorphic	peristalsis	saturated	ultraviolet
metamorphosis	phloem	sedimentary	unsaturated
meter	photosynthesis	sensitivity	urine
meter	pitch	series	uterus
(*length*)	placenta	skeleton	
microbe	planet	sodium	**V**
microscope	plasma	solar system	vacuole
microwave	pollen	solenoid	vacuum
mineral	pollution	solid	valency
mixture	polymer	solubility	vapour
molecule	positive	solute	variable
moment	potential	solution	variation
monohybrid	precipitate	solvent	velocity
motor	predator	species	vertebrate
mucous	prediction	spectrum	vibration
mutation	pressure	sperm	virtual
	prey	stimulus	virus
N	prism	stomata	vitamin
negative	product	stratosphere	volume
neurone	propagation	sublimation	
neutral	proportional	sulphate	**W**
neutron	protein	suspension	watt
newton	proton	symbiosis	wavelength
nitrogen	pyramid	symbol	weight

sociable and less daunting is to use cards of various kinds to go with a piece of text. This can involve a lot of preparation and adaptation by the teacher but can pay off not just for pupils with 'special needs' but for all learners of the written word! The following examples should help to explain:

(a) *True/false cards:* Statements from the text are either transcribed straight onto laminated cards or adapted slightly so that they are false. Using the text, such as a page from a book, students have to sort the cards into two categories – true or false. They discuss these and then perhaps compare their results with another group or present them to the teacher.

(b) *Agree/disagree cards:* On a more value-laden, sensitive or controversial topic, statements from, for example, different pressure groups or parties can be made into cards and then, during group discussion, placed into disagree/agree/not sure categories.

(c) *Matching pairs:* A variety of activities can be done with cards that form matching pairs. The pairs might be:

- a part of a body and its function
- part of any device, such as a car, and its function
- types of teeth and the job they do
- a picture and a word
- a common name and its scientific name
- a material and a common use for it
- a chemical name and its symbol (elements or compounds)

There are many other possibilities in science. The activity can then involve lining the cards up as a group, or it could be done as a memory game often called 'Pelmanism'. This involves placing all the cards face down on the table in two separate groups, such as name in one group, chemical symbol in another. By gradually uncovering cards, players form pairs which they then keep if they form a pair but replace (face down) if they don't.

(d) *Putting words or terms into groups:* Words can be placed onto cards, such as names of a range of animals, and then sorted into classes or groups with a heading on another card (underlined or in upper case) at the top of each group, for example mammals/non-mammals. This could be done with metals and non-metals; solids, liquids and gases; conductors and insulators; vertebrates and invertebrates, and so on.

(e) *Sequencing:* Sentence cards describing, for example, a process or an experiment are jumbled up. They are placed by groups into their version of the correct sequence.

There are many other examples of reading activities that can be done with cards, such as sorting the 'odd one out' and explaining why. They are all specific examples of DARTs (Directed Activities Related to Text), which are discussed further in Chapter 9 on language.

And now to repeat the point made earlier: the guidelines and practical examples listed above allow for individual differences in teaching a group. But in truth, what is 'good practice' for some is good practice for all; the strategies are useful for all pupils. To sum up: 'There is nothing special about teaching pupils with special needs . . . Good teaching for them is simply good teaching.' (Postlethwaite 1993: 39).

References and further reading

Assessment of Performance Unit (APU) (1988) *Science at Age 15: A Review of APU Findings*, London: HMSO.
APU (1989) *National Assessment: The APU Science Approach*, London: HMSO.
Dickinson, C. and Wright, J. (1993) *Differentiation: A Practical Handbook of Classroom Strategies*, Coventry: National Council for Educational Technology (now BECTA).
Ditchfield, C. (ed.) (1987) *Better Science for Young People with Special Educational Needs*, Secondary Science Curriculum Review Curriculum Guide 8, London/Hatfield: Heinemann/Association for Science Education.
Duerden, B., Fortune, D. and Johnson, M. (1992) 'Access and progress in science', *British Journal of Special Education*, vol. 19, no. 12, pp. 59–63.
Duerden, B. and Jury, A. (1993) 'Pupils with special needs in mainstream schools', in Hull, R. (ed.), *ASE Secondary Science Teachers' Handbook*, Hemel Hempstead: Simon & Schuster.
Dyson, A. (1991) 'Special needs teachers in mainstream schools', *Support for Learning*, vol. 6, no. 2, pp. 51–60.
Hall, S. (1997) 'The problem with differentiation', *School Science Review*, vol. 78, no. 284, pp. 95–8.
Hoyle, P. (1993) 'Race, equality and science teaching', in Hull, R. (ed.), *ASE Secondary Science Teachers' Handbook*, Hemel Hempstead: Simon & Schuster.
King, V. (1989) 'Support teaching: the practice papers: 11', *Special Children*, October 1989.
National Curriculum Council (NCC) (1989) *A Curriculum for All – Special Needs in the National Curriculum*, NCC Curriculum Guidance 2, York: NCC.
NCC (1992a) *The National Curriculum and Pupils with Severe Learning Difficulties*, NCC Curriculum Guidance 9, York: NCC.
NCC (1992b) *Teaching Science to Pupils with Special Educational Needs*, NCC Curriculum Guidance 10, York: NCC.
Naylor, S. and Keogh, B. (1998) 'Differentiation', in Ratcliffe, M. (ed.) pp.167–74.
Pask, G. (1975) *The Cybernetics of Human Learning and Performance*, London: Hutchinson.
Postlethwaite, K. (1993) *Differentiated Science Teaching*, Milton Keynes: Open University Press. (The early pages of this chapter draw heavily from Postlethwaite – readers are strongly recommended to explore his book in full.)
Reid, D.J. and Hodson, D. (1987) *Science for All: Teaching Science in the Secondary School*, London: Cassell Education.
Robertson, J. (1990) *Effective Classroom Control*, London: Hodder & Stoughton.
Smail, B. (1993) 'Science for girls and boys', in Hull, R. (ed.), *ASE Secondary Science Teachers' Handbook*, Hemel Hempstead: Simon & Schuster.
Stradling, R., Saunders, L. and Weston, P. (1991) *Differentiation in Action: A Whole School Approach for Raising Standards*, London: HMSO. (Gives strategies for raising the attainment of all pupils by a whole school approach. It also gives practical guidance for a range of learning needs of secondary school pupils.)

Thorp, S. (ed.) (1991) *Race, Equality and Science Teaching*, Hatfield: ASE.

Tunnicliffe, S.D. (1987) 'Science materials for special needs', *British Journal of Special Education*, vol. 14, no. 2.

Westwood, P. (1993) *Commonsense Methods for Children with Special Needs*, London: Routledge.

Widlake, P. (ed.) (1989) *Special Children's Handbook*, London: Hutchinson Education/ Special Children.

Wood, K., Lapp, D. and Flood, J. (1992) *Guiding Readers Through Text: A Review of Study Guiders*, London: Delaware International Reading Association (a practical guide to ways of encouraging active, structured reading).

The *Science Wordbank* in poster and A4 sheet form can be obtained from: ASE Book Sales, Hatfield, AL10 9AA (£3.00 cash with order).

The National Association for Special Educational Needs (NASEN, Stafford ST17 4JX) produces a range of useful publications, including:

Barthorpe, T. and Visser, J. (1991) *Differentiation: Your Responsibility*

The ASE manual, *Race, Equality and Science Teaching*, contains a number of ideas and activities for teaching science to pupils with different needs.

Dyslexia

There is a huge range of literature on dyslexia – four books which explore the issues and offer practical approaches are:

Broomfield, H. and Combley, M. (1997) *Overcoming Dyslexia: A Practical Handbook for the Classroom*, London: Whurr Publishers.

Hulme, C. and Snowling, M. (eds) (1994) *Reading Development and Dyslexia*, London: Whurr Publishers.

Riddick, B. (1996) *Living with Dyslexia*, London: Routledge.

Snowling, M. and Stackhouse, J. (eds) (1996) *Dyslexia, Speech and Language: a Practitioner's Handbook*, London: Whurr Publishers.

Chapter 7

Practical work in science education

> . . . teachers need to be aware of the goals, potential, merits and difficulties of the school laboratory.
>
> (Tamir 1991: 20)

Practical work is one of the distinctive features of science teaching and one of the great expectations of pupil learning. How best should practical work be organised and conducted? What types of practical work can and should be done? Why do we do practical work at all in the science curriculum? These questions are all interwoven. We start with the most fundamental but least asked: Why do practical work?

Why do practical work in science lessons?

An enormous amount of time and money is invested in making practical work an element of secondary school science. Schools employ lab technicians, consume consumables of all kinds and invest large sums in pieces of apparatus that most pupils have never seen elsewhere and are never likely to encounter again after school. In the current era of local management and devolved budgets, it is inevitable that the traditional expense of practical work will be questioned by someone running the school. Science teachers need to be able to justify the time and money spent on practical work not only for this reason, but also in order to answer the two further questions of 'what?' and 'how?'

In 1963, Kerr organised a survey of 701 science teachers from 151 schools in order to find out why they did practical work in school science. He suggested ten aims or purposes which those in the survey were asked to rank for importance in relation to three different age ranges: lower secondary, upper secondary and 'sixth form'. The aims presented to teachers are shown in Table 7.1.

Table 7.1 Ten possible aims of practical work

1	To encourage accurate observation and careful recording.
2	To promote simple, common-sense, scientific methods of thought.
3	To develop manipulative skills.
4	To give training in problem-solving.
5	To fit the requirements of practical examinations.
6	To elucidate the theoretical work so as to aid comprehension.
7	To verify facts and principles already taught.
8	To be an integral part of the process of finding facts by investigation and arriving at principles.
9	To arouse and maintain interest in the subject.
10	To make biological, chemical and physical phenomena more real through actual experience.

Source: Used by Kerr 1963.

It is interesting to note that those aims are still largely relevant today, four decades on. Before reading further, consider each of those aims carefully and rank them for yourself for different ages of pupils. Jot down your own ranking for: years 7, 8 and 9; years 10 and 11; years 12 and 13 (the 'sixth form').

The full analysis of results is well worth reading in full (Kerr 1963). Here is my own potted summary of the responses:

- there was a change in emphasis in practical work as pupils move through the secondary school, for example, away from arousing interest towards careful recording;
- however, observation and scientific thinking were ranked highly throughout;
- aim 9 was highest for years 7–9;
- aim 1 was highest for years 12–13.

Taking all teachers and all age groups into account, the overall ranking of aims was: 1 (first), 2 and 8 (joint second), 6, 10, 9, 7, 3, 4, 5 (last). How do these compare with your own ranking?

The role and potential of practical work

The place of practical work in science *needs* to be justified; fortunately, there are many useful discussions which help by giving us a framework for practical work by outlining its purpose and potential. These can be summarised only briefly here.

Woolnough and Allsop (1985), in an excellent discussion on practical science, suggest that in the past four types of aim have been given by teachers and curriculum developers for small-group practicals:

1 motivational, i.e. that practical science can motivate and interest pupils (cf. Kerr 1963);

2 the development of experimental skills and techniques, such as observation, measurement, handling apparatus, etc.;

3 simulating the work of a real scientist – 'being a real scientist for the day' (a phrase from the early Nuffield days);

4 supporting theory, i.e. using practical to 'discover', elucidate or illuminate theory; and improving retention in line with the other catch-phrase of practical work: 'I hear and I forget, I see and I remember, I do and I understand.'

(The latter two groups of aims are wide open to criticism, as Woolnough and Allsop themselves point out, and their problems will be considered shortly.)

They go on to examine and discuss their own view of the purposes of practical work and then put forward their own three 'fundamental aims':

1 developing practical skills and techniques
2 being a problem-solving scientist
3 getting a feel for phenomena

The types of practical work in school science associated with these aims are discussed in detail by Woolnough and Allsop, who label the three types Exercises, Investigations and Experiences, respectively. Their full description of each type is well worth reading (Woolnough and Allsop 1985: 47–59), but examples would include:

Exercises: using a microscope, estimating, measuring, heating, manipulating, performing standard tests, e.g. food tests, setting up apparatus and equipment, e.g. a cathode ray oscilloscope, an electric circuit.

Investigations: often of the what, which or how variety, e.g. what causes rusting? which material is best for X? how do shampoos affect hair strength? (investigations are given a whole section later).

Experiences: studying, observing, handling, holding, exploring, watching, growing, e.g. plants, crystals; pushing and pulling, feeling etc.

This is a useful classification for classroom teachers – it will not only enable them to plan practical work for range and variety, but also help them to consider why they are doing a practical.

In a later discussion, Millar (writing in Woolnough 1991: 51) unpicks the idea of 'practical skills'. He divides the skills which he feels can be taught and improved into:

Practical techniques: e.g. measuring temperature to within certain limits, separating by filtration or other 'standard' procedures.

Inquiry tactics: e.g. repeating measurements, tabulating data and drawing graphs in order to look for patterns, identifying variables to alter, control, etc.

By developing these skills, pupils will develop their 'procedural understanding' of science (in contrast to their conceptual understanding). Millar argues that pupils can *progress* in practical science by increasing their competence in a wider range of techniques and by enlarging and extending their 'toolkit' of tactics for investigational work. These are the dual aims of practical science.

We only have space to consider a third framework for practical work. This is the Predict-Observe-Explain (P-O-E) pattern suggested by Gunstone (in Woolnough 1991: 69). He offers as a framework for demonstrations a constructivist approach to practical work which includes P-O-E tasks. Gunstone offers it as a framework for demonstrations but I have adapted it as a possible scheme for work with small groups too:

1   *Predict*: students are shown a particular situation and asked to predict what they believe will happen. They are asked to give reasons for their prediction, preferably in writing.
2   *Observe*: the demo or class practical is then performed and all students write down what they observe.
3   *Explain*: the third (probably most difficult stage) is to consider the P and O stages and to attempt to explain, or reconcile, any conflict between prediction and observation.

The latter stage is, in my view, by far the most difficult stage to handle, especially if this framework were used for a class practical! Gunstone elaborates fully on this interesting approach and other strategies which he has suggested in Woolnough (1991) and previous work cited there.

These frameworks for practical work are a selection of many offered regarding the purpose of practical work. I offer my own summary of the reasons for practical science in Table 7.2. Readers are invited to look critically and carefully at this table before we move on to the issue of organising practical activity.

Types of practical work and how to organise them

Different types of practical activity will be appropriate for the different aims shown in Table 7.2. There are at least six possibilities for organising and carrying out practical work in the average school situation with its usual constraints:

1   demonstrations;
2   class experiments, all on similar task, in small groups;
3   a circus of experiments, i.e. small groups on different activities in a 'carousel', spread over chunks of a lesson or over several lessons;
4   simulations and role-play;
5   investigations;
6   problem-solving activities.

The latter three are given special treatment in separate chapters. Aspects of the first three are considered briefly here.

Table 7.2 The role of practical work in science

1 *To develop skills:*

- practical techniques
- procedures
- 'tactics'
- investigation strategies
- working with others
- communicating
- problem-solving

2 *To illuminate/illustrate ('first-hand' knowledge):*

- an event
- a phenomenon
- a concept
- a law
- a principle
- a theory

3 *To motivate/stimulate:*

- entertain
- arouse curiosity
- enhance attitudes
- develop interest
- fascinate

4 *To challenge/confront:*

e.g. 'What if . . .?', Predict-Observe-Explain, 'Why . . .?'

Demonstrations

A Why use demonstrations?

Demonstrations can be useful in meeting aims 2, 3 and 4 of Table 7.2. They can be used to illustrate events or phenomena, e.g. chemical reactions, especially if those events are too *expensive*, or too *dangerous* or too *difficult* or too *time-consuming* to be done by all. There is still a valuable place in science teaching at all levels for the interesting, sometimes unforgettable, demonstration that may form an important *episode* in a pupil's learning. Thus a good demo can excite, intrigue, fascinate and entertain, especially if it has the advantage of *scale*, i.e. bigger, better, more visible, clearer and with more impact than a class experiment.

B How should demonstrations be used and carried out?

All good demonstrations need a framework so that pupils are active and can participate – in short, learners need to be *occupied* during a demo. Passive entertainment is not enough. The Gunstone framework of *predict-observe-explain* is one excellent possibility, especially in achieving aim 3 of Table 7.2. At a simpler level pupils could engage in just one of these stages, using a pencil and 'jotter'. They could be asked to record results and begin to tabulate them. In short, there needs to be an activity, preferably involving writing and recording, to structure every demo. This is essential not only on educational grounds but also for management and control. Finally, as said before, demonstrations need to go for *impact*. This means, to state the obvious, that every pupil needs to be able to see what is happening. Careful management of seating and/or standing is well worth the investment in time.

Whole-class practical work

A Why?

The reasons for class activity in small groups relate closely to almost all the aims of Table 7.2: to develop practical skills and techniques, to illuminate and illustrate, to give a feeling for sizes and orders of magnitude, to generate results for analysis, to entertain, and to challenge.

B How?

There are several aspects to managing and organising whole-class practicals, most of which can only be learnt adequately from observation and experience. But there are certain key points to be remembered: apparatus needs to be carefully distributed around the lab if pupils are to fetch it themselves – this will avoid bottlenecks; the teacher is in a supervisory role at all times and needs to be in a position to see the whole room – discussing the finer points with a small group with his or her back to the rest of the class is not good practice; always allow more than enough time for clearing away.

In planning for and structuring class practicals there are several important, necessary stages in addition to the actual activity:

- setting the scene, i.e. the pre-experiment discussion, discussing and giving instructions, arranging groups and managing the room;
- gathering results: are the pupils given a free hand or a set results table? will the results of everyone be recorded centrally, such as on an OHP or blackboard? or will they record individually or as a small group without sharing widely?;
- discussing the experiment and its results;
- interpreting and concluding: this is the most problematic and widely discussed aspect of practical work (see further reading on the problems of 'guided discovery' and the handling of pupil results);
- should conclusions be elicited from pupils or given to them? who should interpret their data – the pupil or the teacher? This element of practical

work relates very closely, of course, to the initial aim of the activity in the first place;

- writing up and reporting: this is another area of science activity that has caused great debate (see Chapter 9 on Language). Indeed, should practicals always be written up? Can they not be recorded and stored for posterity in other ways, such as audio tape, video, photograph or picture? Using solely written work for reporting strongly disadvantages those who may be good at practical science but poor at writing (for whatever reason).

A circus of experiments

A Why use this way of organising a practical?

A circus can be useful in allowing hands-on activity for all when the number of certain pieces of apparatus or other resources, such as computers and software or specialised equipment is limited. By arranging a carousel, every pupil or group can see and use the resource in turn. It can also be valuable in providing a fairly quick, highly varied set of experiences relating to one topic, such as energy or forces. Thus circuses often fulfil the experiential aim of practical work.

B How can a circus be organised?

Initially it requires a great deal more preparation from teacher and technician to provide a carousel of (say) ten different activities labelled A to J for a group of 25 children than planning a single task which all do at the same time. But this initial planning and organisation can pay dividends and save time in the long term. Additional preparation is needed to ensure:

- all work-places/activities are prepared, set out and labelled before children enter;
- each activity occupies roughly the same amount of time;
- the change-over from one activity to the next is carefully planned and the sequence written down for all to see;
- consumables can be restocked as time goes on;
- instructions for each stage are clear and readable – a work card or sheet at each station will be invaluable;
- each activity is self-contained, as the sequence through which pupils go through the carousel will be different for every group;
- extension activities are given at each station to allow for time differences (between activities and children) and the ability range.

Simulation as part of practical science

Active work in science need not always involve the 'real thing', indeed much of real science involves experiments with models and simulations of real events, for example, river flow in tanks, study of flight in wind tunnels. Pupils should therefore learn that in order to study and understand reality we often need to model it and simplify it. Thus the use of models, analogies and simulations is not only a valuable way of learning but also an important part of scientific exploration. Simulation can involve:

1   the use of ICT, for example a computer simulation, an interactive videodisc (discussed fully in a Chapter 10);
2   physical models, for example a ripple tank, marbles in a tray, molecular models, an orrery, a planetarium, analogues of electric current (such as water flow);
3   secondary sources, e.g. tables of data, graphs and charts, news cuttings, scientific articles, video tape, photographs, images from remote sensing;
4   role play, for example of processes such as melting and boiling or conduction, convection and radiation, molecular movement, etc.

These four types of simulation can achieve many of the aims outlined in Table 7.2, such as illustrating phenomena, clarifying theory. Indeed they can often be more effective than the 'real thing' because of increased clarity and simplicity.

General rules

The usual rules for all practical work apply to all the types listed above:

• the activity must be SAFE. Use whatever is necessary to ensure safety, such as goggles for heating, a safety screen for some demos, etc.;
• always try out the class practical, circus, or demo in advance;
• give a clear list of all requirements to technical/support staff well in advance;
• manage any movement around the room carefully and safely;
• give clear instructions for the activity, using different approaches. Possibilities are: oral (just telling from the start, or oral instructions arising from a class discussion); a worksheet; an overhead transparency; pupils rearranging a jumbled list of instructions into the correct order (which is then checked before starting!). A variety of approaches is needed both for reinforcement (to avoid the 'I've told them so now they know' syndrome) and to cater for all needs and styles in a mixed class.

Oh . . . by the way, remember to count everything out and count it all back in again in as visible and systematic a way as possible, Certain bits of science kit, like magnets and crocodile clips, have a habit of sticking to people!

Pitfalls and problems to watch for

Practical work in science has enormous potential for exciting pupils, giving first-hand knowledge (almost unique to science as a curriculum subject) and

Table 7.3 Pitfalls and problems with practical work in science

I Can we mimic 'real science'?

   (a) Can scientific method he broken down into a set of discrete processes?
   (b) Can scientific processes be caught and taught?
   (c) Is 'discovery learning' a con?

2 Does practical work illuminate or confuse learning in science?

3 The observation problem: Which comes first – the theory or the practical? Can children observe without a framework?

4 Does an insistence on (and a pupil expectation of) practical work limit and restrict the range of topics covered in science and the teaching strategies used?

5 Group work: what are the consequences if we simply put pupils into small groups and let them get on with it?

supporting theory. However, I would like to finish with a summary of some of the pitfalls and problems of practical work, which is very brief simply because so much has been written on it elsewhere. Table 7.3 provides a summary: each issue is considered in turn with an indication of further reading.

First, science teachers may create problems for themselves if they suggest that pupils in school science are really behaving like 'real scientists'. Few scientists can make explicit the processes that they themselves are engaged in:

> Ask a scientist what he conceives the scientific method to be and he will adopt an expression that is at once solemn and shifty-eyed: solemn, because he feels that he ought to declare an opinion; shifty-eyed because he is considering how to conceal the fact that he has no opinion to declare.
>
> (Medawar 1969: 11)

What chance then do science teachers have of accurately mimicking or assessing the processes of scientists, even if such an aim were desirable? (see Driver 1983, on the pupil as scientist; several contributors to Wellington 1989, and a critique of the 1970s and 80s enthusiasm for discovery learning in Wellington 1981 and Atkinson and Delamont 1977).

Second, it may be the case that practical work, especially if things go wrong, can actually confuse rather than illuminate laws and theories. This has led to the tweaking, fiddling and stage management that has become one of the unwritten skills of the science teacher (see Nott and Wellington 1997).

This links to the third point – observation, like the truth, is rarely pure and never simple. Learners often need to be told what to look for, i.e. the framework precedes the practical. This is as true for looking down microscopes as it is for 'observing' magnetic fields or viewing convection currents in air or water. There are at least three points about observation that emerge from current views on the nature of science:

- observations rarely form the *starting point* for a practising scientist;
- observations are theory-dependent, i.e. theory normally precedes observation;
- if more than one person (be it pupil or scientist) observes the *same* phenomenon, their observations may well be different, i.e. people see through their theories (see Hodson 1986).

The practical point for teachers is that it makes little sense to either teach or assess *observation* in isolation.

The fourth point is that an insistence on practical work as an essential feature of school science can actually restrict the science curriculum: 'We won't teach that topic because we can't do practical work in it.' This has led to an often hidden reluctance amongst science teachers to include a topic in a scheme of work because they cannot find a way of including a traditional practical. Thus topics like cosmology, earth science and astronomy, and many of the controversial issues which involve science, have often been neglected. This has led in turn to the use of a very restricted range of teaching strategies amongst science teachers (see Woolnough and Allsop 1985; Wellington 1998).

The final problem considered here is the issue of group work. Teachers commonly place pupils in small groups and assume that the group will *work*. Close observation shows that this is often not the case, especially in groups of three or more. One pupil may dominate while others play little part, e.g. in planning, predicting or carrying out a practical. Pupils may willingly adopt different roles, some of which may have nothing to do with the science: for example one member may simply record and tabulate results with no clue as to what they mean or where they came from. There are many other issues connected with group work – my general point here is that we cannot assume that groups are teams or that pupils share or rotate their roles in a group. In short, group work must be managed, it cannot be taken for granted.

References and further reading

A fairly recent collection of 16 chapters which looks at different types of practical work, justifications for it, the use of ICT, and alternatives to practical work is:

Wellington, J. (ed.) (1998), *Practical Work in School Science: Which Way Now?*, London: Routledge.

General discussions on the aims and conduct of practical work

Bentley, D. and Watts, M. (eds) (1989) *Learning and Teaching in School Science*, Milton Keynes: Open University Press (pp. 21–41 especially).
Driver, R. (1983) *The Pupil As Scientist*, Milton Keynes: Open University Press.
Gunstone, R.F. (1991) 'Reconstructing theory for practical experience', in Woolnough, B. (ed.) (1991) *Practical Science*, Milton Keynes: Open University Press.

Kerr, J. (1963) *Practical Work in School Science*, Leicester: Leicester University Press (a classic enquiry into the nature and purpose of school science practical work, based on a study of 701 teachers in 151 schools).

Medawar, P. (1969) *Induction and Intuition in Scientific Thought*, London: Methuen.

Millar, R. (1991) 'A means to an end: the role of processes in science education', in Woolnough, B. (ed.) (1991) *Practical Science*, Milton Keynes: Open University Press.

Solomon, J. (1980) *Teaching Children in the Laboratory*, London: Croom Helm.

Tamir, P. (1991) 'Practical work in school science: an analysis of current practice', in Woolnough, B. (ed.) (1991) *Practical Science*, Milton Keynes: Open University Press.

Woolnough, B. (ed.) (1991) *Practical Science*, Milton Keynes: Open University Press (a range of useful chapters on school practical work).

Woolnough, B. and Allsop, T. (1985) *Practical Work in Science*, Cambridge: Cambridge University Press.

Safety aspects

ASE (1996) *Safeguards in the School Laboratory* (10th edn.), Hatfield: ASE.

Borrows, P. (1992) 'Safety in secondary schools', in Hull, R. (ed.), *ASE Secondary Science Teachers' Handbook*, Hemel Hempstead: Simon & Shuster. (This highlights the common accidents in labs most of which involve chemicals in the eye or mouth or on the body; and describes five 'main danger areas' such as burns from alcohol fires and alkali metal explosions.) More recently Borrows has written: 'Safety in science education', in Ratcliffe, M. (ed.) (1998).

DfEE (1996) *Safety in Science Education*, London: HMSO.

Everett, K. and Jenkins, E. (1991) A *Safety Handbook for Science Teachers*, London: John Murray.

Critical comments on the value of school science practicals

Atkinson, P. and Delamont, S. (1977) 'Mock-ups and cock-ups: the stage management of guided discovery instruction', in Woods, P. and Hammersley, M. (eds), *School Experience*, London: Croom Helm.

Hodson, D. (1986) 'The nature of scientific observation', *School Science Review* vol. 68, no. 242, pp. 17–29.

Hodson, D. (1990) 'A critical look at practical work in school science', *School Science Review*, vol. 71, no. 256, pp. 33–9.

Millar, R. (1989) 'What is scientific method and can it be taught?', in Wellington, J. (ed.), *Skills and Processes in Science Education*, London: Routledge.

Nott, M. and Wellington, J. (1997) 'Producing the evidence: science teachers' initiations into practical work', *Research in Science Education*, vol. 27, no. 3, pp. 395–409.

Osborne, J. (1997) 'Practical alternatives', *School Science Review*, vol. 78, no. 285, pp. 61–6.

Wellington, J. (1981) 'What's supposed to happen, Sir?: some problems with discovery learning', *School Science Review*, vol. 63, no. 222, pp. 167–73.

Wellington, J. (1989) (ed.) *Skills and Processes in Science Education*, London: Routledge (various chapters).

Chapter 8

Investigations in science

Click, click, click (the school clock). We were supposed to be reading the instructions for an experiment we were going to perform in class that day. Now there's another stupid thing. Year after year, this same teacher makes his students perform the same experiments. Well, if the experiments have been done so many times before, how can they still be experiments? The teacher knows what is going to happen. I thought experimenting meant trying *new* things to see what would happen. We weren't experimenting at all. We were playacting.

(*Claudia and the Great Search*, by Ann Martin, New York: Scholastic)

What are 'investigations'? Are they the same as problem-solving? What types of investigations are there? How should they be carried out and organised? What help can we provide to pupils to guide them and to structure the investigation? Do they present any problems in the classroom? Can they really reflect the way that science and scientists work? These are the questions that this chapter raises.

What are investigations?

Examples of investigations

Below are listed some examples of investigations that I have either seen, used, read or heard about:

- How much rainfall do we get in each month throughout the year?
- What conditions do wood lice like best?
- Design an instrument to make the best spectrum.

- What are the best conditions for yeast growth?
- Which kind of paper is best for mopping up water?
- Design a machine for exercising a dog.
- Design a machine for weighing an elephant.
- Which ball is most bouncy?
- Which surface is best for bouncing a ball on?
- What makes sugar dissolve faster?
- Which factors affect the frequency of the note from a stretched string?
- Study the reaction times of different people.
- How do people's reaction times vary with different stimuli and conditions (for example, after drinking coffee, late in the day, etc.)?
- Which is the best detergent/washing powder?
- Investigate the composition, structure and strength of local soils.
- Which trainer sole is best?
- What factors determine how fast a car can travel?
- What happens to the boiling/melting point of water if you add solvents?
- Can people tell the difference between margarine and butter?
- Separate a mixture of iron filings, salt, sand, and polystyrene chips.
- Design and make a device for enabling an egg to fall 3 metres without breaking.
- Build a tower to a height of 1 metre, using drinking straws, which can support an egg/coin/marble.
- Which factors affect the speed at which different things dry?
- Which fuel (from a safe selection!) produces the most heat.
- Which insulating material is best for keeping hot water hot?
- Imagine a village is threatened by an erupting volcano. Devise ways of protecting it.

Different types of investigation

These are all investigations that have been suggested for, or tried in, the classroom. Varying degrees of structure and guidance will have been given. Some have a 'correct' answer; some don't. Some will take weeks or even months; some a few minutes. Some involve imaginary situations; most involve real situations. Some contexts are 'everyday'; some will be new to pupils. Some involve design-and-make skills (technological?); some do not. Some are 'problem-solving activities', but clearly not all investigations need be of a problem-solving kind.

In an attempt to make some sense of the wide range of investigations now being used or suggested, I have tried a 'typology of investigations', which is shown in Table 8.1. This classification can be helpful in considering suggested ideas for investigations and published examples; it can also be useful in considering a department's policy and planning for investigational work.

Table 8.1 A typology of investigations

'*Which*' type investigations

- Which factors affect X?
- Which *design* is best for ...?
- Which X is best for ...? (for example, insulator, sole of trainers, floor covering, paper-towel for absorbing, soil, washing-up liquid, hamster food ...This can often involve critically testing manufacturers' claims!).

'*What*' type investigations

- What happens if ...?
- What is the connection between X and Y? (for example, shape and strength, aperture of a pinhole camera and image, length of pendulum and period time, temperature and dissolving etc.).

'*How do*' investigations

- How do different Xs affect Y?
- How does X vary with Y?
- How does X affect Y?

General investigations

- A survey, for example historical (nuclear energy, the chemical elements); local (pond study).
- A long-term project, for example local stream pollution, air quality, soil or path erosion.
- (These will often involve secondary sources, such as books, the media, extensive research and reading.)

Problem-solving activities

- Design-and-make, for example a dog-exercising machine, a desalination device.
- Solve a practical problem, for example bridge a gap, build a structure, make an alarm system.
- Simulations.

Open and closed, pupil-led and teacher-led

A second framework for reflecting on the types of investigational work done in science lessons is given in Figure 8.1.

The three axes shown are not independent, of course. The first, teacher-led to pupil-led, indicates a continuum from one extreme at which pupils pose the questions to investigate to the other, in which all the questions are set, posed and restricted by the teacher. In practice, different work at different times will lie at different points along this axis – indeed, it must do if teachers are to meet the requirements of their curriculum.

The second axis, open to closed, shows a second continuum from one extreme in which an investigation or a problem-solving activity will have only one 'correct' answer and only one route for reaching it, to the other in which many possible solutions are equally acceptable, with many routes to them. In between these extremes lie many permutations and possibilities.

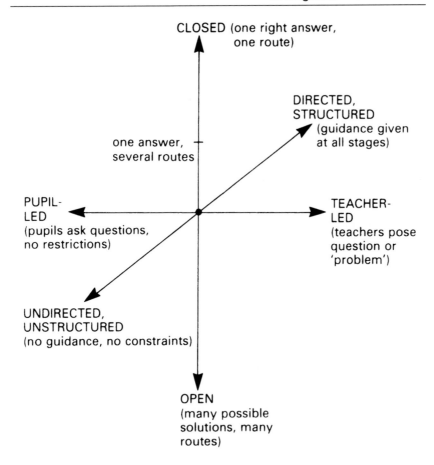

Figure 8.1 Dimensions of investigational work.

The third axis (obviously not independent of the others but still worth separating), is from undirected and unstructured to directed and structured. At one extreme, pupils will be given guidance, constraint and structure all along the way, i.e. in planning, designing, carrying out and evaluating. At the other no guidance, structure and restriction will be placed on them. Neither extreme is very likely to occur in practice.

The main purpose of this framework is to help teachers in planning for and reflecting on the type of investigational work they do in schools. It should help to increase variety and to clarify assessment.

Another way of categorising investigations was put forward by Watson *et al.* (1999: 105). They suggest six categories with certain key features: classifying and identifying; fair testing; pattern seeking; exploring; investigating models; and, finally, making things or developing systems.

Why do them?

There are many good reasons for using an investigational approach to science teaching, in addition to the pragmatic one of 'it's in the curriculum'. For many pupils it can be a great motivator, particularly if they really 'get into' a long-term investigation. Many pupils who are not successful in, and motivated by, other aspects of science work, such as learning content or written work, can sometimes be surprisingly successful at and therefore 'turned on by' investigational work. It can also be extremely enjoyable, perhaps leading more pupils to choose science once they reach the age of choice and consent. It can lead to teamwork and co-operation in science learning, which may be difficult to develop quite so actively in other ways. For many teachers of science, the introduction of investigational work can change entirely the way they approach the teaching of science generally: for example, the teaching of content (conceptual understanding) and process (procedural understanding) can be geared entirely towards an investigation as the end point or motivator. Certain critics of the investigational approach argue that it will leave 'less time for content', but this need not be the case – on the contrary, it could provide the motivation for learning content.

Coping in the classroom

Pitfalls and problems to watch for

We have already seen that investigational work can have a number of benefits in learning and teaching science. But there are, of course, a number of pitfalls and problems that teachers (and pupils) need to be aware of:

- *What is an investigation?*: There is little agreement or clarity in the use of words such as 'investigation', 'experiment', etc. amongst teachers. 'Investigation' and 'experiment' are best seen as lying on a continuum, rather than as separate activities. The framework and typology shown in Figure 8.1 and Table 8.1 respectively may help.
- *Who does what in a group?*: Group dynamics must be considered because most practical work is carried out collectively. What is the role of each team member? Do they contribute equally or do some assume minor subsidiary roles? Do they all learn equally or are some participating within a clerical role, with little or no understanding of the underlying principles? If plans are produced individually, whose plan is followed in a group investigation?
- *How should the 'process' of investigational work relate to learning 'theory' or content?*: Process skills interact closely with children's prior knowledge and understanding – they cannot be separated from them. This has implications for the type of investigation that children can be expected to carry out and is important in considering progression, assessment, and the linking of investigations with work on content.

- *What is progression?*: Progression in investigation work is difficult to identify, observe and measure.
- *When and how should the teacher interfere?*: How much input should a teacher make in an investigation? When and how should she or he intervene – at the planning stage? At the interpretation stage?
- *'Right' and 'wrong' answers*: How should teachers deal with 'incorrect answers' (i.e. scientifically unacceptable) to a closed-ended investigation? (Pupils will often look for the 'right' answer to certain kinds of investigation.)
- *Planning*: The planning part of an investigation is one of the most difficult aspects for pupils.
- *Evaluating*: This seems to be an even more difficult activity for students to do well.

Investigational work rarely reflects the 'true nature of science' (indeed, how could it possibly be expected to?). It may promote the 'data first, theory second' view of science, i.e. the 'Sherlock Holmes in a white coat' notion. In addition, assessment of investigations is (to put it mildly) not easy.

For pupils to carry out investigations successfully in the classroom, most teachers feel that they will need guidance and structure of some sort – the only difference of opinion is to what degree. The next section offers some practical possibilities that have been put forward.

Giving guidance and help

Many schools and education authorities use structured sheets with questions for pupils to follow and fill in at different stages, for example:

My question or idea to investigate is _____

This is what I think will happen. _____

This is why. _____

This is what I am going to do. _____

What things will you keep the same during the investigation? _____

What will you change during the investigation? _____

How will you make sure it is a fair test? _____

What equipment will you need? _____

What will you measure, count or look for? _____

Another education authority (Wakefield) produced an attractive leaflet for all pupils explaining the steps in investigation under a framework of Planning, Doing and Reporting. Here is a short excerpt:

Planning

- Think of the question you are trying to answer.
- What do you predict will happen?
- Have you a reason or hypothesis for your prediction?

Doing

- You must look closely (observe) what happens.
- Make careful measurements using the right instruments.
- Say what you need to change and keep the same – the variables.

Reporting

- Say what your results mean.
- Try to explain or interpret them.
- Could you have done better?
- How might you change your plan?
- Evaluate your work.

Many other frameworks and guidelines for pupils have been produced – the above selections are a tiny sample. They will certainly help to overcome at least some of the pitfalls and problems outlined above. The main general feeling is that pupils will need guidance and structure for at least part of the time during their investigational work. What does seem to vary from one school to another is the amount of guidance given to pupils, which of course has implications for assessment.

Developing a model/structure for investigational work: three levels

One of the aims of doing investigational work in the classroom, of course, must be to develop in pupils some sort of understanding of science procedures as well as the more specific 'kitbag' of skills and techniques. The latter can be taught almost as rules of thumb and can quite rightly involve training as much as education. Thus pupils can be taught how to read a range of measuring instruments, how to set up data-logging equipment, how to record results manually, and how to set up certain common types of apparatus, such as for distillation. This is all part of basic practical science education, verging on training.

At a slightly higher level pupils can be taught the importance of accuracy, the limitations of certain measuring instruments and the need to repeat measurements, i.e. take lots of readings. They can also learn the ideas of identifying and controlling variables and therefore the notion of a 'fair test'.

Eventually, the aim must be to develop a general model of 'investigational work' which pupils can use and apply in a number of different situations. Some curriculum models imply a *linear* approach to investigation i.e. Plan, Do, Observe, Analyse, Evaluate . . . finish. This is often forced upon teachers/

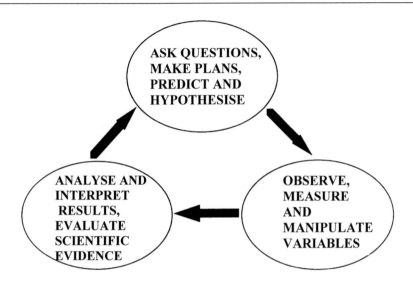

Figure 8.2 A cyclic view of investigational work.

learners by the constraints of an external curriculum, the school timetable and lab organisation. In an ideal world, however, a model of investigational work (and the practice of 'real science') should follow a cyclic approach. The process of interpreting and evaluating results should not be the end-point. Rather it should lead back to the first activity of asking new questions, making revised plans and revisiting predictions. This ideal, cyclic model is shown in Figure 8.2.

The ultimate aim in investigational work, therefore, must be to encourage (or even inculcate) a generalised pattern or model of such work. To develop this, pupils must be able to see each investigation task at some level of abstraction. They must be able to pay attention to the general, structural features of the task as well as its context-embedded, surface, specific features. This must be the justification or rationale for expecting thousands of pupils to spend thousands of hours on investigations in science, i.e. to develop a pattern or model for tackling investigations and problems. How else could we justify the time spent?

This has implications for teaching. As well as providing pupils with interesting investigations in exciting, often everyday contexts, teachers also need to spend time on the general features of each task. What are the pupils doing and why? What types of variable are they controlling? What is this idea of a 'fair test'? Why is it important to repeat measurements? What limits does their experiment and others like it have? Only by considering the general structural features of each specific task will the model develop, a model which might then be transferred to other contexts and other tasks, including perhaps those outside the science classroom. In this way pupils may also learn something about the nature, purpose and limitations of science itself.

Can pupils learn about the nature of science by doing investigations?

My view is that they can, but curriculum statements and guidelines often reflect only one view or model of science. It may be a reasonable mirror or representation of how some scientists actually work (although certain critics might not even admit this). However, it is certain that it could never be a model of scientific procedure, method or practice which mirrors 'real science' in all its forms – indeed, what model ever could be? Perhaps the answer is to allow several different models of scientific investigation which pupils in labs could follow for different types of work. This would certainly get round the following problem: the current statutory guidelines present only one view of science that teachers will inevitably adhere to; therefore, pupils will receive the message that this is 'the nature of science'. This is not a useful, let alone a truthful, message. Despite the complexity and controversy in all the current debates on the history, philosophy and sociology of science, one message is clear: Scientists have, do and will work in a variety of different ways at different times in different disciplines for different reasons.

References and further reading

A very good introduction is:

Qualter, A., Strang, J., Swatton, P. and Taylor, R. (1990) *Exploration – A Way of Learning Science*, Oxford: Basil Blackwell.

An excellent overview of research is: Gott, R. and Duggan, S. (1995) *Investigative Work in the Science Curriculum*, Buckingham: Open University Press.

Laws, P.M. (1996) 'Investigative work in the science national curriculum', *School Science Review*, vol. 77, no. 281, pp. 17–25.

The ATLAS (Active Teaching and Learning Approaches in Science) materials contain many valuable ideas and useful guidance for teachers in doing investigations (from Collins Educational, London, W6 8JB).

Watson, R. and Wood-Robinson, V. (1998) 'Learning to Investigate', in Ratcliffe, M. (ed.) pp. 84–91.

For a critical look at approaches to investigational work try:

Wellington, J. (ed.) (1998) *Practical Work in School Science: Which Way Now?*, London: Routledge.

Woolnough, B. (ed.) (1991) *Practical Science* (various chapters), Milton Keynes: Open University Press.

Woolnough, B. and Allsop, T. (1985) *Practical Work in Science*, Cambridge: Cambridge University Press.

The AKSIS project, based at King's College London, is studying investigations in school science. One of several publications is:

Watson, R., Goldsworthy, A. and Wood-Robinson, V. (1999) 'What is not fair with investigations?', *School Science Review*, vol. 80, no. 292, pp. 101–6.

Various publishers produce resources for the classroom on investigational work. *The Pupil Researcher Initiative* (PRI) based at Sheffield Hallam University is one of the best sources for new ideas and developments.

Finally, keep your eyes wide open for new publications – this continues to be a changing, hotly debated area.

A glossary of terms and variables

Terms

Conceptual understanding/knowledge: Concerned with the ideas and concepts of science, for example force, energy, magnetism, humidity, evolution, reaction.

Hypothesis: A reasoned explanation put forward for an observed event, or events. It should be testable (falsifiable) by investigation.

Procedural understanding/knowledge: Concerned with the procedures of experimental, investigational work, i.e. identifying variables and understanding their importance; planning and designing an investigation; understanding ideas of measurement such as accuracy, reliability and 'repeatability'; recording, displaying and interpreting data.

Qualitative approach: One that does not involve measurement, for example, using terms like quickly/slowly or large/small.

Quantitative approach: One that involves measurements to make observations more precise and put numbers against them.

Variables

A variable is a quantity that can take different values. It can be categoric, discrete, continuous or derived.

Categoric: A categoric variable is a classification, such as colour (red, green, yellow, etc.); shape (square, oblong, round).

Continuous: A continuous variable can have any value, such as mass, weight, volume, length, temperature, time.

Control*: Control variables are those that must be controlled and held constant by the investigator and which make the investigation a 'fair test'. (Sometimes the control variable is confused with 'the control' in an experiment, particularly in biology. A control, such as a plant which is not given any of the nutrients being tested, can be considered as one value of the independent variable.)

Dependent*: The dependent variable is the effect or outcome of interest to the investigator. It is measured or judged in the investigation. In the example under **Independent** below it would be the length of the spring.

Derived: A derived variable has to be calculated from more than one measurement, for example speed from distance travelled and the time taken, acceleration; work.

Discrete: A discrete variable can only have an integer value, such as the number of layers of insulation or the number of germinated seeds.

Independent*: The independent variable is the one which the investigator chooses to change systematically. For example, in an investigation into how different springs stretch, the independent variable is the mass chosen to hang on the spring. **Interacting:** Two independent variables whose effects on the dependent variable are not easily separated, such as the effect of water and air on rusting.

Key: Key variables define an investigation. They are the independent variable and the dependent variable.

*Independent is 'the one you change'; dependent is 'the one you keep an eye on'; control is 'the one you keep the same'.

Chapter 9

Language in science teaching and learning

> Children solve practical tasks with the help of their speech as well as their eyes and hands.
>
> (Vygotsky 1978)

Although science is a 'practical' subject, science teaching occurs extensively through the medium of language, both spoken and written. The purpose of this chapter is to focus on that language and the way that teachers, texts and children use it. We start from three basic premises: (i) language is a major barrier in learning science; (ii) we can identify the main sources of difficulty; (iii) there are teaching strategies which can help to lower the language barrier.

Watch your language: the world of secondary science

In the school science lab pupils meet all sorts of strange objects and devices which they will never encounter elsewhere: they meet the world of the conical flask, the pestle and mortar, the bunsen burner, the evaporating dish, the gauze and the watch glass, not to mention the pipette and the burette. To enter the lab is akin to Alice's passage down the rabbit hole into a new world. This is equally true of pupils' strange encounters with a new world of discourse.

> Twas brillig and the slithy toves,
> Did gyre and gimble in the wabe;
> All mimsy were the borogoves,
> And the mome raths outgrabe.
> . . . Somehow it seems to fill my head with ideas – only I don't exactly know what they are!
>
> (*Through the Looking Glass*, Lewis Carroll)

How many pupils, confronted by a science textbook or by a blackboard covered in scientific prose, are as confused as Alice was when she first read 'Jabberwocky'? Their heads may be full of ideas but they may not be quite sure what those ideas are, or where they came from. In many ways, the language of science resembles the language of Carroll's poem.

Classifying the words of science

Consider the random selection below of words used in science textbooks and by science teachers:

momentum	inertia	acceleration	power
photosynthesis	gene	speed	couple
fruit	wave	electric current	isotope
parasite	particle	critical angle	trachea
electron	substance	force	meniscus
neutron	material	pressure	mass
proton	photon	work	field
amoeba	velocity	energy	

Their only shared characteristic *could be* that each has a precision or 'fixedness' in its meaning. Science words *might be* considered to mean the same whatever the context and whoever the user. But do they? Certainly the 'fixed' meaning of science words is being questioned (Sutton 1992).

But it is the *difference between* the words of science rather than their *shared* features that I would like to concentrate on here, for the words in the above list do vastly different jobs. Take 'trachea' and 'inertia', for example. The word 'trachea' simply *names* a real object or entity: a windpipe ('trachea', like many scientific words, is thus a synonym). It has meaning because it names or 'points to' a real entity. But how does a word like 'inertia' acquire meaning? It does not refer to an object or an entity. Surely then it must signify a *concept*. This concept is somehow derived from experience – the observation that 'heavy things tend to keep going', or a 'steam roller is hard to get started' or similar personal experiences.

Unfortunately, many concept words in science do not, and cannot, acquire meaning as easily as a word like 'trachea'. Take the word 'atom', for example. Your, and my, meaning for this word can never be derived from experience. The same is true for other so-called unobservable entities. There are even greater problems for the meaning of many terms used in physics: 'frictionless body,' 'point mass' and 'smooth surface', for example – not derived from experience, nor unobservable entities, but non-existent idealisations! The terms of Schrodinger's wave equation and De Broglie's statement of wave/particle duality present problems at an even higher level of abstraction. I find it impossible to conjure up even a vague mental image of a particle being a wave all at the same time.

Table 9.1 A taxonomy of the words of science

Level 1   Naming words

    1.1   Familiar objects, new names (synonyms)
    1.2   New objects, new names
    1.3   Names of chemical elements
    1.4   Other nomenclature

Level 2   Process words

    2.1   Capable of ostensive definition, i.e. being shown
    2.2   Not capable of ostensive definition

Level 3   Concept words

    3.1   Derived from experience (sensory concepts)
    3.2   With dual meanings, i.e. everyday and scientific, for example, 'work'
    3.3   Theoretical constructs (total abstractions, idealisations. and postulated entities)

Level 4   Mathematical 'words' and symbols

This all indicates that it can be useful to divide the words of science into various types or categories. Through doing this, science teachers can become more aware of the language they use in classrooms. I have put forward a classification or 'Taxonomy' of the words of science in Table 9.1.

Each category of words acquires meaning in a different way, and it is this complexity that teachers of science need to be aware of:

- The first category can be called *naming words*. These are words that denote identifiable, observable, real objects or entities: words like 'trachea', 'oesophagus', 'tibia', 'fibula', 'fulcrum', 'meniscus', 'vertebra', 'pollen', 'saliva', 'thorax', 'iris', 'larynx' and 'stigma'. Many of these are simply synonyms for everyday words already familiar to pupils, like 'windpipe', 'backbone', or 'spit'. Thus part of learning in science involves giving *familiar* objects new names. At a slightly higher level, some learning in science involves giving new names to *unfamiliar* objects, objects which pupils may never have seen before – perhaps because they cannot be seen with a naked eye (such as a cell) or because they belong to the world of school science laboratories, for example beaker, conical flask, bunsen burner, spatula, gauze, and splint.

- The second category of scientific words, at a new level of abstraction, can be called *process words*. These are words that denote processes that happen in science: words like 'evaporation', 'distillation', 'condensation', 'photosynthesis', 'crystallisation', 'fusion', 'vaporisation', 'combustion' and 'evolution'. Clearly, some of these process words acquire meaning for a pupil more easily than others. A teacher can point to a reaction on the front bench and say 'there, that's combustion', or demonstrate red ink losing its colour and say 'that's distillation'. Thus certain processes are in a sense visible, or at least 'showable'. Their meaning can be learnt by *ostensive definition* (from the Latin *ostendo*, 'I show'). Other processes belong to a higher level within this category. One cannot point to something happening and say 'That's evolution'. Through education and language development, 'evolution' may also become a concept (i.e. level 3.3).

- The third, and largest, category of words in science are *concept words*. These are words that denote concepts of various types: words like 'work', 'energy', 'power', 'fruit', 'salt', 'pressure', 'force', 'volume', 'temperature', 'heat' and so on. This area of learning in science is surely the one where most learning difficulties are encountered, for concept words denote ideas at gradually ascending levels of abstraction.
- We should also note that many words can start as a name but, through language development in science, gradually be used as a concept. For example, fuel may be a name for petrol or paraffin, but gradually it acquires a general, conceptual meaning, such as 'a flammable material yielding energy'. Similarly with the terms 'salt' and 'gas'.

At the lowest level, certain concepts are directly derived from experience. Like certain processes, they can be defined ostensively by pointing out examples where the concept pertains. Colour concepts, such as 'red', are almost certainly learnt in this way. These can be neatly termed *sensory concepts*. The next category contains words that have both a scientific and (perhaps unfortunately) an everyday meaning: examples include 'work', 'energy', 'power', 'fruit' and 'salt'. The existence of the two meanings causes pupils difficulties and confusion. It also explains the seemingly strange yet often perceptive conceptions (alternative frameworks) that pupils possess of 'heat', 'plant nutrition', 'pressure', 'energy', 'work' and so on. The same word is being used to denote two different ideas. In these cases the invention of totally new words (such as 'anode' and 'cathode' coined by Faraday) might have made life easier for generations of school science pupils. Finally, concept words belonging to a third level are used to denote what I will call *theoretical constructs*: words like 'element', 'mixture', 'compound', 'atom', 'electron', 'valency', 'mole', 'mass', 'frictionless body', 'smooth surface', 'field' and so on. Some of these theoretical constructs, such as atom and electron, people may prefer to call unobservable entities because in a sense they exist. Others are simply idealisations, or total abstractions, which cannot possibly exist, such as point masses or frictionless bodies, except in the language of mathematics.

The language of mathematics, its 'words' and symbols, can be placed at the fourth and highest level of abstraction in a hierarchy of scientific words. The mathematical language used in advanced physics is neither derived from, nor directly applicable to, experience. Its meaning is so detached as to become almost autonomous.

Using a taxonomy of words in science teaching

This hierarchy or classification is all very well, you might say, but of what possible use can it be to the science teacher? What implications does it have? I will suggest four areas where it might be applied:

1 Beware of meaning at the higher levels

Different scientific words *mean* in different ways. The word 'iris' has meaning by labelling or pointing out an observable entity; similarly with many other words in level 1 of the taxonomy. But the meaning of words in higher levels is not as clear. At best they denote, or refer to, some mental image or abstract idea.

Words in the highest level of the taxonomy, such as 'electron', can *only* have meaning in a theoretical context. The meaning of 'electron' belongs to a theoretical world of nuclei, atoms, electric fields, shells and orbits – an imaginary, almost make-believe world to pupils starting science. Yet 'electron' can acquire meaning, just as the words in a far-fetched fairy tale do. The problem of meaning (or rather lack of it) at these higher levels of abstraction must be a major cause of failure in science education.

2 Are pupils 'ready'?

The lack of meaning for many pupils of scientific terms in level 3 of the taxonomy particularly may explain why many pupils fail to make sense of science. Perhaps they meet these words too soon – indeed the hierarchy in the taxonomy could be closely related to Piagetian stages of development. Is it possible, for example, for a pupil to acquire any meaning for a term denoting a theoretical construct before he or she has reached the formal-operational stage? (See Chapter 4.) More positively, can science teaching help achieve the required readiness and development?

3 Language development

A conscious awareness of gradually ascending development of meaning can often be useful to the science teacher in classroom teaching and lesson preparation. By developing word meanings for pupils – for example, from a word (say 'gas') being simply a name to becoming a concept – children's understanding, thought and language are enhanced. Word meanings can develop in a child's mind through both appropriate teaching and wider experiences.

4 Teaching for shared meaning

Science education must, to some extent, be initiation into new language. With naming words this can be quite simple. But the more abstract a term becomes the more it must be taught by analogy or by the use of models. If there is no *entity* to which a term corresponds, then clearly meaning becomes more difficult to communicate. But there are dangers.

Encouraging children to make the words of science meaningful *to them* should not imply encouraging them to develop *their own meanings* for scientific words. As Wittgenstein pointed out (1958), there can be no such thing as a private language. Languages are, by definition, public. In short, meanings in science need not be *impersonal* but they must be *interpersonal*. We need to teach for shared meaning (Edwards and Mercer 1987).

These are just four areas where the taxonomy of Table 9.1 has relevance to science teaching. The taxonomy also has important uses in considering teachers' written material and in assessing the readability of science texts. These are both considered in later sections.

Teacher talk

Science teachers spend a lot of their time talking. Inspection reports in the past have shown that the dominant teaching style has been exposition from the teacher, and this is still common. It follows from this, and the discussion above on the complexity of scientific words, that teachers of science need to be especially careful of their spoken language.

One of the most valuable studies published on school language came from Barnes *et al.* (1969).The study identified three types of language used by teachers:

- *specialist language presented*: words and forms of language unique to the subject which teachers are aware of as a potential problem and therefore present and explain to their students;
- *specialist language not presented*: language special to the subject which is not deliberately presented either because it has been explained before or teachers are unaware that they are using it;
- *the language of secondary education*: terms, words and forms of language used by teachers which pupils would not normally hear, see or use except in the world of the school, i.e. not the language of the world outside.

This an important classification and one of which all science teachers should be aware. It is invaluable as a framework for reflecting upon both teacher talk and (discussed shortly) teacher writing. Table 9.2 gives a summary of the categories, with examples from science; readers are invited to examine this table and see if they can add any further examples.

The right-hand column of the table, i.e. specialist language, can be further classified in terms of the taxonomy presented in Table 9.1. Which of the specialist terms are naming words, which are process words and which are concept words? It would seem that, in watching their language, teachers should be especially wary of those in level 3.3 of my taxonomy.

Table 9.2 Watch your language

Can you add to the following lists?

The language of secondary education	Technical language/ specialist language
criterion	regular
in terms of	equilibrium
relatively	calibrate
factors	proportional to
specifically	uniform
complex	force
assumption	work
ideally	energy
initially	power
related to	moment
subject to	miscible
recap	random
determines	diverges
distinguish between	exert
effectively	secrete
theoretically	saturated
becomes apparent	mass
	trachea

Barnes and his colleagues went on to analyse some of the teacher and pupil talk that occurs in science lessons. Some of their extracts are superb; for brevity's sake I present just one below, said to be from a class for pupils who had recently moved into secondary education:

T: Now what we want is a method whereby we can take off this . . . um . . . green material . . . this green stuff off the grass and perhaps one or two of you can suggest how we might do this . . . yes?

P1: Boil it.

T: Boil it? What with?

P1: Some water in a beaker and . . .

T: Yes, there's that method . . . we could do it and . . . um . . . I think probably you could guess how we might be able to do it by what we've already got out in the laboratory. How do you think we might do it? (Pestle and mortar are on bench.)

P2: Could pound it. . . .

T: Pound it up with water and that's exactly what we're going to do.

T: We're going to cut the grass into small pieces and then we're going to put it into the . . . what we call a mortar . . . this is what we call a mortar . . . this bowl . . . and anyone know what we call the other thing which we're going to pound it in?

T: Now I don't know whether any of you could jump the gun a bit and tell me what actually is this green stuff which produces green colour ...

P: Er ... em ... water.

T: No ... have you heard of chlorophyll?

T: Put that into the distillation flask and then distil off and then we get thermometer recording the correct temperature which is the boiling point for acetone. Then we collect the acetone which came over as a distillate.

Look carefully at the talk here. Which words and terms can be classed as the language of secondary education? How is the specialist language being handled? It is also interesting to note the questioning going on here: is it closed or open? Is the teacher asking the pupil to 'guess what's in my head' (what Barnes calls a pseudo-question)?

The Barnes study contains many similar extracts and is thoroughly recommended; little has changed since its publication. It would be a valuable activity for any teacher to record his or her discourse with a class in the same way and then to analyse it using the frameworks above.

In the thirty years or more since Barnes' first work a number of important studies have been made of classroom language and the discourse of science in the UK, USA and Australia. That research cannot be summarised here (see further reading), but my own analysis of it shows that certain words come up again and again. Table 9.3 shows my own potted summary of some of the difficult words identified in research on pupils' understanding.

Overcoming language barriers

Chapter 6 on the different needs of pupils suggested several practical strategies for helping pupils to get to grips with some of the language of science strategies such as wordbanks, and word games using laminated cards. Other strategies for teachers are presented later in this chapter. One strategy which I have been trying out in schools involves pupils in using a glossary or a dictionary of all the scientific words they are likely to encounter in their pre-16 curriculum. Figure 9.1 shows one page from a Science Dictionary which contains explanations of

Table 9.3 Some 'hard' words in science

factor	average	concept
abundant	adjacent	contrast *
incident *	composition *	contract *
complex	component	rate *
spontaneous	emit	exert
relevant	linear	negligible
valid	random	sequence

(* indicates words with double meanings for pupils).

Prism

A prism is a piece of glass in the shape of a 3D triangle which can do interesting things with light. Some prisms can split light into the seven colours which make up white light.

In a rainbow, raindrops act like tiny prisms and split sunlight into the colours of the **spectrum**: RED, ORANGE, YELLOW, GREEN, BLUE, INDIGO, VIOLET (remember: 'Richard of York gave battle in vain')

90° RIGHT-ANGLED PRISM

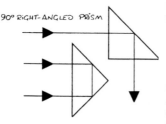

If the seven colours are painted evenly onto a disc and the disc is spun quickly, it appears to be white.

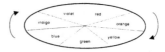

Prisms shaped so that one angle is 90° and the others are 45° can be used to reflect light, or change its direction completely. Prisms like this are called right-angle prisms and are used in cameras and binoculars.

Protein

Protein is a body building food. It is used for growth (especially for young people or for pregnant women), or for repairing damaged or worn-out body tissue. Proteins can also be a source of energy. They are in foods like meat, fish, eggs, cheese and Soya beans; and also flour, rice and oatmeal.

SOURCES OF PROTEIN

Vegetarians can get all of the proteins they need if they eat a wide variety of plant foods such as beans, peas, brown rice, pasta and nuts.

Proteins have very large molecules made up of lots of different amino acids joined together.

When our body digests proteins it breaks them down into amino acids. Like protein, most of the human body is made up of the four elements: carbon, oxygen, hydrogen and nitrogen.

Figure 9.1 Entries from a *Science Dictionary*.
© J.J. Wellington.

190 science words – there could be many more but these are a selection of the key words used in the curriculum of countries such as the UK, USA and Australia. Each word is explained (rather than defined) and illustrations for each entry help to give it meaning. Many of the words are related and cross-referenced. A photocopiable glossary of this kind can be used in many ways in the classroom. For example, the entries can be copied and pasted on to laminated cards. These 'word cards' can then be kept in an index box for pupils to use when reading, revising, writing or discussing.

More specifically, teachers could use a glossary or dictionary of this kind to:

- highlight new words which will occur in teaching a topic e.g. electricity, energy, food, water, plant growth etc. The words could be singled out, photocopied and made into a poster.
- many teachers are teaching outside their own subject specialism and it will be useful to them if they need 'refreshment', reminder or in some cases if the word is completely new to them. A bit of pre-lesson revision is always useful (even in our *own* specialism) and also helps to remind us of the importance of language in science teaching.

Pupils can use the dictionary:

- for revising or simply refreshing their memory;
- when writing about science, e.g. a story, a description, an account of an investigation, a write-up of an experiment: the dictionary will help them to use words accurately and to stimulate new ideas and vocabulary to use in writing;
- in reading about science, e.g. a science textbook, a story about science, a newspaper article or a piece in a magazine: the dictionary can help readers to understand the writing, to check its accuracy and to look for other words and ideas which connect with it (these are highlighted in **bold**);
- in discussing or just talking about science, e.g. to clarify words; to look for new words, or to connect words and ideas together.

Teacher writing for learning and understanding

One of the essential skills of the teacher is to present and explain the processes and the content of science in a palatable and interesting way. This is true of teacher talk but is equally applicable to teacher writing – whether it be on the blackboard, the OHP or a worksheet. All the above cautions and frameworks for care in language apply to the written word perhaps even more than to the spoken word. Writing is in some ways more permanent, more open to scrutiny and less flexible and interactive. The aim of this section is to offer guidelines on writing material for pupils. Teacher writing is worthy of long discussion (see further reading), but for brevity here I begin simply by offering guidelines for writing, aimed principally at worksheet writing although many of the points apply equally to (say) blackboard or assessment writing.

Table 9.4 Writing for learning in science: guidelines and checklist

Why write?

- To give experimental instructions
- To transmit information
- To structure a film, video, slides, etc.
- To ask questions, or to test (using, for example, all questions; information then questions; fill in the blanks; crosswords)
- To provide your audience with ready-made notes

Writing good material

- Write clearly and directly
- Do not present too much information or too little
- Try it out in rough first
- Make the reader think!
- Use plenty of structure such as an appetiser; headings that stand out; summary/key points
- Print neatly or type it – don't write
- Use a ruler
- Use graphs, diagrams and illustrations to break up the text where possible
- Do not write to a Readability formula

Watch your language

- Avoid long sentences (i.e. more than twenty words)
- Try to keep to one idea per sentence
- Beware of technical terms which have not been introduced (such as 'mass', 'current', 'pressure', 'momentum', etc.)
- Avoid the 'language of secondary education' (Barnes): terms like 'relationship with', 'recapitulate', 'exert', 'becomes apparent', 'derived from', etc.
- Avoid too many short, staccato sentences
- Address the reader as 'you' (don't use the royal 'we')
- Keep language brief and concise (use a colleague as your editor)

Getting it right

- Have somebody from your target audience in mind as you write (for example, Jane Bloggs from Year 9)
- If possible, try it out on a member of your target audience first
- Always ask a colleague or friend to check your writing before letting it loose (i.e. use a proof-reader)
- Misspellings and poor grammar are not acceptable

Readers are invited to look closely at these points – there may be guidelines here that you disagree with. If so, it is well worth drawing up your own list or adapting the one here: whichever guidelines you use, it is essential to have some pointers to clear and effective writing.

There is excellent further discussion of the use of writing in teaching and communicating science in Newton (1990), Sutton (1992) and Shortland and Gregory (1991).

The language of the science textbook

In my view it is good practice for teachers to write some of their own material at least some of the time. It can help them, for example, to understand a topic more clearly themselves and to structure it and present it to pupils. Writing clear, readable material should be seen as one of the skills of a teacher. However, in the real world, teachers will commonly find themselves searching for, using and evaluating textual material written by others. The published scheme has proliferated and now is beginning to dominate – leading, unfortunately, to a reduced need for teachers to be able to write for pupils. The increased need now, however, is for teachers to be able to assess carefully, critically and to some extent objectively the texts they will be using and paying for. Many of the following features of science text can be assessed fairly quickly and intuitively:

- its 'appeal'
- its structure and layout
- the style of the writing
- the use of illustrations (photos and artwork)
- the use of colour where appropriate

Subjective, intuitive judgement is valuable in looking at science texts. There are, however, also a number of tried and tested formulae for assessing quantitatively the 'readability' of a piece of text. These should not be seen as alternatives to the intuition of (especially) an experienced teacher with a critical eye for text, but they can be useful extensions and checks of subjective judgement. They are well worth trying on a range of texts, from the *Sun* newspaper to the A-level science text. They first became well known in a science context in the late 1970s and early 1980s (see Johnson 1979) when the commonly used textbooks of the time, such as Abbot's *O–Level Physics* and Mackean's *Biology* text, were shown to have reading ages of 18 and 19 respectively.

There are a number of readability measures with different features, all of which are discussed in full in Harrison (1980: 51–83). A summary of just four tests is given in alphabetical order; these have been chosen because they are fairly easy to apply, have reasonable validity and over the years have proved to be quite accurate. Generally, they look at sentence length and word length, judged by the number of syllables. The steps for applying each test are shown in Table 9.5. These are all tests of readability which can be easily applied by teachers and have been shown to be reasonably valid and accurate. However, as noted above, they should be seen as an addition to intuition, not a replacement for it. Furthermore, they do not help in assessing how difficult a science text is to understand. This is where the taxonomy suggested in Table 9.1 can help.

Measurements of readability are largely preoccupied with counting syllables and sentence lengths and hunting for polysyllabic words. Is this the most accurate way of assessing the *difficulty* or 'transparency' of a text? An excellent

Table 9.5 How readable is text? Four measures to use

1 The Flesch formula

- Select at least three samples of 100 words.
- Count the average number of syllables in each 100–word sample (Y).
- Calculate the average length of the sentences in the samples (X).
- Calculate the Reading Ease Score (RES) using the Flesch formula:
- Reading Ease Score = 206.835 – {(X x 1.015) + (Y x 0.846)}
  where X = average sentence length in words
  Y = average number of syllables per 100 words.
  Examples: RES 90+: very easy, e.g. comics
  60–70: standard, e.g. mass non-fiction
  30–50 : academic prose
- Change the Reading Ease Score to a US grade level using this table:

Reading ease score (RES)	Flesch grade level (FGL)
Over 70	((RES – 150)/10)
Over 60	((RES – 110)/5)
Over 50	((RES – 93)13.33)
Under 50	((RES – 140)16.66)

  Add 5 to the Flesch grade level to give the reading age of the text.

2 THE FOG ('frequency of gobbledegook') TEST

- Select sample passages of exactly 100 words.
- Calculate the average sentence length (S), i.e. the average number of words per sentence.
- Calculate the percentage of polysyllabic words (words of three syllables or more) in each sample and find the average (N).
- Calculate the US grade level using the formula:
  US grade level = 0.4 (S + N).
- Find the reading age by adding 5 to the US grade level.

3 The FRY readability graph

- Select random samples of exactly 100 words (at least three samples and preferably more).
- Count the number of sentences in each sample. For a part sentence count the number of words and express as a fraction of the length of the last sentence, to the nearest one tenth.
- Count the number of syllables in each 100–word sample. (For numerals and abbreviations count one syllable for each symbol, e.g. ASE is three.)
- Mark a dot on the graph (Figure 9.2) where the average number of sentences and the average number of syllables in the samples intersects. The dot's position gives the US grade level.
- Add 5 to the US grade level to give the reading age.

Table 9.5 (continued)

From the Fry graph (Figure 9.2) it is possible to tell the relative difficulty of vocabulary or sentence length. The curve of the Fry graph is meant to represent normal texts and therefore a point below the line (bottom left) will indicate material of greater than average sentence length and hence difficulties of sentence structure. Points above the line, top right, indicate higher than average vocabulary difficulty.

4 The SMOG formula

- Select three sample passages, each consisting of ten sentences – one from the beginning, one from the middle and one from the end of the text.
- Count the total number of words of three syllables or more in the thirty sentences selected.
- Find the square root of the total.
- Add 8 to give the reading age in years.

Note: Cloze Procedure

Teachers can also carry out a Cloze procedure test. A passage is selected from a text and words omitted regularly, such as every fifth or sixth word. The pupil has to read the passage and fill in the correct word (any word that makes complete sense): 60% success means the pupil could use the material independently; 40–50% means the pupil could use the material with teacher support; below 40% indicates the 'frustration level', i.e. too difficult. This is a useful technique for matching pupil and text.

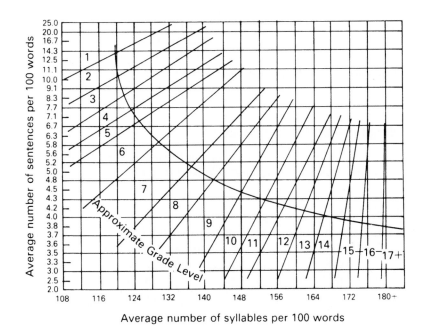

Average number of syllables per 100 words

Figure 9.2 Fry's extended readability graph.

example of lack of transparency in a sentence is given by T.H. Savory (1953): 'If there are more cows in the world than there are hairs in the tail of any one cow, there must be some cows with the same number of hairs in their tails.' It is extremely difficult to see *through* these words to the objects and facts involved. The sentence is almost opaque. Similarly with many of the words and terms of the physical sciences. Yet the 'opacity' of certain words is not taken into account by any measure of readability.

Opacity is partly related to the taxonomy in Table 9.1 (although not wholly, as Savory's example shows). Naming words are most transparent because they point directly to their referent, usually an observable entity. Words in the higher levels, meanwhile, are the most opaque: it is far more difficult to 'see through' these words to any clear meaning or referent.

Consider the word 'oesophagus'. With its five syllables it will be judged less readable than the words 'electron', 'valency' and especially 'mole' (indeed the word 'mole' has the same readability when used to refer to a little furry beast as it does when referring to the most difficult and discussed concept in chemistry). This is surely an unfair way of judging the difficulty or *understandability* of scientific prose.

Recent concentration on the readability of science textbooks has certainly done a useful job in making them more *readable*. But surely a measure of 'understandability' is also appropriate for the pupil? As this is clearly related to the taxonomy in Table 9.1, some sort of weighting could be given to words depending on which level they belong to – the presence of a word in level 3.3, for example, could be given the added weighting of two extra syllables.

At present, readability measures are unfair on biology textbooks (with their predominance of long naming words in level 1) yet give a deceptive underestimate of the difficulty of many physics texts (with their abundance of short words like 'work', 'energy', 'field', and 'mass' belonging to level 3.2).

Reading for learning in science

> Since reading is a major strategy for learning in virtually every aspect of education . . . it is the responsibility of every teacher to develop it.
>
> (Bullock 1975)

Reading is by and large a neglected activity in science classes. Textbooks are often used to provide homework (if schools can afford such a luxury), to guide a practical, to keep pupils busy if they finish too soon or at worst to prop up a piece of apparatus. Traditionally science teachers have had little concern for text. This is unfortunate for many reasons: practising scientists spend a lot of their time reading; much science can be learnt more efficiently from reading than from (say) observing or listening; many pupils enjoy reading; and there is a wide range of reading on science available in children's books, magazines and newspapers.

The starting point in this section is that reading is an important but neglected activity in science education and that one of the responsibilities of science teachers is to teach pupils to read actively, critically and efficiently. This point is also followed up in a later chapter on using newspapers in education.

How can pupils be encouraged to read in science for longer periods? How can their reading become more active, reflective, critical and evaluative? A project described in Lunzer, Gardner *et al.* (1984) suggested that passive reading occurs when reading tasks are vague and general, rather than specific; and when reading is solitary rather than shared. In contrast, active reading involves reading for specific purposes and the sharing of ideas and small-group work. The project therefore developed a number of strategies for use by teachers. These were called Directed Activities Related to Text, or DARTs (Lunzer and Gardner 1984; Davies and Greene 1984).

Directed reading activities make pupils focus on important parts of the text and involve them in reflecting on its content. They involve the pupils in discussion, in sharing ideas, and in examining their interpretations of a text. DARTs fall into two broad categories.

1 Reconstruction (or completion) DARTs

These are essentially problem-solving activities that use modified text – the text or diagram has parts missing (words, phrases or labels deleted) or, alternatively, the text is broken into segments which have to be re-ordered into the 'correct' sequence. These activities are game-like and involve hunting for clues in order to complete the task. Pupils generally find them very enjoyable and the results can feed in to pupil writing.

2 Analysis DARTs

These use unmodified text and are more study-like. They are about finding targets in the text. The teacher decides what the 'information categories' of the text are and which of these to focus on. These are the targets which pupils are to search for; this involves the pupils in locating and categorising the information in the text. When the targets are found they are marked by underlining and/or labelling.

The search for targets can be followed by small-group and class discussion in which the merits of alternative markings are considered and pupils have a further opportunity to modify or revise their judgements.

In each case the text has to be prepared for pupils, or small groups of pupils, so that they can work with it. Many DARTs will involve marking or writing on the text itself. Table 9.6 shows a classification of the various DARTs that could be used with a piece of writing in science.

Notice that the analysis DARTs can be done with the straight, unmodified text – by, for example, underlining certain types of work; labelling segments of

Table 9.6 DARTs table: a brief summary of directed activities related to text

Reconstruction darts (Using modified text)	Analysis Darts (Using unmodified text)
1 Completing text, diagram or table	*1 Marking and labelling*
(a) *Text completion* Pupils predict and complete deleted words, phrases, or sentences (cf. Cloze procedure).	(a) *Underlining/marking* Pupils search for specified targets in text, e.g. words or sentences, and mark them in some way.
(b) *Diagram completion* Pupils predict and complete deleted labels and/or parts of diagrams using text and diagrams as sources of information.	(b) *Labelling* Pupils label parts of the text, using labels provided for them.
(c) *Table completion* Pupils use the text to complete a table using rows and columns provided by the teacher.	(c) *Segmenting* Pupils break the text down into segments, or units of information, and label these segments.
2 Unscrambling and labelling disordered and segmented text	*2 Recording and constructing*
(a) Pupils predict logical order or time sequence of scrambled segments of text, e.g. a set of instructions, and re-arrange.	(a) Pupils construct diagrams showing content and flow of text using, for example: a flow diagram, a network, a branching tree, or a continuum.
(b) Pupils classify segments according to categories given by teacher.	(b) *Table construction* Pupils construct and complete tables from information given in text, making up their own headings (rows and columns).
3 Predicting Pupils predict and write next part(s) of text, e.g. an event or an instruction, with segments presented a section at a time.	(c) *Question answering and setting* (i) Teachers set questions; pupils study text to answer them (ii) Pupils make up their own questions after studying text (either for the teacher to answer, or other pupils).
	(d) *Key points/summary* Pupils list the key points made by the text and/or summarise it.

the text; making up questions to ask about the text. Text from any source – government pamphlets, leaflets, the newspapers of the Internet could be used for this purpose. The reconstruction DARTs require modification before use – by, for example, deleting key words from the text or labels from a diagram; chopping up a passage into segments which need re-sequencing to make sense. Figure 9.3 shows one example of a DART.

The pupils' writing

The debate on pupils' writing in science is as long and important as that on reading. We cannot do it justice here (see further reading), but the main questions concern the style in which pupils should write and the purpose of their writing in science education.

Reasons for writing

Until quite recently there seemed to be general agreement in science teaching that the main reasons for writing in science lessons were either to take notes on the content/knowledge required or to write up a piece of practical work (Sutton 1989). On the latter there was also a consensus that it should follow the pattern: Aim . . . Method/procedure . . . Results . . . Conclusions. This consensus has lasted for at least three reasons:

1   Generations of pupils, some of whom become teachers, feel familiar and comfortable with it.
2   It provides a convenient structure for reporting the kind of practical work that has often been done in schools, i. e. verifying or proving a law, fact or principle.
3   It was believed to reflect the nature of science and the way that scientists actually proceed and write up.

The latter two assumptions are now wide open to question. Practical work (see Chapter 7) is less commonly of the 'To prove . . .' or 'To verify . . .' or 'To demonstrate that . . .' kind. For example, investigational work, which requires a completely different structure in which to write it up, is becoming more common, even if not every teacher is comfortable with it. Second, there have been a number of excellent, readable publications (see Chapters 7 and 8) to show this kind of write-up is a false reflection of the way that scientists actually work and report. In short, a theory or 'conclusion' does not actually follow an experiment and the collection of results. On the contrary, it precedes and shapes the experiment: observation is theory-led. The reality is not a case of 'data first, theory later' (Sutton 1989). Experienced scientists such as Medawar (1979) showed a long time ago that reports which portray science in this clean, logical, methodical, inductive way are simply a fraud.

Thus changing views on the role of practical work and the nature of science mean that teachers need to rethink the 'writing up' which pupils do. There is also growing recognition that pupils can actually learn science through writing and therefore that modes and styles of writing in science lessons should be tried other than either note-taking or write-ups of practicals.

Styles of writing and alleged reasons for each

There is a strong case for widening the range of writing which pupils do in science lessons, beyond the traditional formal report style. Writing could be

Put the heads (▶) on the arrows to show the correct direction for the cycle of decay.

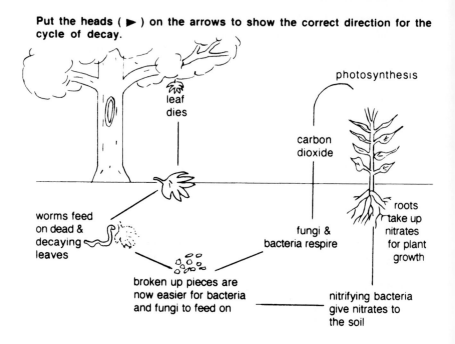

photosynthesis

leaf
dies

carbon
dioxide

worms feed
on dead &
decaying
leaves

roots
take up
nitrates
for plant
growth

fungi &
bacteria respire

broken up pieces are
now easier for bacteria
and fungi to feed on

nitrifying bacteria
give nitrates to
the soil

Complete the passage by choosing the best words from the list:

bacteria   warm   carbon dioxide   dry   damp   worms

fungi   smaller   hot   cold

Dead material decays (rots) when _____ and fungi feed on it. When this

happens _____ gas is given off.

Decay works best if the conditions are _____ and _____ , with a good

supply of air.

The decay process is helped by _____. They break the dead material into

smaller pieces so that bacteria and _____ can get into the material.

Why is it important that dead animals and plants decay?

On your diagram, show two places where respiration is taking place (mark the spot with the following sign 'R - - - - - - ->')

Sort this list out into things which can be broken down by bacteria and fungi and things which can't. Put each object into the following table:

banana skin   apple   tyre   leather shoe

glass bottle   wooden crate   cardbord box

drink can   polythene

Things which can be broken down by bacteria	Things which can't be broken down by bacteria

Figure 9.3 An example of a DART: 'The cycle of decay'.
Source: Based on Partridge 1992: 78.

broadened first of all to allow (on some if not all occasions) subjective and creative reporting – asking for experiences and feelings. Writing could be further extended by asking for imaginative and creative work based on the pupils' learning in science, such as a letter to an MP or the PM/the police/a pressure group, a newspaper report, or any other writing which might involve written role play. Pupils should use their science knowledge and 'specialist science language' (see Table 9.2) in this kind of writing, for example, with teachers offering them key words or scientific terms to be included.

In short, three styles of writing, each with a different purpose, are summarised below:

1   the impersonal, the third person, i.e. the formal report, objective and factual;
2   the personal, the first-person report, i.e. subjective, creative, interpretative reporting of, for example, observations, experiences, feelings, impressions;
3   imaginative, expressive writing, for example 'a day in the life of . . .', 'a letter of complaint', 'how it feels to be . . .', 'a journey into . . .', 'shrunk to a millimetre . . .', which makes use of science knowledge and learning. This might also include imaginative drawing, as in Edward De Bono's well-known 'Design a dog-exercising machine/elephant-weighing machine' activity.

To encourage and stimulate different types of writing it will often be valuable to show pupils different models, such as writing from past scientists or past pupils, newspaper reports, science stories. Different types of reading will enhance different styles of writing (Sutton 1989; Sheeran and Barnes 1991).

There are so many other issues about pupil writing that cannot be covered here that we will finish with a brief mention of just four:

1   Writing has a range of purposes: it may be a way of keeping a record of content or practical work for future reference, such as revision; it may be used by a teacher to assist classroom control – pupils are almost as quiet when they write as when they eat; it may be a way, for pupils, of learning and clarifying; it can be a way of sharing, if pupils write in a small group. Teachers need to recognise these different purposes and use them.
2   The use of word-processors (on notepad, notebook, laptop or desktop) can be a great aid to some people's writing, whether they have special needs or not. ICT can aid presentation, allow drafting and redrafting, encourage people to get started, allow spell-checking and encourage collaborative writing. In short, the use of ICT can change writing and marking quite radically. This is discussed further in Chapter 10.
3   There are various methods of note-making and note-taking that pupils can follow, ranging from the totally passive (straight from the teacher's head to the pupil's notepaper) to the active. The continuum of possibilities is shown in Figure 9.4.

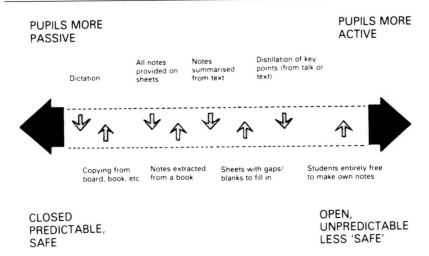

PUPILS MORE
PASSIVE

PUPILS MORE
ACTIVE

Dictation

All notes
provided on
sheets

Notes
summarised
from text

Distillation of key
points (from talk or
text)

Copying from
board, book, etc.

Notes extracted
from a book

Sheets with gaps/
blanks to fill in

Students entirely free
to make own notes

CLOSED
PREDICTABLE,
SAFE

OPEN,
UNPREDICTABLE
LESS 'SAFE'

Figure 9.4 Ways of note-making and note-taking.

Teachers should at least be aware of these different possibilities and examine the reasons why and when they might use them. For example, dictation might be a good means of classroom control but does it have any other value?

4   Why not *start* a lesson with some writing? This is an activity worth trying:

> Give each pupil a small piece of blank rough paper as they walk in (small and rough because it is less daunting). Ask them to write on it one of the following:
>
> - a summary of what they did last lesson (perhaps with comment)
> - 'Everything you already know about . . .'
> - their views on . . .
> - what they would like to know about X – for example, food, health magnetism, nuclear energy, etc.
> - the answers to five questions that you pose, such as on the previous lesson
> - the key words, say five, that you will use today
> - the plan for the day's lesson
>
> You could also give them a sheet of drawings or diagrams on which they are asked to write or comment – for example, illustrating situations where forces are being used and asking pupils to mark in and describe the forces.

Activities like this can be useful to start a lesson for a number of reasons: they are good for classroom control; they can help teachers to start 'from where the pupils are at'; they allow a recap and revision of the previous lesson; they can be a good source of feedback; they allow the use of open questions in a more manageable way than orally. They can also be enjoyable and amusing, especially if pupils write in twos.

Communicating science: more than words

> What use is a book without words and pictures
>
> (*Alice in Wonderland*, Lewis Caroll)

Finally, we all need to remind ourselves that there is far more to science communication than verbal language, i.e. the spoken and written word. Words are important but in science more than any other subject we rely on a combination and interaction of words, pictures, diagrams, images, animations, graphs, equations, tables and charts. They all convey meaning in different ways and they all have their own importance and their own limitations. For example, the old saying that 'A picture is worth a thousand words' is probably true but it does not go far enough. There are certain meanings we wish to convey in science that cannot possibly be put across in words alone. Messages and meanings in charts and graphs, for example, can never be replaced by the written word, whether we use one thousand or two. The smells of science (which adults remember most vividly of all from their science lessons) or the touch and feel of practical work cannot be put into words. Gestures and other body language can convey scientific ideas more effectively and memorably than chalk and talk, or a passage in a textbook.

In the jargon of linguists, there are a range of *semiotic modes* available to the science teacher (*semiotics* can be defined as the study of how we make meaning using words, images, symbols actions and other modes of communication). The onus on the good teacher is to employ these modes appropriately, i.e. in the right place at the right time for the right reasons. For example, chalk and talk might be fine for teaching some ideas, but others, e.g. change of state, may require animation (perhaps with multimedia or maybe simpler teaching aids like marbles or ball bearings). The movement of plates in Plate Tectonics can be described in words but it may be better conveyed using gesture and hand movements.

Equations and mathematical symbols can sum up for some pupils in a nutshell some difficult ideas which are very lengthy in words (although symbols may not suit every learner). Ideas such as rate of change, proportionality and decay might best be shown on a graph. Cyclical processes, e.g. the carbon cycle, can best be shown using a diagram with arrows; while sequences, e.g. the manufacture of a chemical, can be seen visually with a flowchart.

We all know this and in some ways it is no more than common sense. But the art of good communication in science teaching would seem to involve at least three skills, some of which can be deliberately trained for and developed or coached, while others just seem to be part of the 'tacit', hidden knowledge and ability of the 'born teacher':

1   *The recognition that teaching does involve a range of modes of communication*. In science, we have at our disposal:

- the spoken and written word;
- visual representation;
- images, diagrams, tables, charts, models and graphs;
- movement and animation – either of physical models, e.g. beach ball for the Sun, a pea for the Earth, or using multimedia, or using gesture or other body language;
- practical work with its feel, touch, smell and, of course, sounds;
- mathematical symbols, either as shorthand or in the form of equations to convey a connection.

2   *The awareness of these different modes and the recognition that different modes suit different learners*, i.e. learning styles vary. Some modes work best for some learners, other ways of conveying meaning work better with others.

3   *The ability* (which is often described as tacit or intuitive) *to switch from one mode to another when teaching*. If one way is not working then good teachers switch to another way according to the teacher's awareness of, and alertness to, the class. Even within a mode e.g. the spoken word, one line of explanation or one analogy may not be working with a group of pupils. The teacher's knack is to move to a different approach within that mode . . . or even a new mode completely, e.g. to use a physical model instead of talk or chalk. Each mode has its value and its limitations.

In summary then, once again science teaching presents both a challenge and an opportunity. It offers a range of ways of communicating (visual, verbal, graphical, symbolic, tactile) which can be exploited to engage with different learning styles or abilities and to provide a variety of teaching approaches. (We cannot expand further here but the work of Jon Ogborn and Gunter Kress, and Jay Lemke in the USA is particularly useful in this area.)

In conclusion

The ideas and findings of Barnes' work are still as important as ever for science education. Little has changed. Textbooks have become more 'readable', certainly in terms of standard readability tests (although I have heard teachers say that many of them look like colourful comics). In addition, teachers have become more aware of the language they use in speaking and writing. But for the pupil, the language barrier remains as real as ever in science and for many continues to be the main obstacle to their learning. Teachers still need to concentrate on how language is interpreted rather than just its 'delivery'. It is hoped that the practical strategies offered here will help in overcoming some of the language barriers in learning science.

References and further reading

The words of science

Vygotsky, L. (1978) *Thought and Language*, Cambridge, Mass.: MIT Press.
Two excellent and influential pieces of research were carried out on pupils' understanding of non-technical words in science in the 1970s (words like 'pungent', 'significant', 'average', 'propagate', and 'valid'). They are still useful today.
Cassels, J.R.T. and Johnstone, A.H. (1978) *Understanding of Non-technical Words in Science*, London: Chemical Society Education Division.
Gardner, P.L. (1972) 'Words in Science', part of the Australian Science Education Project, Melbourne.
Clive Sutton's work in this area is excellent, ranging from:
Sutton, C. (1980) 'Science, language and meaning', *School Science Review*, vol. 218, no. 62, pp. 47–56,

to more recently:
Sutton, C. (1992) *Words, Science and Learning*, Milton Keynes: Open University Press.

One of the classics of twentieth-century philosophy which discusses the way language is used is:
Wittgenstein, L. (1958) *Philosophical Investigations*, Oxford: Blackwell.

In the science field, another classic from the same era is:
Savory, T.H. (1953) *The Language of Science*, London: Andre Deutsch.

The book which really opened up the language-in-education debate is:
Barnes, D., Britton, J. and Rosen, H. (1969) *Language, the Learner and the School*, Harmondsworth: Penguin.

Another important book is:
Stubbs, M. (1983) *Language, Schools and Classrooms* (2nd edn.), London: Routledge.

An excellent general book on classroom language and ritual, drawing on the work of Vygotsky, is:
Edwards, D. and Mercer, N. (1987) *Common Knowledge*, London: Methuen.
The ASE manual *Race, Equality and Science Teaching* (1991), Hatfield: ASE, gives a useful discussion on terms such as 'Third World', 'black', 'under-developed' and 'race' which are sometimes used thoughtlessly (see their Appendix 2, p. 176). It also contains activities for teachers on 'Language and learning in science' (pp. 85–8) and 'Children's writing' (pp. 89–93).
Gill, D. and Levidow, L. (1987) *Anti-Racist Science Teaching*, London: Free Association (also contains practical discussions of racism in the language of science and pseudo-science).

Three interesting studies of 'difficult words' from different parts of the world are:
1   Meyerson, M., Ford, M., Jones, W. and Ward, M. (1991) 'Science vocabulary knowledge of third and fifth grade students', *Science Education*, vol. 75, no. 4, pp. 419–28.
2   Pickersgill, S. and Lock, R. (1991) 'Student understanding of selected non-technical words in science', *Research in Science and Technological Education*, vol. 9, no. 1, pp. 71–9.
3   Marshall, S., Gilmour, M. and Lewis, D. (1991) 'Words that matter in science and technology', *Research in Science and Technological Education*, vol. 9, no. 1, pp. 5–16.

Writing, and teaching with, text

Barlex, D. and Carré, C. (1985) *Visual Communication in Science*, Cambridge: Cambridge University Press (discussion and guidelines on using visual material in science teaching).

Chall, J. and Conard, S. (1991) *Should Textbooks Challenge Students?*, New York: Teachers' College Press (argues that textbooks should not be so hard that students cannot read and understand them, nor so easy that students are un-challenged and bored by them).

Lloyd-Jones, R. (1985) *How to Produce Better Worksheets*, Cheltenham: Stanley Thornes (a useful guide on producing classroom material with examples that can be photo-copied).

Newton, D.P. (1990) *Teaching with Text*, London: Kogan Page.

Partridge, T. (1992) *Starting Science: Book J*, Oxford: Oxford University Press.

Shortland, M. and Gregory, J. (1991) *Communicating Science: a Handbook*, Harlow: Longman.

Reading and readability

Bullock, A. (1975) *A Language for Life*, London: HMSO.

Carrick, T. (1978) 'Problems for assessing the readability of biology textbooks for first examinations', *Journal of Biological Education*, no. 12, pp. 113–21.

Harrison, C. (1980) *Readability in the Classroom*, Cambridge: Cambridge University Press.

Johnson, K. (1979) 'Readability', *School Science Review*, vol. 60, no. 212, pp. 562.

Knutton, S. (1983) 'Chemistry textbooks: are they readable?' *Education in Chemistry* vol. 20, no. 3, pp. 100–5.

Long, R. (1991) 'Readability for science', *School Science Review*, vol. 262, no. 73, pp. 21–33.

Zakaluk, B. and Samuels, J. (1988) *Readability: Its Past, Present and Future*, Newark, NJ: IRA.

An excellent website, created by textbook author Keith Johnson, gives the reading ages and the 'human interest scores' of all the major science texts for 11–16 in the UK. The website is at: www.timetabler.com.

Encouraging active reading

Three accounts of active reading containing discussion and valuable classroom ideas are:

Bulman, L. (1985) *Teaching Language and Study Skills in Secondary Science*, London: Heinemann (this also includes useful sections on readability, pupils' writing, teacher talk and writing worksheets).

Davies, F. and Greene, T. (1984) *Reading for Learning in the Sciences*, London: Oliver and Boyd.

Lunzer, E. and Gardner, P.L. (eds) (1984) *Learning from the Written Word*, London: Schools Council/Oliver and Boyd.

Pupils' writing

Hand, B. and Prain, V. (1995) 'Using writing to help improve students' understanding of science knowledge', *School Science Review*, vol. 77, no. 278, pp. 112–17.

Medawar, Sir Peter (1979) 'Is the scientific paper a fraud?', reprinted in Brown, L., *et al.* (1986) *Science in Schools*, Milton Keynes: Open University Press (a Nobel Prize winner tells us what scientific write-ups are really like). See also: Medawar, P. (1979) *Advice to a Young Scientist*, London: Harper & Row.

Sheeran, Y. and Barnes, D. (1991) *School Writing*, Milton Keynes: Open University Press. (has an excellent chapter on 'Writing in science').

Sutton, C. (1981) *Communicating in the Classroom*, London: Hodder & Stoughton (Chapters 1 and 2 on writing).

—— (1989) 'Writing and reading in science', in Millar, R. (ed.), *Doing Science: Images of Science in Science Education*, pp. 137–59, Lewes: Falmer Press.

General

Henderson, J. and Wellington, J. (1998) 'Lowering the language barrier in learning and teaching science', *School Science Review*, vol. 79, no. 288, pp. 35–46.

Osborne, J. (1996) 'Untying the Gordian Knot: diminishing the role of practical work', *Physics Education*, vol. 31, no. 5, pp. 271–8.

Wellington, J. (1998) 'Dialogues in the science classroom', in Ratcliffe, M. (ed.) (1998) pp. 146–58.

Resources

The *Science Wordbank*, in poster and A4 sheet form, can be obtained from: ASE Book Sales, College Lane, Hatfield, Herts, AL10 9AA (£3, cash with order).

The *Science Dictionary* (ISBN 1–898149–84–4) can be obtained from: Questions Publishing, 27 Frederick Street, Birmingham B1 3HH.

Theme C

Enriching science teaching

Chapter 10

Using ICT in teaching and learning science

This chapter is about the use of information and communication technology (ICT) in the teaching and learning of science in the secondary school. We start by looking at the nature of science and science teaching to see where ICT might help. Then we look at what 'computers are good at', to link science as a subject to computers as a learning tool. The chapter then goes on to look at the issues involved in *managing ICT in the school environment*. The specific areas of use of ICT for science are then considered: spreadsheets, databases, data-logging, simulations, multimedia applications and the Internet. Each is examined practically and critically. The key question is the one of *'added value'*, i.e. what value can the use of ICT add to the teaching and learning of science. Teachers need to be able to judge when the use of ICT is effective and *beneficial* and when its use is ineffective or inappropriate.

What can ICT offer to science education?

The use of IT in science can involve: word-processing and desk-top publishing; database and spreadsheet use; communications; data-logging; simulations and modelling; multimedia of any kind; and control hardware and software. The possibilities are summarised in Table 10.1 – the list will grow as IT itself progresses and becomes more cheaply available to schools.

This chapter considers these various uses. But first, we need to consider why, how and when IT can be of value in science education.

What's special about science and science teaching?

The emphasis here is to first look at the nature of science and science teaching and learning, and ask what is distinctive about it – *then go on* to ask what ICT can (and cannot) do for science education (as opposed to starting from the technology, then trying fit it into science teaching, as many approaches in the past have done).

Table 10.1 Some potential uses and applications of IT in science education

Word processing/desk-top publishing	*Control*
e.g. in presenting data	e.g. controlling experiments; controlling external devices
Databases and spreadsheets	*Simulations and modelling*
e.g. in pattern searching; hypothesising; recording and presenting data; accessing and organising data	e.g. predicting and searching for patterns
Communications	*Data-logging*
e.g. identifying the features of a transmission system; data coding and handling	e.g. using sensors; gathering and recording data
Interactive media *(CD, Internet, video-disc etc.)*	*Graphics*
e.g. accessing data; searching etc.	e.g. presenting data

The first point is that science and especially school science, is often a very *practical subject*. It involves *doing things*, which is often one of its attractions to learners. It involves observing, measuring, communicating and discussing, trying things out, investigating, handling things, watching and monitoring, recording results . . . these are all things we see happening in the science classroom. ICT can help in virtually all of these activities, as we see shortly.

But as much as science is a practical discipline, it is equally *a theoretical subject*. It involves, and always has done: thinking, inferring, having good ideas and hunches, hypothesising, theorising, simulating and modelling. Thinking and thought experiments are as important as hands-on activity. ICT can help as much in this aspect of science as it can in the practical aspect.

We also need to see science from two different angles when we talk about learning and teaching it. The two viewpoints involve *process* and *content*. Both are equally important to science education. The content of science – its facts, laws, theories and understanding of them – needs to be taught alongside its processes. ICT can help in learning the *content of science* – information sources such as the Internet and material on CD-ROM can play a part (as can traditional books). ICT can also help in learning the content and facts of science by using it in revision or tutorial mode (discussed later). But equally, ICT can help in learning the *processes* of science – measuring, recording, processing data, hypothesis, and communicating. These skills and processes are vital to science itself, as well as to science education.

The tables below sum up some of the areas of activity in science and the specific item of ICT which can enhance them:

Table 10.2 Pupils' science activities and the ICT tools which enhance them

Pupils' science activity	What ICT tools will help?
Planning an investigation	Word processing
Researching/learning about a topic	CD-ROM, databases, tutorial programs, Internet
Taking measurements	Data-logging
Making results tables	Data-logging, spreadsheets
Drawing graphs	Data-logging software, spreadsheets, databases
Doing calculations	Spreadsheets, data-logging software
Searching for patterns	Spreadsheets, databases, simulations, modelling programs
Asking 'what if ....?' questions	Simulations, databases, modelling programs
Comparing pupils' results with other people's (reviewing a topic)	CD-ROM, data files, Internet
Presenting information in a report	Word processing, desk-top publishing, spreadsheets

Table 10.3 Processes in science and appropriate uses of ICT

Process in science	ICT use
Measuring	Data-logging
Hypothesising (what if ...?), predicting	Simulation, spreadsheets
Recording, processing data	Data-logging, spreadsheets, databases
Thinking	Simulations, modelling programs
Communicating	Word processing, desk-top publishing, e-mail, Internet, spreadsheets
Observing	Multimedia, data-logging

All these are discussed in more detail later.

So ... why use IT in science education?

We can start to answer this by first listing some of the things that modern IT systems (hardware and software) are good at:

- collecting and storing large amounts of data
- performing complex calculations on stored data rapidly
- processing large amounts of data and displaying it in a variety of formats
- helping to present and communicate information

These capabilities all have direct relevance to the process of education, and they help us to address the key question of *when to use ICT . . . and equally importantly, when not to*. One issue concerns the use of computers as labour-saving devices. As listed above, computers can collect data at a rapid rate and perform calculations on it extremely quickly. But the question arises: should the computer (in an *educational* context), be used to collect, process and display rather than these being done by the learner? For instance, why should data-logging software plot graphs 'automatically', rather than a pupil using pencil, ruler and graph paper? In other words when does the use of a *computer* in saving labour take away an important educational experience for the *learner*? A similar issue appears in the use of computers and electronic calculators to perform complex calculations rapidly. This may be desirable in some learning situations, e.g. if the performance of a tedious calculation by human means actually impedes or 'clutters up' a learning process. But it can also be argued that the ability to perform complex calculations rapidly should be one of the *aims* of education, not something to be replaced by it.

The distinction between what counts as *authentic* (i.e. desirable and purposeful) and *inauthentic* (i.e. unnecessary and irrelevant) labour in the learning process is a central one in considering the use of IT in education. The notions of 'inauthentic' and 'authentic' labour should be remembered when we look at the added value of ICT in the examples later.

It is also worth noting that computers do exactly what they are instructed to do, very quickly, as many times as they are told to do it. On the one hand, this means that they are not (or at least not yet) capable of making autonomous or independent judgements, or personal interpretations. However it is also the case that they do not become tired, bored, hungry, irritable, angry or impatient, or liable to error. This may place them at an advantage in some situations as compared to teachers! It has been said that *one* of the reasons why children appear to enjoy learning with computers is precisely because of their impersonal, inhuman 'qualities'.

One final point on the 'abilities' of computers is worth stressing. Computers can, in a sense, speed up, or slow down, reality. As Kahn (1985) puts it 'they operate outside the viscous flow of time in which humans perform tasks'. This is an important point which will be elaborated upon when the use of computer *simulations* in education is considered.

Planning for the use of ICT in teaching science

The key question for a school is: how best can ICT be deployed and managed in a school setting? Unfortunately, in schools as with any organisation containing human beings, there are a lot of vested interests, power struggles and micro-politics at work. The science teacher (especially the new one) rarely has the power or status to make whole-school decisions about ICT, what should be bought and where it should be located. We will also see later that the use of ICT is not always compatible or easy to reconcile with the nature and organisation of secondary school classrooms.

From a school perspective, teachers need to ask in their own working setting, which factors in their school promote and enhance ICT use in science? And, conversely, which factors act as a barrier or impediment? For example:

- the logistics of the school
- resources and their location
- the role and attitude of the school ICT co-ordinator
- school policies and attitudes to ICT
- home background, e.g. home access to ICT

Science teachers may not always be in a position to decide where resources are situated in a school (unless they become the Head or the ICT co-ordinator!). But they can judge and consider: How does ICT use in science lessons relate to, and stimulate, use of ICT elsewhere, e.g. follow-up learning in the library; home use? How can they manage its use themselves? When should they go for 'whole-class teaching' (the electronic blackboard)? When should they use small-group activities, involving the whole class in what I call 'battery hen mode? – but this would mean booking the computer room; and when should they make it one activity among others? These possibilities are summarised in the crude drawing in Figure 10.1.

The issue for the science teacher is: *Where* is ICT best deployed, e.g. in the science lab, computer room, the library? We can list several modes of use of ICT which are currently in operation, for better or for worse:

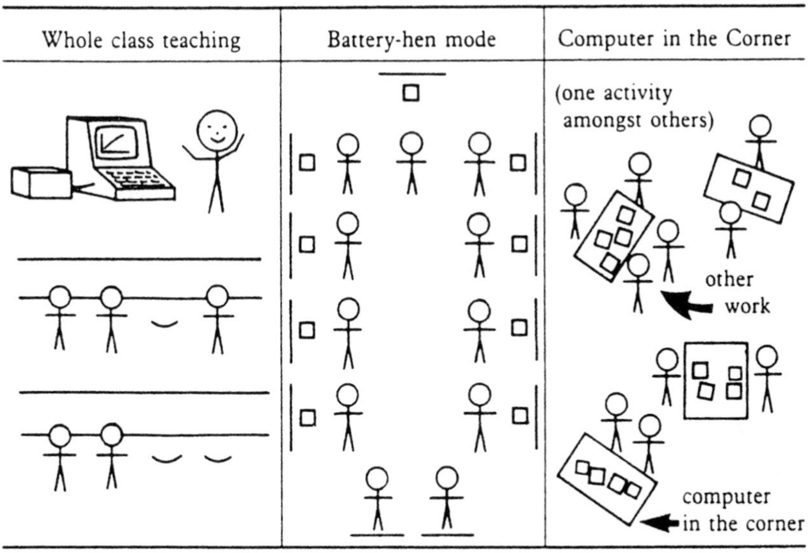

Figure 10.1 Using computers in the secondary school, three possibilities.

Table 10.4 Computers to the classroom versus classes to the computer room

+ FOR	− AGAINST
1 *Classes to the computer room*	
Dedicated room may lead to: • tighter security • easier maintenance • appropriate facilities (e.g. power points; suitable furniture; healthier viewing; distance and positions) • ease of supervision (e.g. technical help on hand) • careful monitoring (e.g. of temperature, dust, ventilation etc.)	• room may be seen as the province, territory or annexe of certain departments • computing seen as a 'special' activity • prior planning, timetabling and scheduling needed (rules out spontaneity) • reduces integration with other aspects of classroom practice or curriculum
2 *Computers to the classroom*	
• more likely integration into classroom practice and curriculum • seen as just another 'learning tool' • not seen as the property of one department more than another • spontaneous, unplanned use made possible	Problems of: • security • maintenance and monitoring • adequate facilities • environmental conditions e.g. chalk dust, water, chemicals • Technical support not on hand

- mode A: as a tool for lecture/demonstration, e.g. using a big screen or projector;
- mode B: using a single PC with one small group, e.g. as part of a circus in the lab;
- mode C: with half a class using up to five PCs;
- mode D: with a whole class, using a suite of computers, e.g. in the computer room;
- mode E: independent use (e.g. at home, in the library, or the learning resource centre) prompted and motivated by seeing ICT used in the classroom.

Which of these modes are best for which teaching or learning purposes in science? Table 10.4 below summarises the pros and cons of the two polarised approaches.

Classroom applications of ICT in science

Introduction: why bother?

The following benefits or 'added value' can be gained by trying and using IT in the classroom: motivation, excitement and pleasure; an improvement in pupils' self-esteem and perseverance; and the opportunity for pupils to produce neater, more accurate work. In science, in particular, the use of IT can extend and enhance learning in many other ways. For example:

- *simulations* can show students phenomena and processes which may be too slow, too fast, too dangerous or too expensive to do in the school lab;
- *data-logging* can assist in the recording of results, making results tables and plotting graphs so that students can spend more time on some of the 'higher-order' skills such as interpreting, discussing and hypothesising;
- *databases* on topics such as mammals, the planets or the periodic table can allow students to search through information in a fast, flexible way, to make connections and to try comparing one set of figures with another, e.g. wing span and speed of flight;
- *spreadsheets*, in the same way, can also offer the removal of drudgery: tedious, repetitive calculations such as taking the *new* length of a spring away from its *original* length every time, and allow students to get on to the more important things in science – asking 'What if . . .?' or 'Why don't we try . . .?'

In the next section, we look at each use of ICT in science, with some illustrations of classroom possibilities. We start with computer simulations.

1 Computer simulations in science education

1.1 Types of simulation in science education

It is useful to make some fairly crude distinctions between types of simulation which should act as a rough guide:

1   direct copies of existing laboratory activities, e.g. titrations;
2   simulations of industrial processes, e.g. the manufacture of sulphuric acid, bridge building;
3   simulations of processes either:
    - too dangerous
    - too slow, e.g. evolution, population growth, an ecosystem of any kind
    - too fast, e.g. collisions
    - too small, e.g. sub-atomic changes

    to be carried out in a school or college environment.
4   simulations involving non-existent entities, e.g. ideal gases, frictionless surfaces, perfectly elastic objects;
5   simulation of models or theories, e.g. kinetic theory, the wave model of light.

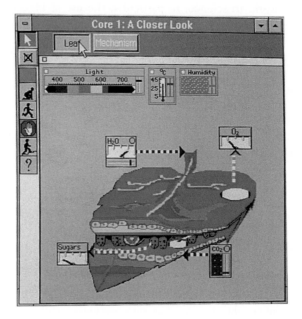

Figure 10.2 An example of a computer simulation.
Source: Capedia Ltd.

1.2 Why use computer simulations in science teaching?

The main advantages of using simulations can be summarised as follows:

1   *Cost*: money can be saved in directly copying some laboratory experiments, either by reducing outlay on consumables, e.g. chemicals, test-tubes, or by removing the need to buy increasingly costly equipment in the first place.
2   *Time*: using a computer simulation instead of a genuine practical activity may save time, although some teachers are finding that a good computer simulation in which pupils fully explore all the possibilities may take a great deal longer.
3   *Safety*: some activities simply cannot be carried out in a school setting because they are unsafe.
4   *Motivation*: there is a feeling, though with little evidence to support it, that computer simulations motivate pupils in science education more than traditional practical work.
5   *Control*: the use of a simulation allows ease of control of variables, which traditional school practical work does not. This may lead to unguided discovery learning by pupils who are encouraged to explore and hypothesise for themselves.

6   *Management*: last, but certainly not least, computer simulations offer far fewer management problems to teachers than do many traditional activities. Problems of handing out equipment, collecting it back again, and guarding against damage and theft are removed at a stroke. Problems of supervision, timing and clearing up virtually disappear.

1.3 Dangers of simulation

So much for the supposed advantages of computer simulations. What of the dangers in using computer simulations in science education? The main dangers of using simulations lie in the hidden messages they convey, classified as follows:

1   *Variables*: simulations give pupils the impression that variables in a physical process can be easily, equally, and independently controlled. This message is conveyed by simulations of industrial processes, ecological systems, and laboratory experiments. In reality not all variables in a physical situation can be as easily, equally, and as independently controlled as certain simulations suggest.

2   *Unquestioned models, facts and assumptions*: every simulation is based on a certain model of reality. Users are only able to manipulate factors and variables *within* that model. They cannot tamper with that model itself. Moreover, they are neither encouraged nor able to question its validity. The model is hidden from the user. All simulations are based on certain assumptions. These are often embedded in the model itself. What are these assumptions? Are they ever revealed to the user? All simulations rely on certain facts, or data. Where do these facts come from? What *sources* have been used?

3   *Caricatures of reality*: any model is an idealisation of reality, i.e. it ignores certain features in order to concentrate on others. Some idealisations are worse than others. In some cases, a model may be used of a process not fully understood. Other models may be deceptive, misleading or downright inaccurate; they provide caricatures of reality, rather than representations of it.

4   *Confusion with reality*: pupils are almost certain to confound the programmer's model of reality with reality itself – such is the current power and potency of the computer, at least until its novelty as a learning aid wears off. Students may then be fooled into thinking that because they can use and understand a *model* of reality they can also understand the more complex real phenomena it represents or idealises. Perhaps more dangerously, the 'micro world' of the computer creates a reality of its own. The world of the micro, the keyboard and the VDU can assume its own reality in the mind of the user – a reality far more alluring and manageable than the complicated and messy world outside. The 'scientific world' presented in computer simulations may become as attractive and addictive as the micro worlds of arcade games as noted by Weizenbaum (1984), and Turkle (1984).

5   *Double idealisations*: all the dangers and hidden messages discussed so far become increasingly important in a simulation which uses a computer model of a scientific model or scientific theory which itself is an idealisation of reality, i.e. the idealisation involved in modelling is doubly dangerous in simulations which involve a model of a model. A simulation of kinetic theory, for example, is itself based on a model of reality.

1.4 Safeguards in using simulations

Given that science teachers will continue to use simulations, what safeguards can be taken to reduce these dangers? First, all teachers and, through them, pupils, must be fully conscious that the models they use in a computer simulation are personal, simplified and perhaps value-laden idealisations of reality. Models are made by man, or woman. Students must be taught to examine and questions these models.

Second, the facts, data, assumptions and even the model itself which are used by the programmer must be made clear and available to the user. This can be done in a teacher's guide, or the documentation with the program. All sources of data should be stated and clearly referenced. Any student using a simulation can then be taught to examine and question the facts, assumptions and models underlying it.

1.5 Examples of simulation programs

A wide range of simulations is now available for school science ranging from simulations of chemical collisions, the manufacture of ethanol or the siting of a blast furnace to the simulation of electric and magnetic fields, electricity use in the home, wave motion, floating and sinking, a 'Newtonian' world of frictionless movement and the construction of bridges. For the life sciences, simulations are available on pond life, the human eye, nerves, the life of the golden eagle and predator–prey relationships.

2 Multimedia use in science education

What is Multimedia?

A simple definition is that 'multimedia' (on either CD-ROM, or via the Internet) should involve at least three of the following:

- speech or other sound
- drawings or diagrams
- animated drawings or diagrams
- still photographs or other images
- video clips
- text, i.e. the printed word

This mix of media is illustrated by *The Chemistry Set* which uses a mix of media to provide information on the elements of the periodic table (Figure 10.3). It has a large number of still photos of elements and compounds; sounds made by different reactions, e.g. caesium being dropped into water; video clips of such reactions; text and tabulated data; drawings and diagrams which can be seen from different angles, e.g. of models of molecules.

Value-added ... or value (including smell) taken away

A number of CD-ROMs for science now allow quite detailed 'virtual experiments' to be done successfully and repeatedly on screen, without using up any of the consumables which science teachers can ill afford to buy (although chemistry teachers lament the loss of smell). The key issue is whether this devalues scientific activity by removing some of the real, hands-on, authentic business of science and placing it in the realm of multimedia.

Should experiments which can be done 'for real' in the lab be done on the screen? The key issue in deciding on any ICT use is whether it adds value to teaching and learning of science. Table 10.5 below sums up the aspects of multimedia (from CD-ROM or Internet) which teachers should examine carefully in deciding when (and when *not*) to use it.

Home-school convergence, or divergence, with multimedia

With the advent of multimedia systems entering homes almost as quickly as schools, we will be forced to consider the links and liaison between the two. This is given more urgency by the growing number of publishers now producing CD-ROM titles for both the home and school markets – something which has never really happened before in IT. How will the organisational structures of the school (timetables, bells, teacher-centredness, etc.) manage situations where pupils may know a CD-ROM inside out (such as *The Ultimate Human Body* from Dorling Kindersley) from using it at home? Will pupils be able to use school discs at home, and teachers use home discs at school? How will teachers be able *to keep control* of children's learning as they do now? Will teachers be flexible enough to exploit home use? How can we hope to create equal opportunities? Will pupils be as excited and motivated by the school discs as they are by those in the home . . . and so on? The number of questions is limitless – but teachers and schools are certain to face them as the number of multimedia systems at home far exceeds the number in schools.

3. Word-processing (WP) and desk-top publishing (DTP)

Why use word-processing in science education?

Most pupils and students still write by hand. Write-ups of experiments, evaluations, project work and so on are more likely to be handwritten than typed on

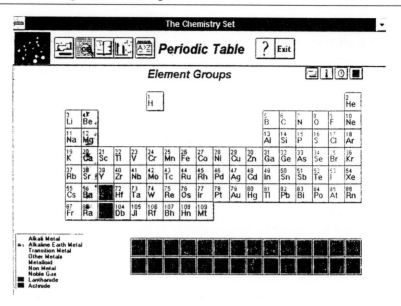

Figure 10.3(a) The Chemistry Set uses a range of media in a disc which can be used as a database, a tutorial program or 'virtual laboratory'.
Source: New Media.

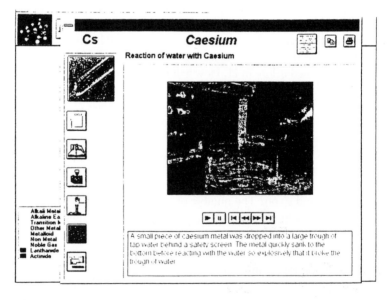

Figure 10.3(b) A still from a *Chemistry Set* video clip (with sound) of caesium being dropped into water – a 'virtual demonstration'.
Source: New Media.

Table 10.5 Points to consider when looking at multimedia for the classroom

What added value can multimedia provide?

What can CDs provide that, for example, a book cannot?

... and therefore why should people use them?

This is an issue which many teachers pose for themselves and rightly expect a satisfactory answer to. A crude list of what multimedia can provide which a book cannot shows the technical differences between the two:

1   **Audio:** a CD-ROM can provide speech and sound effects. Does this help or hinder? e.g. poor readers.

2   **Animation:** books can include diagrams but cannot provide the animation which a computer program or multimedia package can. Does animation help explanations?

3   **Video:** many CD-ROMs provide short video clips although their quality is (as yet) commonly quite poor. Do they help learning?

4   **Interactivity/tutorial help:** books are non-interactive in that they cannot provide feedback on a learner's progress – CD-ROMs can also be interactive in other ways although not always (see later).

5   **Substitutes for practical work:** a CD-ROM can provide many possibilities for practical or 'field' work which a book cannot, for example:
    • virtual experiments
    • simulations
    • real-life situations to study
    • surrogate walks
    • demonstrations

Teachers need to recognise these attributes and possibilities, and examine each disc to see what 'added value' they do provide.

a keyboard. Most people would argue that writing with a pen or a pencil is an essential skill and should be preserved. Few would disagree. A small minority would go further and suggest that the use of a keyboard to write words, a computer to process and store them, and a printer to print them will actually hinder or stunt the development of handwriting and even writing generally. I have heard this point of view expressed at meetings, courses and in discussion. Will the keyboard oust the pen?

In fact there is little or no evidence to support this understandable fear. In a project where schools and homes were virtually saturated with computers (the Apple Classroom of Tomorrow project, or ACOT) it seemed that pupils' writing was enriched and certainly increased through the use of computers. Pen and pencil were still used. The nature of writing was also changed.

The use of WP can provide the following enrichment and benefit:

1   Pupils are given the opportunity to draft and redraft their own work much more readily. This is well known, and all those who have used a WP system will have experienced it. It seems to affect different users in different ways. Some are much more inclined to actually make a start on a piece of writing (arguably the hardest part of the process), knowing full well that it can easily be changed or edited. Some are actually much more inclined to keep going, just to get their thoughts down onto paper or the screen, knowing that they can easily be redrafted. This aspect of WP is often said to enhance the writing of so-called 'lower-ability' students – but it affects writers at all levels.

2   Pupils are able to collaborate (work co-operatively) on a piece of writing much more easily with a computer system than with pen and paper. Partnership in writing is encouraged. This occurs for perhaps two main reasons: first, the writing is up there on the screen for all partners to see. This enables them more easily to take an equal share in it. Second, the writing is actually physically done by a shared keyboard, there on the desk or bench. It often does not 'belong' to one person more than another as, say, a pen does.

3   Marking of work done on a WP system can be so much more painless. Again, this applies equally at all levels of education and writing. Writers are far more inclined to seek feedback and critical comment if they know that alteration, addition and editing are relatively simple. This is again said to apply especially to those most likely to make spelling or grammatical mistakes, which is certainly true: the use of WP does remove the need for marks and corrections all over a script. But it can have an influence on people's writing attitudes and habits at all levels.

4   The final product of a piece of writing can be so much better through the use of WP and DTP, as we will see later. This can produce a positive feedback loop, in turn influencing the earlier stages.

5   Finally, writing done with a WP system can be easily stored and exchanged. On the one hand this may encourage malpractice with exam coursework (though I know of no cases). Its positive effect is to allow a person or a group to stop writing at a convenient point and take it up again more easily later.

Teachers' use of WP and DTP

These are some of the main general points connected with the use of WP in science education. A further aspect of interest in the use of WP in schools is that teachers who are otherwise reluctant about using IT are often willing users of WP and DTP. Their activities tended to focus on the production of teaching materials such as worksheets, assignment sheets and tests, as well as general course and departmental documentation. The seemingly anomalous situation of a teacher owning several boxes of floppy discs while never using a computer in a lesson seems not to be uncommon. One possible interpretation of this is that as WP is an extension of something familiar, namely typing, and the user is firmly in control of events, the technology is therefore relatively non-threatening to the user. It is accepted by IT sceptics because the pay-off outweighs the threat.

When used by teachers to produce teaching materials and professional documentation, WP can contribute to departmental teamwork (as can e-mail). It is much easier to circulate draft copies to colleagues and accommodate their suggested changes when the document is stored on disc. In this sense, IT is an aid to management processes in schools, and within science departments.

Two key practical issues with WP

Over the brief history of ICT in schools (about seventeen years) two key issues related to the use of WP have constantly surfaced and resurfaced:

1   Should pupils be taught *keyboard skills*, using the ubiquitous QWERTY layout at an early age? One of the barriers to the use of WP (and databases) has been pupils' slowness in typing in text. Should keyboard skills be taught to *all* pupils as a matter of course?

    Research shows that these skills are certainly one of the main requirements of employers in connection with IT (see Wellington 1989, for past research on this question).

2   A second barrier to use, as with many aspects of IT, is access to a computer system. What will be the effect of increased use of portable/laptop computers on the incidence and use of WP? Should they be introduced into science lessons on a wide scale, especially as pupils increasingly acquire their own laptops and have ICT at home?

Desk-top publishing (DTP)

Word-processing programs are designed to manage text made up of letters, numbers and other symbols such as those found on typewriters. The layout of the text can be altered in several useful, but strictly limited ways. Desk-top publishing (DTP) programs are more flexible. DTP can accommodate line drawings and sprites (pictures made of groups of pixels: a pixel is a small area of the screen) as well as data from other programs. The DTP user might utilise newspaper format in columns, text flowing round graphics, attractive data display such as a three-dimensional pie-chart, text enhancements including a variety of fonts, headings and borders. DTP programs can also operate as simple word-processors, which is not as retrograde as it appears because printing can be much quicker in this mode of use.

Pupils' presentation of work can be greatly enhanced with DTP and WP, which raises many issues for assessment (discussed later).

4. Spreadsheets

Introduction

A spreadsheet is a program which deals with information in the form of a table, with rows and columns. The rows are often given numbers and the columns are given letters so that any particular cell or element of the table can be identified, for example as C5 or J2. Data can be changed or linked to other data by specifying which elements are to be changed and what the nature of the change is to be. An example would be to multiply every number in column D by the corresponding number in column E and put the results in column F. If column D contained data about speeds and column E contained data about time intervals, then column F would represent distances. This facility for data manipulations is a key characteristic of spreadsheet programs. Spreadsheets can also be used for sorting and displaying stored data and for creating and manipulating mathematical models.

Some manipulation processes can be carried out by using either a spreadsheet or a database. Which one is preferable? A rough guide might be that databases tend to offer more powerful search and sort options while spreadsheets tend to be easier to inspect, update and edit.

Uses for spreadsheets in teaching science

A simple form of spreadsheet may be dedicated to accepting only one type of data, for example, the food consumed by every pupil in a class in one day. The data are manipulated in prescribed ways, with the aim of communicating information in a pre-programmed format. Although restricted in use, such programs are accessible to students and they can be a gentle introduction to the use of more versatile spreadsheets.

The more flexible and powerful the spreadsheet, the more the user is required to make decisions about the way the data are stored and manipulated. These decisions may include the user having to classify the data into groups and identifying the relationships between groups of data.

Any activity in science which involves students looking at or building up tables of information might be considered as a candidate for spreadsheet use. Learners can then go on to do modelling activities, by asking 'What if?' questions (i.e. the conjectural paradigm). Examples might include: investigating a predator–prey relationship; correlating experimental data, such as current, voltage, resistance and power; looking at food intake over a period of time.

Spreadsheets: pros and cons

The use of spreadsheets can enhance students' learning in science, but what is the balance between pay-off and cost to the teacher? The cost, in its broader sense, involves acquiring and learning to use the software, at least so as to

Spreadsheet jargon

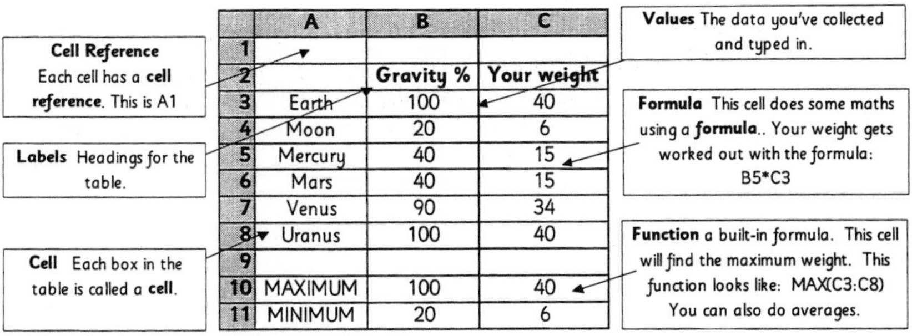

Figure 10.4(a) Spreadsheet jargon.
Source: Roger Frost.

	A	B	C	D	E
1	Food	Carbohydrate as %	Protein as %	Eat as as %	Energy content in kJ per 100 g
2	peas	17.3	6.9	0.5	404
3	sugar	100	0	0	1700
4	skimmed milk	5	3.4	0.1	35
5	chocolate bar	56.3	5.8	29	2130
6	baked beans	10	5	0.5	268

	A	B	C	D
1	Temperature in °C	Quantity of enzyme in cm³	Quantity of starch in cm³	Time taken to break down starch in seconds
2	10	20	10	50
3	20	20	10	40
4	30	20	10	30
5	40	20	10	20
6	50	20	10	30

Figure 10.4(b) Two examples of spreadsheets being used in science activities.
Source: Chapman and Lewis 1998.

remain one step ahead of the students (or only one step behind!). It also involves building IT into schemes of work and lesson plans, and booking a computer at the right time, in the right place. Finally the students must be shown how to use the software. The pay-offs from using spreadsheets must include the potential for improved student learning and motivation, otherwise they would have no place in the classroom. Additional advantages include the following:

- *Flexible learning*: students can work independently and at their own pace.
- *Working co-operatively in groups.*
- *Teacher–pupil relations*: pupils will notice and value the fact that the teacher has bothered to introduce a new and interesting activity.
- *Improved teacher competence in IT*: teachers may find uses for spreadsheets in their professional work other than with their classes. Departmental accounting and stocktaking, and collation of assessment schedules and examination results are two likely areas.
- *Increased teacher confidence in IT*: teachers who have hitherto been wary of computers may find that simple spreadsheets are much easier to use than they feared.
- *Emancipation*: spreadsheets can allow *modelling* and predicting to take place (the conjectural paradigm) while also taking away the drudgery of laborious calculations of rows and columns of figures.

5 Data-logging

Data-logging typically involves using a computer to record and process readings taken from sensors. Perhaps the simplest data-logging system is shown in Figure 10.5.

The sensor plays the part of a translator. It responds to some property of the environment and sends a message to the computer. The message, or signal, has the form of a voltage at one of the computer's input ports. The computer is programmed to record the value of the input signal. Temperature is an example of an environmental property which can be sensed in this way.

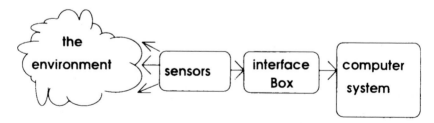

Figure 10.5 A basic data-logging system.

With modern data-logging systems, sensors can identify themselves, logging rates are automatically optimised, and interfaces match the type of information given by the sensor to the type which the computer can accept. Teachers should expect many of these features in new data-logging equipment. The result should be that the 'inauthentic labour' of matching the computer to the environment is removed from the teacher and is incorporated in the hardware and software design of the system.

Here are a few practical examples of using sensors in science:

- temperature sensors to study cooling curves or insulation, e.g. heat loss from the building;
- a light sensor to study the rate of the reaction where a precipitate forms;
- light and temperature sensors as simple meters to compare habitats;
- a data-logger to measure light, temperature and oxygen readings in an aquarium, pond or greenhouse;
- light gates to measure speed, time and acceleration;
- a position sensor to monitor the movement of a pendulum;
- sensors to study current–voltage relationships.

What added-value comes from data-logging?

The following advantages have been claimed:

- *Speed*. Computers can often log much faster and more frequently than humans.
- *Memory*. Computers have enormous capacity for retaining and accessing a large body of data in a compact form.
- *Perseverance*. Computers can keep on logging – they do not need to stop for food, drink or sleep.
- *Manipulation*. The form in which data are gathered may not be the form in which we want to communicate. Computers come into their own when it comes to fast manipulation of large bodies of data.
- *Communication of meaning*. Computers can present data when gathered, in realtime, using graphic display to enhance the meaning which is communicated to the observer.

Some of these advantages are aimed at transferring 'inauthentic labour' from the human to the machine. (see Barton's Chapter 14 in Wellington 1998). The change of emphasis away from the routine process of logging towards the use of interpreting skills can enhance scientific thinking, creativity and problem-solving ability. However, this view is not universally shared by teachers. It has been pointed out that perseverance, ability to organise data systematically and calculating skills are part of science and that students should go through these processes in practical work.

6 Databases

What is a database?

In its simplest form a database is nothing more than an organised collection of information. Thus an address book, a telephone directory, a card index, and a school register are all examples of databases. They all contain data, which can convey information to people, and which is organised in a more-or-less systematic way, e.g. in alphabetical order. The advantage of organising data is partly for ease of use and access to information, but also depends on the fact that well-organised and structured data can be used to show patterns and trends and to allow people to make and test hypotheses or hunches. Therein lies the *educational value* of a database. Having an organised and clearly structured collection of data allows and even encourages users to derive information and knowledge from it.

The key skill to develop in pupils is the ability to *search* for information in a logical and systematic way. This is true for not only databases but also CD-ROM, the Internet and spreadsheet use.

Searching skills and computer databases

The advantages of storing, organising and retrieving information from a computer system are worth considering briefly. First, using magnetic or optical media (e.g. floppy discs, 'laser discs', CD-ROM, etc.) huge amounts of data can be stored in a relatively compact form. Second, data can be retrieved from a computer database quickly. Third, data retrieval from a computer database is relatively flexible. For example, to find a number in a paper-based telephone directory from a name and initials would be almost as quick as finding it from a computer-based directory: but consider the situation in reverse. How long would it take to find a person's name and initials with only their number? With a suitable computer database this could be done as quickly as a search in the other direction. Fourth, changes (editions, additions and subtractions) to a computer database can be made more easily and more painlessly than to, say, a card- or paper-based database – this is, in a way, similar to the use of word-processors in amending and redrafting text.

Important terms used with databases

A *file* is a collection of information on one topic, e.g. dinosaurs, planets, trees, birds. Files are organised into separate *records* (e.g. each type of dinosaur with its own name). Within each record data might be stored on each kind of dinosaur and this can be organised into *fields*. One field might contain data on what the animal eats, another on its size, another on its weight, and so on. In setting up a file as part of a database, people can decide how many records they wish to include (e.g. how many different dinosaurs, and how many fields they wish to

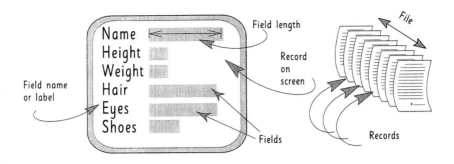

Figure 10.6 Database jargon.
Source: Roger Frost.

use in storing information on each animal). Of course, they can always add records (e.g. if we hear about more dinosaurs, or more fields or if we decide to store new or more complex data). Thus records and fields can be added to, edited, or even removed.

Why use databases in science education?

1 *For recording data collected during an investigation or an experiment.* Data can be entered directly onto the database and stored on a computer-based medium (e.g. a disc).

2 *In allowing students to sift or browse through their own, or someone else's data using the computer.* This kind of serendipitous learning (learning by browsing) can often be very valuable and is commonly underestimated.

3 *Students can explore data in a more systematic manner.* They can:

- look for patterns
- put forward hunches
- make predictions
- suggest and test hypotheses
- draw and discuss interpretations

4 *Better display.* With suitable software the computer system can be used to display and present data so that it conveys information in an attractive and clear way (cf. spreadsheets).

The use of databases in science supports and enhances many of the so-called process skills in the science curriculum such as classifying, hypothesising and testing. It can also take away some of the 'inauthentic labour' or drudgery discussed earlier.

7 Using the Internet in science teaching

The value and potential of the Internet in science teaching

The Internet provides a way of:

- sharing and exchanging information
- communicating
- accessing information
- providing a local exchange of information on resources, e.g. for pooling
- linking with industry
- giving *current* information to pupils/students
- improving study skills and search skills
- giving pupils the excitement of on-line computer information
- allowing collaboration in science: between pupil and pupil, school and school, teacher and teacher (see Sc-I Journal later)
- downloading material, e.g. data (particularly valuable for certain special needs pupils)
- setting up a forum for debate and queries amongst teachers of science

Words of warning

Most people agree that the Internet is *potentially* a powerful resource for education – but as critical teachers we need to avoid being carried away by the hype which often surrounds it. It certainly has educational value, which lies in three areas: in exchanging and sharing ideas and information, e.g. between teacher and teacher, pupil to pupil or a mixture of both; in enhancing and facilitating communication, e.g. by e-mail; and third, in providing a source of information for learners and teachers on almost any topic from football to photosynthesis. The value of the first two uses for schools is beyond doubt. Initiatives such as ScI-Journal (see addresses below), for example, allow all sorts of ideas about investigational work to be shared and exchanged world-wide. But use of the Internet as a vast source of information for schools is more problematic. Yes, there is a huge supply of data on every topic – but this is at once its potential and its downfall. How much of that information has been checked and edited, or even proof-read? How accurate and reliable is the information? Who has written it and what were their motives? We should, quite rightly, treat all material on the Internet with a healthy scepticism, just as we would (or should) regard data in the national newspapers. This scepticism should be central to both the attitude of teachers and the message conveyed to learners.

Equally, the amount of information available is now so vast that it is extremely difficult for teachers to contain, or harness it, in order to meet the needs of a statutory curriculum. This is why so many teachers on courses which I run on multimedia always come up with three major, interconnected concerns: 'containing', vetting and drawing boundaries round material; similarly, structuring and guiding learners through material; and last but probably foremost, *curriculum relevance*. If learners are let loose on the Internet where will it all end? What relevance will it have to the 'delivery' of the curriculum which, in the 1990s, has become the classroom teacher's main driving force? And who can blame them, given the external pressures?

The Internet does have *curriculum relevance*. The challenge for teachers is to 'map' Internet sources onto the curriculum and then their schemes of work – this takes time, but some of the links listed below may help as a pointer.

Useful sites for science

In science, there is now a wide range of sites in areas such as: the human body, space, mini-organisms, the periodic table, health, plants and biotechnology. The ASE journal, *School Science Review*, now has a regular section describing these sites and giving their addresses which is well worth looking out for. The Science Museum also provides a rich source of educational materials for teachers at http://www.nmsi.ac.uk/education/stem.

One example of a site which meets curriculum requirements in several *different* areas is the Arthur C. Clarke website (www.acclarke.co.uk) which provides a comprehensive history of modern communications, computing and media, using text and images which are appropriate for key stages 3 and 4. In science, for example it covers large sections of the statements on electricity and magnetism and a good chunk on waves.

Worthy of a special mention is the *Schools Online Project* at *http://sol.ultralab. anglia.ac.uk/pages/schools_online*. This is a project with some excellent pages for science teachers, many containing good classroom ideas.

Other useful sites are:

ScI-Journal
http://www.soton.ac.uk/~plf/ScI-Journal: an award-winning on-line publication. It gives science students the opportunity to publish their work so that other students around the world can read about it. Each edition consists of a number of science investigation reports written by students. They are mostly at KS4 level but cover a range of topics and approaches.

BECTA, (Science Park, Coventry CV4 7JJ)
http://www.becta.org.uk

Pupil Researcher Initiative
http://www.shu.ac.uk/schools/sci/pri/index.html

The ASE site
http://www.ase.org.uk/

Note: Website addresses are subject to changes.

Practical issues and concerns expressed by teachers

When I ask a group of teachers: 'How would you use the Internet?', their replies could be crudely summarised as: For a research tool for teachers and pupils – almost all said 'Yes'. As a teaching aid e.g. in front of a whole class, almost all said 'No!'

Other concerns which have been expressed to me by teachers are:

- the front end/usability;
- need for more teacher experience in using the Net – requirement for more teacher time to get to know it;
- need to share experiences with other teachers, e.g. on a list of useful sites;
- access by pupils and teachers – will access be equal, especially as home use increases. What about the notion of entitlement?
- slowness of the system, i.e. time taken (e.g. in gaining access to something valuable);
- curriculum relevance;
- urgent need for pupils (and teachers) to develop search skills, e.g. use of search engines; discrimination/ evaluation of information;
- is *more* information necessarily a good thing?
- what will happen if pupils get access to obscene or pornographic material – who will get the blame . . . probably the classroom teacher;
- ownership/copyright of material (including pupils' material);
- vetting/refereeing/filtering of material before it goes on the Net;
- viruses;
- plagiarism, quoting without attributing;
- accuracy of information;
- partiality of information;
- vastly extended audiences for a pupil's (or teacher's) work;
- people's motives for putting material on the Net;
- the language level of the material (most of which is text-based) and the text handling difficulties it presents;
- the 'haphazard'/uncontrolled learning which will take place if pupils are allowed free access;
- the cost, i.e. who will pay the phone bills?

Developing students' searching skills

One of the key aims when using either CD-ROM or the Internet is to develop in learners the ability to search a large source of information. A good search needs to be efficient and focused. There is perhaps something to be said for learning by 'browsing' (or 'serendipity', to use the pretentious term), and surfing the Internet is a common pastime. But for school learning with curriculum relevance the search needs to be refined in order to maximise effectiveness in the use of valuable computer (and phone line) time. Here are some valuable strategies which have been suggested:

- *Focus* the search by making it as specific as possible, rather than using wide, general terms. For example, searching on the word 'Planet' on the Internet will produce nearly half a million 'hits'. Similarly with a topic like pollution: gradually focus it to (say) global warming (which will still produce thousands of hits) or 'acid rain'.
- *Purpose*: a good search has a specific purpose in mind, and clearly framed or articulated questions.
- *Vetting*: teachers should check or 'vet' sites before a lesson (or the start of a topic). Sites can be 'bookmarked' using searching software.
- *Structure*: structuring the search and giving guidance, e.g. on the use of 'and', 'or' and 'not', will help to focus and refine. A prepared worksheet, setting out what information learners are expected to find can help, or even a kind of treasures hunt/treasure trail.
- The *Schools on Line* science pages are a good starting point to help you search or 'surf' in the right direction.

Searching skills also include the higher order skill of selecting *information*, i.e. deciding what is relevant and valuable (and therefore what to print); and the ability to *assess and evaluate information* for its worth and potential accuracy, i.e. to establish where the information came from, who put it there, and why, e.g. do they have vested interest's; or is it likely to be biased?

Further reading

The use of the Internet is a huge topic which we have only touched upon here. For a valuable further discussion see: John Wardle's chapter entitled: 'Virtual science: a practical alternative?', pages 271–81 of Wellington (ed.) (1998): *Practical Science Which Way Now?*, published by Routledge, ISBN 0–415–17493–7. The same book also contains a chapter on data-logging (by Roy Barton) and multimedia simulations (by Linda Baggott).Also, see Jackson and Bazley (1997) 'Science education and the Internet – cutting through the hype' in *School Science Review*, December 1997, vol. 79, no. 287, pp. 41–4.

The teacher's role in using ICT in science

Matching teaching and learning objectives with ICT applications

One thing is certain with ICT in the future: the teacher's role will change as a result of ICT in school and in the home. My argument here is that the teacher's role is an extremely complex one – it will require flexibility and reflection, and often a change of attitude. We look at the teacher's job closely in the next sub-section.

But the first issue is to become clear about the teaching objectives in science and how they can be matched to, or *enhanced by*, the use of ICT. We have seen how several applications of ICT can help in learning and teaching science: spreadsheets, data-logging, word-processing, multimedia, and so on. The first job of the science teacher is to match these applications to their learning and teaching objectives. For example, data-logging can help pupils to observe, study and interpret data, and take away some of the drudgery of manual recording and processing, such as drawing a graph with pencil and graph paper. Spreadsheets can help to tabulate data clearly, and enable 'what if?' questions to be asked. Word-processors can help pupils to produce a well-presented report, e.g. of an investigation. Simulations, on a CD-ROM for instance, can allow people to do experiments that are either too dangerous, too fast or too slow to do in a school.

The key question which teachers need to address is the question of what is the authentic or important learning objective. To take a crude example, if a teacher wants pupils to learn how to use a mercury-in-glass thermometer, then using a temperature sensor and a data-logger is not a good idea! There are numerous examples like this, which classroom teachers can reflect upon for themselves. The teacher's job, not an easy one, is to ask: what can ICT do to help particular learning objectives in science . . . and (as the football managers say) to *take each one as it comes.*

The changed role of the teacher: observing, intervening, monitoring and supporting learning

The teacher's job is a tough one. As well as the educational question of matching objectives with ICT use there are plenty of practical issues to consider too (as we saw in the earlier section on managing ICT use in school). Some of these difficulties are hard to overcome, not least the issue of having the right resources available at the right time. My own research (with Collins and Hammond 1997) shows that, even with the resources available, the teacher still has to decide: when to stand back and let the pupils get on with it, or when to intervene and steer them; similarly, how much structure and guidance should be given e.g. worksheets to go with CD-ROMs, or free-rein learning.

The effective teacher's role seems to involve carrying out several demanding, complex and time-consuming tasks including:

- assessing proposed ICT for relevance and content (see next sub-section);
- gaining a level of confidence and competence in using the material for oneself;
- organising access to the technology in an equitable way;
- organising access to other relevant material *away from the computer* to support children's learning;
- providing a structure or a framework within which the group will work – in many cases this will be an open-ended task and discussed with the group;
- assessing pupils' ability to teach others about the workings of the machine and making the need to hand over skills explicit to the pupil expert;

- assessing the work of the group and suggesting appropriate activities which may lead to progression in students' learning;
- reflecting on the activities of the class as a whole and acting on suggestions for amendments next time round.

Central to the teacher's facilitating role is the dialogue which goes on between teacher and the students working on the computer. This does not mean standing over the children at all times – such a task would be impossible – but it does mean engaging with learners at key moments and guiding their learning.

Reviewing and evaluating software

One of the skills which teachers need to develop with ICT is the ability to judge or evaluate items of software both *before* and *after* they have used it. Being able to assess its value *before* use is vitally important for financial means. If you don't like it or it won't 'work' in your department, don't buy it. Teachers also need to develop the ability and experience to *look back* on an application of ICT and evaluate its success.

Judging and evaluating software (just like assessing 'good' science textbooks) comes with intuition and experience but it can also be valuable to have a set of points or a *checklist* to aid your intuition. The points below (some obvious, others not so obvious) are designed as a framework to help in reviewing ICT, before and after you use it:

- Does it fit the curriculum? Does it support your learning goals?
- Does it fit the learners? Is the depth of treatment right for the audience? Does it suit the ability range within a class?
- Does it fit the time slot? For example: does it suit a five-minute demonstration, pupils taking short turns, or whole-lesson use in a computer room?
- Does it fit the hardware? If the software is on CD-ROM, can it be used with a network of computers? Does it need demonstrating on a large screen?
- Does it enhance science education? Can it do things better than we can normally? Does it encourage problem-solving, investigating, modelling, classifying, sorting, questioning, pattern-finding, data-exploring, researching, group work, out-of-class work?
- Does it fit the teacher? Is it easy to get started? Does the effort put in to use it produce a pay-off? Does the manual say how you're supposed to teach with it? Is it possible to customise the software to suit your approach?

The key question of course is what added-value does it offer in learning *and* teaching science?

The various criteria can be divided (somewhat arbitrarily) into five areas:

Table 10.6   A checklist for judging ICT

Technical
- Will it run on your machine?
- Any special requirements? (e.g. extra memory: high-resolution graphics; peripherals)
- Is there valuable use of colour, graphics, and animation?
- What use is made of sound? Can the sound be controlled, or even switched off?

Practical
- Is it robust?
- Can it cope with various levels and abilities?
- Does it give clear instructions?
- Is the screen well presented and laid out?
- How much text appears?
- Is it useful for individuals, small groups, or whole classes?

Subjective
- What are the reactions of teachers and pupils to it?
- Is it interesting and motivating?
- Does it get them talking?
- Do pupils find it too difficult or too easy?
- Does it build confidence . . .or shatter it?

Educational
- Is the content accurate, relevant and appropriate?
- Are the program and its instructions pitched at the right level?
- What educational aims does it develop: skill and drill; factual recall; understanding; analysis; evaluation?
- Can learners use it *independently*?

Accompanying materials
- What materials come with the program: a simple users' guide; teachers' guide; documentation?
- Are there suitable and readable pupils' materials to use with, or alongside the program?

Assessing work done by ICT: additional demands and teacher expectations

Using ICT can improve pupils' work (especially those with special needs), but in assessing it teachers need to be aware of new issues which have cropped up as a result of ICT (both at home and at school).

(a) Plagiarism, and giving references

A number of teachers have complained to me of science homework done with the aid of ENCARTA (or a similar CD-ROM, or the Internet) which has gone 'straight from the computer and onto printer paper without any intervention by the pupil's brain'. Teachers are rightly suspicious of such work, especially when the Microsoft copyright logo is still on the bottom of the page! Teachers need to demand that the work can be shown to be the pupil's own, even if a CD-ROM or the Internet was used as a source. Pupils must acknowledge the source of their work and *be taught the correct way to give references* (a skill which has rarely been taught in the past below undergraduate level).

b) Work enhanced by the use of ICT

Word-processed work can now be spell-checked and this becomes an additional issue for teachers, especially as few of their science pupils who use word-processors at home or school will be allowed to use them in the Examination Hall. Should some work also come in hand-written e.g. reports of investigations? Similarly, with the ability of ICT (in the right hands and using a DTP package or similar) to make a pupil's work look highly professional: how should teachers view this and assess it? Scanning in images and drawing graphs with a computer package can make some pupils' work look superb? But is it all style and no substance?

Several pieces of research have indicated that word-processed work can be of most assistance for pupils with special needs, e.g. poor writers: those who have difficulty in writing by hand. This is where ICT can be of great value to pupils who may be good at *science*, but whose writing ability does not do their scientific skill justice. But an issue at the other extreme for teachers assessing work is whether they can be 'conned' by superbly presented work.

The first question, raised above, is: whose work is it? The second question is: what is the quality of the *content* of work which has been presented in an all-singing, all-dancing style? Teachers (more and more in future with the growth in home use of ICT) will need to make careful judgements in these two areas, i.e.:

- whose work is it? are outside sources acknowledged?
- is the quality of the *science* work being disguised – or enhanced – by the quality of the presentation?

(c) Collaborative work

One of the excellent features of ICT is that it permits, or rather *enhances*, collaborative group work. Pupils can often write collaboratively using a computer whereas writing collaboratively with a pen is more difficult! Increasingly, there will be assignments and coursework, at *all* levels of education, which have been done as a collaborative team effort. This trend will be fuelled by the demands of employers whose requirements of staff in new forms of employment always include 'team-work' and 'collaboration' near the top of the list. It is interesting to observe that collaborative work is commonplace in primary school and in Higher Education – but seems to be almost taboo in some secondary schools.

ICT will enhance collaborative work but the issue of how it should be assessed remains a controversial one:

- should all partners receive equal credit, or the same mark?
- have any pupils had a 'free ride'?
- will pupils who (quite rightly) want a good mark avoid and exclude certain other pupils who might 'lower the grade'?

These issues will occur at all levels, from primary school to university. But they should not be allowed to prevent collaborative work from being done. Through careful observation of group work (who is doing what, when and for how long?), through record-keeping, and through discussion with pupils, teachers can ensure that collaborative work will be assessed fairly and individual pupils do not see it as a soft option.

Summary

We started this chapter by considering the nature of science and science education and then asking: 'How can ICT enhance and improve it?' By looking at what computers are good at it becomes clear that ICT can *add value* to learning and teaching in science. The chapter has outlined several applications of ICT which can be particularly beneficial (e.g. simulations, data-logging, the Internet).

One of the key jobs of the teacher is to ask what counts as *authentic* or appropriate use of ICT in science (as opposed to *inauthentic* or inappropriate use). This question can only be answered when we become clear on our *learning and teaching objectives*. For example, if our objective is to teach graph-drawing with paper and pencil then a data-logging package is not appropriate. However, using a sensor with good data-logging and graph-plotting software can remove some of the drudgery and take pupils quickly to the higher-order skills of discussing and interpreting graphical results. The chapter has also considered the important business of *managing* ICT in a school setting. This relates closely to the *teacher's role* in using ICT, including the important issue of taking account of and managing *home use* of ICT, which is growing at a rapid rate. The use of ICT at home and at school raises vital issues for the teacher's task of judging and assessing ICT work, including work done collaboratively. Key points in assessment were listed, with practical suggestions for teachers.

Finally, the teacher's role in reviewing and evaluating ICT as part of science education was discussed. The ability to review and evaluate software for its *educational value and curriculum relevance* is a key aspect of the teacher's repertoire of skills in using ICT. Ideas and a checklist for evaluation of ICT applications were put forward which should be valuable to teachers in *critically* considering ICT in education. Indeed, the main theme of this chapter is that teachers should look forward to the use of ICT in teaching and learning where it can give *added value*. There are enough examples available of 'value-added' activities – in data-logging, in simulations, in spreadsheet and database use, and in text processing – to show that ICT can genuinely enhance science education.

References and further reading

Blease, D. (1986) *Evaluating Educational Software*, London: Croom Helm.

Chapman, C. and Lewis, J. (1998) *IT Activities for Science: 11–14*, Oxford: Heinemann.

Collins, J. Hammond, M. and Wellington, J.J. (1997) *Teaching and Learning with Multimedia*, London: Routledge.

DfEE Statistical Bulletins (published annually).

Frost, R. (1998) *The IT in Secondary Science Book*, Hatfield: ASE.

Frost, R. (1998) *Software for Teaching Science*, Hatfield: ASE Publications (ISBN: 0–9520257–5–2).

Hoyles, C. (ed.) (1988) *Girls and Computers*. London: Bedford Way Papers.

Kahn, B. (1985) *Computers in Science*, Cambridge: Cambridge University Press.

Loveless, T. (1996) 'Why aren't computers used more in schools?' *Educational Policy*, December 1996, pp. 448–67.

McFarlane, A. (ed.) (1997), *IT and Authentic Learning*, London: Routledge.

Merali, Z., Blamire, R. *et al.* (1995) *Highways for Learning: An Introduction to the Internet for Schools and Colleges*. NCET: Coventry (now BECTA).

Owen, M., Pritchard, J. and Rowlands, M. (1992) *Information Technology in Science*. Wales: MEU, Cymru. (A useful pack of ideas, information and case histories of IT use in science).

Rogers, L. (1990) 'IT in science in the national curriculum', in *Journal of Computer Assisted Learning*, no. 6, pp. 246–54.

Sanger, J. with Wilson, J., Davis, B. and Whittaker, R. (1997) *Young Children, Videos, and Computer Games*, London: Falmer Press.

Scaife, J. and Wellington, J.J. (1993) *IT in Science and Technology Education*. Buckingham: Open University Press.

Sewell, D. (1990) *New Tools For New Minds: A Cognitive Perspective on the Use of Computers with Young Children*, Hemel Hempstead: Harvester Wheatsheaf.

Turkle, S. (1984) *The Second Self: Computers and the Human Spirit*. London: Granada.

Underwood, J. and Underwood, G. (1990) *Computers and Learning*. Oxford: Basil Blackwell.

Weizenbaum, J. (1984) *Computer Power and Human Reason*. Harmondsworth: Penguin.

Wellington, J.J. (1985) *Children, Computers and the Curriculum*. London: Harper and Row.

Wellington, J.J. (1989) *Education for Employment: the place of information technology*, Windsor: NFER-Nelson.

Wellington, J.J. (1998) (ed.) *Practical Work in School Science: Which Way Now?*, London: Routledge, especially Chapters 14, 15 and 16.

The December 1997 issue of *School Science Review* was devoted to ICT in Science and contains several useful articles (SSR, vol. 79, no. 287, pp. 15–103).

Chapter 11

Conveying messages about the nature of science: practical approaches

(with contributions by Mick Nott)

Portraying messages about the nature of science, and teaching about it directly, both present a challenge to science teachers. This chapter presents examples of classroom approaches to teaching about the nature of science. Some of these involve using unplanned, spontaneous incidents in the classroom. Others involve planned teaching.

Classroom strategies for the nature of science

School science in many countries is dominated by practical work. Although the value of this work has been questioned (see, for example, Hodson 1990; Wellington 1998), science teachers are used to organising demonstrations and practicals and to setting written work based on them and the theories they are meant to illustrate. However, the nature of science sets new challenges that few science teachers have tried: some may be willing to try, but some may be unwilling to recognise them as appropriate to science at all. Science teachers will need to organise and provide activities which include:

* structured discussion amongst small groups of children;
* structured reading or listening or watching of items which may involve some of the stories of science;
* drama and role play so that children can develop the qualities of sympathy and empathy with people in the past and from different cultures;
* experimental work where children have to engage with the models of science both to explain and predict.

This chapter will provide case studies to illustrate some of these strategies. However, first we consider incidents which arise spontaneously in science classrooms but which can all be used to convey messages about the nature of science.

Responding to 'critical incidents'

Lessons do not always go according to plan. The natural world, and the young people who inhabit it (pupils), do not always play ball. Over a number of years,

Mick Nott and I have been collecting examples of critical classroom incidents which have either happened to us or which have been reported to us by experienced teachers. The list is long and still growing. Below we include a selection. They all force teachers into making on-the-spot decisions and often changing their plans. Teachers' responses to them, in the heat of the classroom, are often spontaneous. However, they are important in that the teachers' responses convey messages to pupils about the nature of science.

The selected incidents are divided up into those occurring during practical work, and those which raise moral questions or classroom discussion. Each incident evokes an on-the-spot decision which is informed by the teacher's views of the nature of science. The incidents below are critical because:

- they occur *despite* sound long-term planning;
- the way they are handled by the teacher can have a profound effect on pupils' views of science.

Please read each one carefully. For each one, think about: (i) what you *would* do in the heat of the classroom in responding to this incident; (ii) what you *could* do, e.g. given more time; (iii) what you *should* do, i.e. the moral course of action.

Practical incidents

A   HEATING MAGNESIUM

A class of 14–15-year-old pupils is heating magnesium ribbon in a crucible with a lid. The purpose of the lesson is to test the consequence of oxygen theory that materials gain mass when burnt.

At the summary at the end of the lesson four groups report a loss in weight, two groups report no difference and two groups report a gain in weight.

B   USING MICROSCOPES

A class of 11–12-year-old pupils are working with microscopes and you want them to observe and draw onion skin cells.

They set up the slides and you check that they have focused the microscopes competently and then they start to look and draw.

You find their drawings to be nothing like your image of onion skin cells.

Onion cells

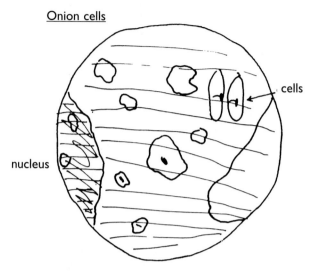

Figure 11.1 A pupil's view of an onion-skin cell.
Source: Barlex and Carré 1985.

C   TESTING FOR PHOTOSYNTHESIS

You have set up a demonstration of the production of oxygen by photosynthesis with Canadian pond-weed. Just before the lesson when the class are to look at the apparatus again, you notice that there is a small amount of gas in the test tube but not enough with which to do the oxygen test.

D   USING CIRCUIT BOARDS

Children are doing experiments with circuit boards. With two lamps in series, many find that one is lit brightly whilst the other appears to be unlit.

E   OBSERVING REFRACTION

You are demonstrating wave phenomena using a ripple tank. The children are unable to observe refraction clearly, and frankly you find it hard to see with the apparatus available.

F   TWO MORE EPISODES FROM PRACTICAL LESSONS

1   A teacher is doing the starch test on leaves. For inexplicable reasons the tests are indecisive.

2   A teacher is demonstrating the non-magnetic properties of iron sulphide. However, the freshly made sample sticks to the magnet.

In both instances, pupils say the following:

'But science experiments never work.'

'Anyway, we'll believe you. Tell us what should have happened.'

Non-practical incidents

G   EXPLAINING THE UNIVERSE

You are conducting a lesson on the big bang theory of the origin of the universe. A pupil at the front interrupts in the middle of your account of the big bang and says: 'My family believe that the Earth was created by God in six days. This is what it says in Genesis and we believe the Bible to be true.'

H   LOOKING AT LIFE

You are well into a teaching unit on 'Life and Living Processes'. One of the pupils asks impatiently at the start of a lesson, 'When are we going to start cutting up rats then?'.

I   THE UNWILLING CHEMIST

You have a particularly reluctant learner in your chemistry class. The pupil is not aggressive but assertive, declaring that this work on chemistry is not something they like doing. When you ask why, the pupil says: 'Because if it hadn't been for chemists, we wouldn't have these chemicals ruining the Earth.'

J   CONTRACEPTION AND CATHOLICISM

You are teaching a group of 13–14-year-olds contraception and the lesson is about different methods of birth control. One of the pupils asks: 'Do you believe it's right for the Catholic Church to say that only the rhythm method is acceptable? The rest are sinful.'

The range of teachers' responses to these incidents

We have used these incidents with many groups of teachers, and asked them to respond by saying what they *would* do, *could* do and *should* do. The first question involves a kind of off-the-cuff, pragmatic reaction to the incident. The second involves a more divergent approach, as it asks what they could do if perhaps they had fewer constraints and more time to reflect. The third category of response leads into the area of what they really ought to do as science teachers (i.e. the moral area).

The incidents where laboratory activities 'go wrong' appear to elicit three categories of response. These are 'talking your way out of it', 'rigging' and 'conjuring' (Nott and Smith 1995). The majority of responses are in the first category of 'talking your way out of it' or, as we would like to say more positively 'talking your way through it'; when science teachers talk their way through practicals that have gone wrong they often engage the children in a critical evaluation of practical work. 'Rigging' is the use of strategies that teachers have learned over the years to ensure that the apparatus or procedure works. The last category, 'conjuring', is where the teacher fraudulently produces the correct result for an experiment by sleight of hand.

The 'conjuring' category, we must stress, is by far the smallest. But we have had the following responses from experienced teachers:

- 'I put my thumb on the scales to ensure that there is a gain in weight' (example A).
- '. . . spike it and it always works' (example C).
- '. . . cheat, use oxygen from a cylinder' (example C).

There appears to be a small set of experiments in the science repertoire that are *regularly* conjured. The pond-weed incident is a case in point: children are *not* told about how the result was produced. We have found that student teachers can start to conjure spontaneously or are inducted into it by science staff and technicians. We suggest that conjuring is a practice which student teachers should discuss and challenge. (Nott and Wellington 1997)

Others say that they resort to 'rigging' or 'tweaking' practicals i.e. carefully adjusting the variables to achieve the 'correct result', e.g. in the pond-weed example teachers might dope the water with 'sodium bicarbonate' or use strong growlights.

But the majority of responses are in the category of 'talking your way through it'. The examples given below are all statements that teachers have actually made. We do not offer them all as examples of good practice, merely as illustrations of what often occurs. When science teachers talk their way through practicals that are going wrong they often engage the children in a critical evaluation of science practical work and therefore teach them about the nature of science.

First, the teacher may criticise the apparatus or the practical procedures:

- 'Blame the fact that the light bulbs aren't identical' (example D).
- 'Check the weighing procedures with the magnesium ribbon' (example A).
- 'Assume the experiment with pond-weed has been done wrongly' (example C).

But the talking can also involve explanations and interpretations of the reliability and replicability of practicals and the way that practical results are negotiated, as the following responses show:

- (With the magnesium strip) '. . . stress the need to repeat experiments' (example A).
- (With the onion skin slide) 'get the children to agree by consensus about what they see' (example B).
- 'Get them to see that negative results can be useful and significant' (example D).
- 'Get the class to discuss why it could have gone wrong with the magnesium ribbon' (example A).
- 'Analyse and average the results – perhaps average the data' (examples A and D).
- (With the onion skin slide) '. . . show them a drawing of a slide and ask them if they can see something like that' (example B).
- '[I] would have to tell them the expected outcome otherwise they wouldn't learn anything [but] say if it's wrong for a reason.'

It is easy to be critical of science teachers who conjure experiments. But how many of us can honestly say we are totally innocent? The constraints of classroom life and the pressure of examinations force teachers into planning, tweaking, rigging or even conjuring practical work so that pupils are not confused by it and that they learn the 'right answer'.

However, it is only by 'talking their way through it' that teachers can use critical incidents of this kind to teach pupils about the nature of science. By discussing the incidents, teachers are conveying messages about real science, i.e. it is an activity:

- where practicals need to be evaluated and this involves repeating experiments;
- where the null result is as important as the positive result;
- that involves sharing results and collectively criticising, negotiating and deciding procedures;
- in which, to learn from and to do practicals, you need to have an idea in your head before you start;
- in which there are reasons why experiments go wrong, and that there is always a rational explanation;
- in which results need to match previously accepted knowledge.

The magnesium ribbon and pond-weed examples can illustrate the procedures that scientists use to check experimental results and show that experiments are as much the result of the experimenters' skills as they are a mirror of nature. The onion skin cells and ripple tank examples can show that the work of scientists is guided by other scientists' images and pictures of what is to be perceived – all observations are theory-laden and newcomers have to be trained to see in the ways of more experienced scientists.

Responding to non-practical critical incidents

In this way, events and demonstrations which don't always go according to plan can be used to illustrate the nature of science. Such critical incidents can be used to positive effect if teachers are alert and ready for them. In this way, much teaching about the nature of science can occur unexpectedly and spontaneously – as opposed to the planned teaching activities presented later.

What of the non-practical critical incidents shown earlier? They present teachers with equally difficult on-the-spot decisions – and they raise equally important questions about the nature of science and scientific activity. Students need to learn that scientists and scientific ideas are strongly influenced by the social, moral, spiritual and cultural contexts in which they live and work. Critical incidents such as examples G–J raise questions about the context of science and the controversies it provokes. In a crowded lesson, teachers rarely have the time to respond fully – hence the need for planned lessons on controversial issues which is discussed in the next section. But groups of teachers we have discussed the incidents with have suggested possible strategies.

In response to the rat incident, one teacher said that she would point out that biology is the study of living things, not dead things, and would perhaps use the incident to prompt or plan a future class debate about the morality of dissection, and perhaps broaden it to discuss animal experimentation.

The big bang incident always prompts a lot of discussion. Several teachers said, in their responses, that the big bang theory should be presented as the 'accepted scientific explanation' but not the only possible explanation: 'It is a theory, not a fact.' Another tactic was to argue that 'religious beliefs are religious beliefs, but scientists have theories which *explain* [the teachers' emphasis]: scientists have theories which are based on evidence'. Another response was that 'theories change with time – they are not held on to for all time'. Thus the main thrust of this response is that religious beliefs are totally different from scientific theories, and that presumably they can exist alongside one another. Scientific knowledge is a way of explaining, but it is not the *only* way of explaining.

The student with 'an attitude' to chemistry elicited responses from teachers that promoted the benefits of chemistry to health and well-being, but there was also talk about scientists not always being in control of the products they create. Perhaps we should also convey the message that the application of knowledge is not the sole responsibility of scientists.

Increasingly, science teachers will be faced with controversial issues which arise spontaneously – one way of preparing themselves (and their pupils) for this is to plan and teach lessons which present a controversial issue and also teach some science *content* at the same time.

Handling controversial issues

Why include them?

There are at least three good reasons for including controversial issues in teaching and learning science:

1   As a way of making 'content' more interesting, meaningful, exciting and relevant, i.e. engaging and motivating pupils.
2   As a way of portraying the true nature of science, i.e. as an activity which is *not always* exact, clear, certain and unproblematic. Indeed, *not* to include controversial issues in the science curriculum would be a serious mis-representation of the subject (see Wellington 1986a and Millar 1996) and lead to public misunderstanding of science.
3   Students can acquire important attitudes, *skills* and understanding of processes by examining controversial issues related to science.

Students can learn to weigh up evidence, to search for information, to detect bias, to question the validity of sources and to present their own considered viewpoint. The skills of communication, listening, working collaboratively and co-operating in group sessions can all be enhanced. (Clearly the development of these skills will depend on the approach of the teacher, which we consider later.) The attitude of 'healthy scepticism' can be fostered.

What are controversial issues?

Many aspects of science are *not* tentative or controversial. I would wager my house that in 50 years' time Newton's second law will still apply on Earth, metals will expand when heated, photosynthesis will still occur in the same way and caesium will react violently with water.

Issues become controversial when there is either: (a) considerable scientific debate or disagreement about causes, theories and evidence, e.g. as in the case of cold fusion, BSE or GM foods, or (b) debate and disagreement about the *applications* of science and its effects on the environment, on people or on animals, e.g. the use of nuclear energy and nuclear weapons; animal experiment-ation; cloning of animals or humans; the spread of GM foods.

Some issues in science are controversial for both the above reasons, i.e. both the science and its applications are controversial. These are perhaps the issues best suited to inclusion in the science curriculum.

Many current controversial issues, and several which have a longer shelf-life, relate closely to the knowledge and content of the science curriculum. For example:

contraception	the origin of life
religious belief	the paranormal
food and diet	smoking, alcohol and other drugs
pollution	farming methods
energy supplies	genetic engineering
the origin of the Universe	sex and reproduction
evolution	transport

All are subject to: a lack of certainty (in both scientists and the public); a range of different views; different perspectives and responses according to a person's spiritual, moral or cultural standpoint.

The teacher's role

Traditionally, the science teacher has dealt with the 'facts' and left 'values' to the humanities staff. That approach will not do in the twenty-first century (see *Beyond 2000*), even if it ever did hold water. Many scientific issues now involve a complex mixture of facts, values, value-laden facts, and values dependent on people's perceptions of the 'facts'.

The science teacher's job is a difficult one. A teacher will be able to settle disputes on some factual points involved in controversial issues. For example, in a discussion on nuclear energy, a teacher can usefully correct the mistaken belief that a nuclear reactor could explode like an atomic bomb in the event of an accident. But should the teacher act as 'an authority' in settling matters of *value*? Clearly, a teacher who did so would not be acting objectively, neutrally or in a balanced way.

There is a *legal* requirement in some countries (including the UK) that teachers should present a balanced view when dealing with controversial issues. But how does this work in practice? Should the case *for* smoking be presented alongside the anti-smoking arguments? Should teachers balance the evidence against illegal drugs with the evidence for their benefits?

Most teachers are, quite justifiably, wary of exposing their own personal views and values to a classroom full of young people. They are often safer in adopting one or more of the following rules:

- *devil's advocate*: confronting individuals or groups by adopting (tongue-in-cheek) the opposite viewpoint;
- *the neutral chair*: ensuring that all views and values are given an 'equal airing', whilst not disclosing their own values;
- *the advocate role*: presenting all of the available viewpoints as objectively as possible, then concluding by stating his/her position.

The latter role is probably least safe, though it may be seen as safer than openly declaring a position at the outset or (more extremely) propagating a particular view on (say) drugs, contraception, food or nuclear energy (the various roles are presented in Plant and Firth 1995, p.42).

However, it is often essential for a teacher to play some sort of *advocate role*, especially if (as is often the case in classroom discussion):

(a) there is no divergence of view among participants, or the divergence is not equally distributed; or
(b) some important viewpoints are not expressed at all.

My own view is that teachers should challenge and confront different viewpoints (perhaps as a kind of devil's advocate) but they are on dangerous ground if they use the classroom as a platform from which to promulgate and promote their own personal views. Fortunately, there are accepted teaching strategies which can be used.

Practical classroom strategies for controversial issues

Obviously, discussion is likely to be the dominant approach rather than didactic teaching. However, simply asking (or expecting) students to read material on a controversial issue, and then discuss it, may not be appropriate in many classes. More active learning and involvement is often needed. The following activities offer a range of alternatives:

Brainstorming

Brainstorming is useful for starting open thinking on a new topic. This is likely to work best in a small group. It is an effective way of gathering people's ideas, associations and impressions of almost any topic. It will be most illuminating before discussion or teaching has begun. An open, non-evaluative session of this kind can form an excellent starting point for three main reasons:

• Interest and awareness are aroused.
• The teacher is provided with useful information on the views and prior knowledge of the students.
• People learn the attitudes and impressions of others in an enjoyable and non-argumentative way.

With larger or less manageable groups, individuals can be asked to write down the first three words or ideas that come into their mind in response to a given word. (This can be done individually or in small groups.) The responses can be collected and made into a large chart for display. Brainstorming is not a new idea and it may not work well for every teacher with all classes, but it is a good way of making an unbiased, open-minded start to a topic.

Questionnaires

Another way of arousing interest is to ask members of a group to interview each other. This can be done in small groups or pairs. Interviewers can ask about peers' views, attitudes and opinions; about anxieties or worries; or even about their existing knowledge of a subject. Results can remain anonymous, and may prove as interesting to the teacher as to the group members themselves. The results may be collected and displayed. Teachers may wish to devise their own interviews to suit particular classes or, better still, ask the students to make up their own interviews to try out on the others. Questionnaires can also be used to raise consciousness and explore areas similar to those described for interviewing.

The questionnaires can be handed out to each student in the class, and once they are complete the results can be collated to form a 'class profile'. Histograms or pie-charts can be designed to display people's opinions and attitudes visually. Simple computer databases are ideal for collating and displaying results.

Examining pictorial material

Photographs, illustrations, projected slides or OHTs can all be used as alternatives to written material for generating discussion and presenting evidence. Photographs, newspaper cartoons or topical pictures can be used to start a discussion or instigate written work.

To start discussion the teacher can:

- invite general comments from anyone in the group;
- focus on particular aspects of a picture, e.g. people's expressions, the likely time of the photograph, size and scale;
- ask for impressions or associations conjured up by the picture (rather like brainstorming);
- invite speculation on why the picture was made: What point it is trying to make? Why was a cartoon drawn?
- invite discussion on what individuals might be saying or thinking.

Similar ploys can be used to promote written work. Students can be asked to write down three words or ideas which spring to mind when they see a picture. alternatively, students can write down what the characters in a picture might be saying, perhaps incorporating this into a comic strip. The suggested speeches can be compared and discussed. These, and other ploys, are all valuable starting points for using pictorial material to stimulate discussion and written work.

Role play and simulation

Controversial issues are ideally suited to role play and simulation. The actual classroom practice will depend on the style, inventiveness and imagination of the teacher.

Reading and writing

Active reading and writing techniques can also help students come to terms with the wide range of information presented in connection with controversial issues (see DARTs in Chapter 9 on language). One activity to encourage reading and writing is to examine media coverage and controversial issues from different sources, e.g. the Internet, newspapers, leaflets from pressure groups. Wall displays and collages could be made showing both the quantity and quality of newspaper coverage, and in some cases those of magazine articles. Different newspapers could be compared. If possible, old newspapers, or copies of parts of them, could be used to show coverage of present and past incidents.

All the activities described here are fairly simple, and can easily be adopted and adapted by class teachers for their own use. The value in many of the activities suggested is that the existing knowledge and prior attitudes of the group can be revealed, sometimes anonymously. This feedback is as essential to a teacher dealing with a contentious issue as it is in teaching other aspects of the curriculum, e.g. scientific concepts. In short, the teacher can start from where students are, both in their previous information and existing attitudes and use active learning strategies to go forward effectively and sensitively. Neither the teacher, nor any individual pupil in the class, need have their personal viewpoints or beliefs crudely exposed.

By introducing and carefully handling controversial issues in the classroom, science teachers can not only engage and motivate pupils, but also portray many aspects of the nature of 'real science'. They can also develop important critical skills and attitudes such as a healthy scepticism towards information and where it comes from. The next section describes two direct teaching approaches which can be used to illustrate further aspects of the nature of science.

Direct teaching approaches on the nature of science

Case Study I – Experimental work: using the ray model to interpret and predict (Mick Nott)

Children are expected in school science to use and understand the ray model of light. Research (Driver *et al.* 1985) has shown that this model is difficult to assimilate. My own experience of school teaching convinced me of the difficulty children had in drawing ray diagrams because they did not understand the model. The children I taught had not latched on to the idea of the infinite extension of the ray. Figure 11.2 shows a difference between children's science and scientists' science.

Another 'standard' diagram that children find problematic is the pinhole camera. Figure 11.3 shows a standard diagram. Every item in the diagram is represented by lines on paper. Some lines have arrowheads drawn on them, but in my experience children often don't notice them. The real object, the theoretical rays, the real camera and the *ethereal* image are all represented by lines of

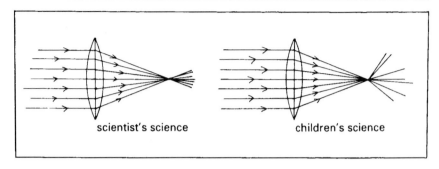

Figure *11.2* Children's science, scientists' science.

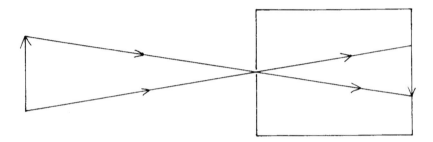

Figure *11.3* Standard design for a pinhole camera.

the same status. It is my hunch that this lack of differentiation may create comprehension problems. The diagram only makes sense if you understand the model already.

An Arabic scientist, Al-Kindi, worked with a ray model to explain the formation of shadows and the production of images in the camera obscura. Centuries later, in another continent, Kepler worked on the problem of image formation through apertures. To understand the phenomenon, Kepler modelled rays of light by using threads. (This use of threads was well known to artists; see Pedoe, 1976.)

One of the diagrams that Al-Kindi drew, using the ray model, was to explain the formation of a shadow by a point source (see Figure 11.4). The point D represents a point source. DE is the height of the source above the bench. AB represents an opaque object, and DAG is the ray which grazes the top of AB. The distance BG then indicates the length of the shadow cast on the bench.

Children can set up a raybox and screen on a bench to see if Al-Kindi's model works, but it may be more effective to have them work with the model first. Children can be given paper cut-outs of a raybox and screen; they could 'borrow' Kepler's use of a thread to model a ray (see Figure 11.5). The teacher could ask questions like:

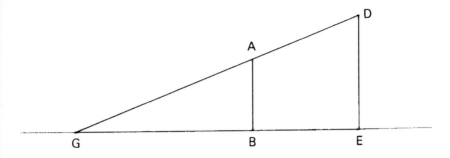

Figure 11.4 Al-Kindi's explanation of shadows.

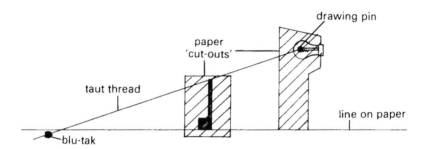

Figure 11.5 Using a thread to model a light-ray.

'What does the model predict will happen to the length of the shadow if you

... move the screen towards or away from the lamp?'
... move the lamp towards or away from the screen?'
... use a smaller or larger size screen?'

The children can use the thread 'ray' to make predictions and then go to the apparatus and see if, according to the model, their predictions were correct. If the teacher judiciously chooses the size of the paper cut-outs to match the size of the apparatus, then the children can make qualitative and quantitative predictions. Also, this particular activity asks the children to work only with one ray.

This idea can be extended to working with two rays to help children understand explanations of the pinhole camera. This time the paper cut-outs can be of a pinhole camera and a carbon filament lamp (see Figure 11.6). If the children use one thread 'ray' from the top of the lamp and the other from the bottom of the lamp, then the teacher could ask questions like:

'How can the light get from the lamp to the screen? Does your model predict where light from the top of the object will arrive on the screen and vice-versa?'

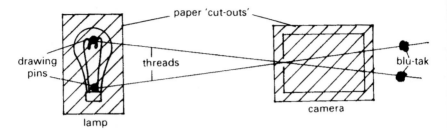

Figure 11.6 Using threads to model a pinhole camera.

'What does your model predict about the size of the image and the orientation of the image? Work with the model first and then go to the apparatus and test your prediction.'

'What will happen to the size of the image as the distance between the camera and lamp is made smaller or larger? Work with the model first to make a prediction and then go and test it with the apparatus.'

There are more possibilities that come to mind. Different colours for the two threads may help some children understand the image inversion, or with some children the teacher may ask them to try and use or adapt the model to see if it can help to explain how the brightness of the image alters with the distance of the object. The teacher may wish some children at some time to explore phenomena that are hard to explain with the model, so that the notion that scientific models have limits is raised.

Children are learning to use and apply standard scientific models. This example draws on the history of science, but it isn't teaching children the history of science. Al-Kindi's and Kepler's work are anachronistically juxtaposed to provide practical work to help the learning of a currently acceptable model. This doesn't stop a teacher telling the story about Al-Kindi or about Kepler and this may help children understand that scientific ideas have been created and developed in different cultures and in different times. These stories about science and scientists are important. Generally children enjoy them, teachers enjoy telling them and would like to know more of them, and they counteract negative images (or no images) of other cultures and people in the past. They also provide an experience appropriate for the later years.

However, the prime motivation for creating the activity is for children to learn, use and understand the ray model of light. The other point of interest here is that the model is provided by the teacher. This is not to say that time shouldn't be spent eliciting children's ideas on how shadows and images are formed, but once they are elicited then the children could test their ideas against the scientists' (teachers') model. It is my belief that children in school laboratories and with school apparatus will not rediscover or uncover many scientific theories. The teachers' role is to offer reasonable explanations which, in most circumstances, can be reasonably tested.

The teachers and children with whom this work was used on a trial basis found it worthwhile; the materials were first published in *Exploring the Nature of Science* (Solomon 1991).

Case study 2 – Discussion work and role play: the story of Edward Jenner (Mick Nott)

The next case study concerns some curriculum materials called 'Jabs for James Phipps', which can be found in Solomon (1991). The specific topic is the story of Edward Jenner's work on vaccination. Teachers have slotted the materials in with units on topics like microbiology or health.

There is a series of programmes produced for schools called *Scientific Eye* (Yorkshire Television 1984). In one particular programme, called 'Minibeasts and Disease', is a short (approximately five minutes) cartoon of the story of Edward Jenner and the famous vaccination of the small boy called James Phipps. The style is 'jokey', but this does not detract from the fact that the main points of this scientific episode are raised. The experimental procedure is described in a clear chronological order. A rationale is also provided for Jenner's actions. The cartoon suggests with its imagery that James was not necessarily a willing volunteer to an 'untested' procedure. This (unintentionally?) raises ethical issues about this work. So here is a resource, common to many schools, which contains information about the introduction of a new idea, clearly describes the experiment and raises ethical and moral issues surrounding the procedure. It forms an ideal stimulus for some classroom activities about the nature of science.

The structure of the materials

The published materials consist of the following:

1 TELLING A STORY

The first part is an activity to process the information in the cartoon story in the video. The children are split into groups of approximately four. Each group is given an envelope with jumbled chunks of text which describe the story. The group task is to put the chunks of text in the right chronological sequence. (See Figure 11.7 for the ten chunks of text.)

If some blanks are included in the envelopes then the children can add any bits of information that they think are important. The children can take part in the 'ordering' and the telling of the story. When the pieces of paper are in the right order they can then be stuck onto a large piece of paper to make an 'instant' poster detailing the events of the story in the correct temporal sequence.

The purpose of this activity is to provide an alternative way of processing the information in the cartoon – in other words, to retell the story in a different manner. If done in mixed-ability groups it provides an opportunity for all children to contribute to the telling of the story.

Jenner's experiment

✂ -

Jenner puts cowpox pus into James's arm.

✂ -

Jenner sees that James doesn't get smallpox.

✂ -

JENNER HEARS THAT THE MILKMAIDS DON'T GET SMALLPOX.

✂ -

Jenner decides that having cowpox stops you getting smallpox.

✂ -

Jenner sees that James suffers from cowpox for a few days, and then gets well.

✂ -

JENNER TAKES SOME PUS FROM A SMALLPOX VICTIM
AND PUTS IT INTO JAMES'S ARM.

✂ -

Jenner thinks that if he gives someone cowpox first
they won't get smallpox.

✂ -

JENNER HEARS THAT MILKMAIDS
OFTEN GET COWPOX.

✂ -

JENNER TAKES COWPOX PUS FROM A MILKMAID

✂ -

**Jenner thinks that having cowpox
might stop you getting smallpox.**

✂ -

Figure 11.7 Jenner's experiment.

2 EVALUATING AN EXPERIMENT

The second part of the activity is to then open a second envelope containing pieces of paper with the phrases 'making a hypothesis', 'observing', 'prediction', 'reaching a conclusion' and 'doing an experiment' (see Figure 11.8). The children's task is then to match these words to the places where they think they occur in the story of Jenner's experiment that they have just put on the poster.

Process words

OBSERVING

Meaning: **To watch carefully what is happening.**

(As well as using your eyes you can observe by listening, smelling, touching and occasionally tasting.)

MAKING A HYPOTHESIS

Meaning: **To have an idea about why something happens.**

(You can use this idea to design experiments.)

DOING AN EXPERIMENT

Meaning: **When you design and carry out a test for your hypothesis.**

PREDICTION

Saying what you think is going to happen.

REACHING A CONCLUSION

Deciding what your experiment shows.

(You might be deciding if your hypothesis is right or wrong.)

Figure 11.8 Process words.

The purpose of this second activity is to help children to analyse the structure of the experiment. Teachers who have used these materials agree that the evaluation of Jenner's experiment happens, but it has also been reported that the analysis of the structure of the experiment has a transferability across to other scientific investigations. The following is an extract from an interview with a teacher:

'The amazing thing for me came in the next module along when the kids ... were planning an investigation . . . One girl came back, she had a series of flow diagrams . . . she had written on little boxes 'hypothesising here', 'testing here' and 'observing here' and I said, "Where did you get all this from then?" She said she remembered it from the last unit that we did on the Jenner story. I went and had a chat with some of the other kids, and they had actually transferred the skills and ideas from ["Jabs for James Phipps"] to another [module], which to me is fairly successful . . .'

(Nott 1992a: 222)

It appears that the children, having analysed (and criticised) the structure of experimental work as exemplified in the Jenner story, learned something about the structure of experiments. That learning had then been transferred to the planning of their own benchwork experiments. It may be that learning 'processes' through stories is as important as learning them by doing experiments. The processes of experimental planning could be seen as the identical processes in the Jenner story.

3   VALUES AND EXPERIMENTS

Lastly, the children can be invited to discuss whether they think Jenner's experiment was a 'fair test'. They can suggest improvements to Jenner's experimental design. They can be asked to discuss whether all improvements would be right and proper in terms of whether they would be allowed to do them, or whether they felt it would be right to do them.

The purpose of this activity is to encourage the children to evaluate the experiment and hence to consider whether there are any ethical and moral limits on the nature of the experiment and hence medical experiments in general.

4   ROLE PLAY

When children watch the cartoon they do so with interest and feeling. The cartoon implies that the procedure involved some risk and possible hurt to James. This is done in a way that is amusing, albeit darkly amusing. The materials contain a role-play activity so that children can sympathise and empathise with the characters in the Jenner story. (For a further introductory discussion on role play and drama in school science, see Bentley and Watts, 1988.)

The characters are the obvious characters in the cartoon – Jenner, James Phipps and Sarah Nelmes, the milkmaid. However, 'new' characters are also added. These are Mr and Mrs Phipps and James's aunt and uncle. These last two characters are fictitious; they are presented as two people who had James's interests at heart, and their views are constructed to represent contemporary arguments for and against Jenner's work.

A role card is available for each character, and questions at the end stimulate discussion amongst the children and make them start to build a character on the information they have (see Figure 11.9 for examples). A class can be split into small groups so that the roles can be built in groups and then one child from each group can act out the role – and even be prompted by her or his colleagues. (A concise background to the organisation of role play in science is contained in Williams, Hudson and Green 1992.)

The pupils should spend time (approximately 15 minutes) 'getting into role' in groups. Then one child from each group can play the part of the character. The scenario suggested in the published materials is a press conference where those not playing a role can act as journalists. This format has been seen to work extremely well – children are familiar with press conferences from the news. It should also be noted that a press conference is an anachronism but the point is to play a role where feelings and values can be explored, not to play a drama that looks for historical authenticity.

Press conferences observed have covered a range of issues that the role cards raise, such as:

- fatalism, i.e. if God chose you to get smallpox then that was your fate versus the motivation of Jenner that God would be benign and want people to be saved;
- authority of experts on the risks of the experiment versus the risk of catching smallpox;
- the ethics of the experiment, including issues of experiments on animals;
- the influence of the employer–employee relationship between Jenner and the Phipp's household;
- the uncertainty whether the cowpox 'agent' would mutate into something more virulent inside James.

And all of this in approximately 10 minutes!

No work has been done with children on following up this classroom experience, but it does indicate that the materials stimulate a broad coverage and, in some cases, expression of some subtle ideas.

Teachers have been inventive and creative with it as well. One teacher reported creating the scenario for the role play as 'the Phipps' family tea' – a familiar occurrence for children to use; and there have been children working the story up into 'the Jenner rap' (Nott 1992a), and even a ballet!

The evidence appears to be that teachers have found this work to be very valuable both in exploring moral and ethical issues and in reprocessing the story and procedures of the experiment itself.

These materials deal only with a very narrow case, i.e. the experiment on James Phipps by Edward Jenner. It is important to add that the textbook impressions that it was solely Jenner who invented a safe technique of immunisation are wrong (see Smith 1987). The story of immunisation in England is one that involves other cultures and a determined woman, Lady Mary Wortley Montague (Alic 1986). There is also available some excellent classroom material, 'The long war against smallpox' (Science Education Group, York

James

You are eight and three-quarters years old and love fishing. You have gone to Sunday school a few times but you usually manage to escape and go down to the river. You don't want to learn to read. You don't want to start work either, but you know you will have to as soon as you are nine.

When you were little you fell out of a tree and broke your leg. Your father got Dr Jenner to set the broken bone and it hurt very badly. You have always been scared of Dr Jenner from that time. Once he gave you a medicine to cure your fever which was made from bitter aloes. You couldn't get the taste out of your mouth for a week afterwards.

You don't know much about smallpox except that your aunt had it. Now her face looks horrible with large deep pits all over it. You cannot even bear to kiss her.

Now decide:

Did you understand what Dr Jenner was going to do?
How would you feel about asking the doctor questions?
Now that you are safe from having smallpox would you advise your friends to have the vaccination too?

James' Mum

You did not go to school but have worked with your husband in the fields for many years. Now that he is gardener to Dr Jenner things are much easier.

You have had nine children but two of them died when they were only babies. You have never forgotten that. Dr Jenner did come and give the babies some medicine but it did not help them. He was not able to help your sister either when she died in childbirth.

James is your youngest and you know you spoil him a little, but you can't help it. He is always out fishing when your husband wants him to help in the garden. A month ago your husband suggested that James should be given smallpox now to prevent him from getting it later. That seemed terribly dangerous. You didn't sleep for a whole week worrying about it.

Now decide:

How do you feel about doctors?
What did you think when Dr Jenner explained what he was going to do to James?
Did you talk it over with your husband? If so what did you say to him?

Figure 11.9 Examples of role cards.

1990), which adds to the historical dimension of the materials above and introduces the multicultural dimension. Both teachers and children learn about the nature of science from this.

Science as story-telling

This last section has provided examples of classroom strategies which allow teachers and children to explore and investigate the nature of science in their classrooms. The intention has been to provide enough detail and information so that the reader can experiment with a range of teaching strategies that teach children science and the nature of science.

The above cases are based on stories of scientists. How many does one need to know? The answer is: not many. A teacher only needs a small range of stories to convey the key ideas of the nature of science to children. Not every lesson is going to be, nor needs to be, based on historical information. An expectation that science teachers will be fully conversant with an accurate sociology, history and philosophy of science is unrealistic. The classroom resources cited and given in further reading below will provide any teacher with a good half-dozen ideas and stories to get going.

It is important to have some stories and to recognise that stories are an important part of the culture of science. As Peter Medawar said: 'Scientific theories are the stories that scientists tell each other.'

References and further reading

Alic, M. (1986) *Hypatia's Heritage*, London: Women's Press.

Barlex, D. and Carré, C. (1985) *Visual Communication in Science*, Cambridge: Cambridge University Press.

Bentley, D. and Watts, M. (1988) *Teaching Science: Practical Alternatives*, Milton Keynes: Open University Press.

Beyond 2000: Science Education for the Future (an excellent report resulting from a series of seminars funded by the Nuffield Foundation, available from: King's College, London SE1 8WA).

Brush, S. (1974) 'Should the history of science be rated X?', *Science*, 183: pp. 1166–72.

Children's Learning in Science Project (CLISP) (1987) *CLIS in the Classroom: Approaches to Teaching*, Leeds: CSSME, University of Leeds.

Driver, R., Guesne, E. and Tiberghien, A. (1985) *Children's Ideas in Science*, Milton Keynes: Open University Press.

Futtock, K. (1991) *Louis Pasteur*, in the *Nature of Science* series, Hatfield: ASE.

Hesse, M. (1973) 'Models of theory change', in Hesse, M. (1980) *Revolutions and Reconstructions in the Philosophy of Science*, Brighton: Harvester Press.

Hodson, D. (1990) 'A critical look at practical work in school science', *School Science Review*, March 1990, no. 71, p. 256.

Hunt, A. (1997) *The World of Science: New SATIS 14–16*, London: John Murray (an excellent set of student material with a Teacher's Resource Book).

Nott, M. (1992) 'History in the school science curriculum: infection or immunity', *Proceedings of the Second International Conference on the History and Philosophy of Science Teaching*, Kingston, Ontario: Queen's University.

Nott, M. and Wellington, J. (1997) Producing the evidence: science teachers' initiations into practical work, *Research in Science Education*, 27(3), 395–409.

Nuffield Foundation (1967) *Nuffield Physics: Guide to Experiments III*, London/Harmondsworth: Longmans/Penguin.

—— (1971) *Nuffield Combined Science*, London/Harmondsworth: Longmans/Penguin.

Pedoe, D. (1976) *Geometry and the Liberal Arts*, London: Penguin.

Rowland, M. (1991) 'The great Brownian motion swindle', *New Scientist*, 3 April 1991: p. 49.

Science Education Group, University of York (1990) *Science: The Salters' Approach. Key Stage 4. Unit Guide: Keeping Healthy*, London: Heinemann.

Shortland, M. and Warwick, A. (1989) *Teaching the History of Science*, London: BSHS/ Blackwell.

Smith, J.R. (1987) *The Speckled Monster*, Chelmsford: Essex Record Office.

Solomon, J. (1991) *Exploring the Nature of Science*, Glasgow: Blackie.

Solomon, J. (1993) *Teaching Science, Technology and Society*, Buckingham: Open University Press.

Solomon, J., Hunt, A., Johnson, K. and Nott, M. (1989) *Teaching about the Nature of Science*, Hatfield: ASE.

Wellington, J. (ed.) (1998) *Practical Work in Science: which way now?*, London: Routledge.

Williams, S., Hudson, T. and Green, D. (eds) (1992) *Active Teaching and Learning Approaches in Science*, London: Collins Educational.

Yorkshire Television (1984) *Scientific Eye*, Leeds: YTV.

Critical incidents

Nott, M. and Smith, R. (1995) ' "Talking your way out of it", "rigging" and "conjuring": what science teachers do when practicals "go wrong" ', *International Journal of Science Education* no. 17, pp. 399–410.

Nott, M. and Wellington, J. (1995) 'Critical incidents in the science classroom and the nature of science', *School Science Review*, no. 76, pp. 41–6.

Nott, M. and Wellington, J. (1996) ' "Probing teachers" views of the nature of science: how should we do it and where should we be looking?', in Welford, G., Osborne, J. and Scott, P. (eds) *Science Education Research in Europe*, London: Falmer Press, pp. 283–94.

Handling controversial issues

Claxton, G. (1991) *Educating the Inquiring Mind: The Challenge for School Science*, London: Harvester Wheatsheaf.

Henderson, J. (1994) 'Teaching sensitive issues in science: the case of sex education', in Wellington, J.J. (ed.) *Secondary Science: Contemporary Issues and Practical Approaches*, London: Routledge.

Henderson, J. and Knutton, S. (1990) *Biotechnology in Schools: A Handbook for Teachers*, Milton Keynes: Open University Press.

Lock, R. and Ratcliffe, M. (1998) 'Learning about social and ethical applications of science', in Ratcliffe, M. (ed.), pp. 109–17.

Millar, R. (1996) 'Towards a science curriculum for public understanding', *School Science Review*, vol. 77, no. 280, pp. 7–18.

Plant, M. and Firth, R. (1995) *Teaching Through Controversial Issues*, Nottingham: Nottingham Trent University.

Ratcliffe, M. and Fullick, P. (1996) (eds) *Teaching Ethical Aspects of Science*, Southampton: Bassett Press.

Sheffield City Polytechnic (1992) *Active Teaching and Learning Approaches in Science*, London: Collins Educational. (now Sheffield Hallam University).

Solomon, J. (1998) 'About argument and discussion', *School Science Review*, vol. 80, no. 291, pp. 57–62.

Stradling, R., Noctor, M. and Baines, B. (1984) *Teaching Controversial Issues*, London: Edward Arnold.

Wellington, J.J. (1986a) *Controversial Issues in the Curriculum*, Oxford: Basil Blackwell.

—— (1986b) *The Nuclear Issue*, Oxford: Basil Blackwell.

Chapter 12

Using out-of-school sources to enrich science education

Many people equate learning in science with the formal science curriculum. Yet much, if not most, of children's learning about science takes place outside the confines of a timetable and a school. There is a mound of evidence to show that this 'informal' learning is both powerful and tightly held onto. Museums, newspapers, magazines, television and the Internet can all be sources of learning outside school. This chapter considers children's out-of-school learning sources and studies in detail two sources which teachers can make use of.

Formal and informal learning

All people learn science from a variety of sources, in a range of different ways, and for a number of different purposes. In other words, the reasons, sources and favoured modes for learning science vary from one individual to the next. There are two different sources of or areas of learning that must be considered in science education – these can be called *formal* and *informal* learning. The main features of the two areas are summed up in Table 12.1.

Formal learning takes place largely through the medium of the curriculum. It is compulsory, highly structured and regularly assessed. In contrast, informal learning is voluntary, sometimes accidental, haphazard and unassessed. Therein lie its advantages as well as its drawbacks. It also has the advantage of being spontaneous, sociable, learner-led and open-ended but with the consequent drawbacks of being unpredictable, unsequenced and undirected. The distinction between them is not always clear-cut, however, nor should we assume that formal learning is always confined to school with informal learning always occurring outside. Much valuable informal learning takes place in school, while some formal learning occurs out of school.

One thing is clear. In future, informal and undirected learning in science will be of increasing importance – the so-called ICT revolution will ensure this. Learning will take place in a variety of contexts and through an increasing

Table 12.1 Features of formal and informal learning in science

Informal learning	Formal learning
Voluntary	Compulsory
Often haphazard, unstructured, unsequenced	Structured and sequenced
Non-assessed, non-certificated	Assessed, certificated
Open-ended	More closed
Learner-led, learner-centred	Teacher-led, teacher-centred
Outside of formal settings	Classroom and institution based
Unplanned	Planned
Many unintended outcomes (outcomes more difficult to measure)	Fewer unintended outcomes
Social aspect central, e.g. social interactions between visitors	Social aspect less central
Low 'currency'	High 'currency'
Undirected, not legislated for	Legislated and directed (controlled)

number of media. Learning outside of school is certain to be of growing importance in relation to the formal school curriculum. This will perhaps be as true in science, in our so-called 'scientific and technological society', as in any of the other curriculum subjects.

Using and understanding informal learning

My view is that the realm of 'informal learning' in science is an under-used and under-studied area. If we knew more about it, or simply took more notice of it, children's science education could be greatly enhanced.

There is already evidence to suggest that 'factors outside of schools have a strong influence on students' educational outcomes, perhaps strong enough to swamp the effects of variations in education practices' (Schibeci 1989: 13). More knowledge of, and attention to, 'informally acquired ideas' (Lucas, *et al.*, 1986) could thus be used to enrich science education and the work of classroom teachers: 'If the process of acquiring these ideas were examined carefully, information could become available that would be of use to teachers in their day-to-day work' (Lucas, *et al.* 1986: 341).

Lucas (1983) provided an excellent review of sources of informal learning and their influence on so-called 'scientific literacy'. His analysis offers valuable guidelines in considering out-of-school learning in science. He distinguished, for example, between intentional and unintentional sources of learning, and between accidental and deliberate encounters with learning sources. These distinctions present various interesting permutations (Figure 12.1). Thus a casual

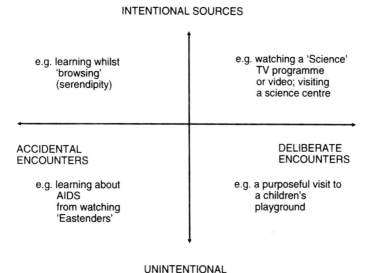

INTENTIONAL SOURCES

e.g. learning whilst 'browsing' (serendipity)

e.g. watching a 'Science' TV programme or video; visiting a science centre

ACCIDENTAL ENCOUNTERS

DELIBERATE ENCOUNTERS

e.g. learning about AIDS from watching 'Eastenders'

e.g. a purposeful visit to a children's playground

UNINTENTIONAL SOURCES

Figure 12.1 Classifying informal sources of learning.

visit to a children's playground may be called an accidental encounter with an unintentional source of learning, for example a roundabout. Interestingly, this encounter may lead children to believe in the centrifugal force on an object which physics teachers later inform them is fictitious. Encounters with science may take place in an interactive, 'hands-on' science centre – these are likely to be deliberate encounters with an intentional source. There is clearly a huge variety of informal sources of learning that impinge on science education:

- everyday experiences, such as slipping on ice; fastening a seat belt; visiting Disneyland or Alton Towers; riding on a bus; eating, drinking, cooking; gardening; riding in a lift; sweating; boiling a kettle, etc., the list is endless;
- the media: television programmes, some deliberately educational, some providing 'accidental learning'; radio; newspapers;
- access to multimedia at home, either via the Internet, CD-ROM, or other platforms;
- visits to museums, science centres, workplaces, etc.

These and many others make up the so-called informal learning which can sometimes support, but occasionally conflict with, the process of the formal science curriculum. In this chapter there is only room to consider briefly two sources of 'informal' learning in science: text and print encountered out of school, be it supermarket, publicity leaflet, advert or news cutting; and interactive science centres of various kinds.

Example 1: Using 'informal' sources of text in science teaching

This section discusses the way in which print and reading from any outside source can be used in science education, although the main focus is on text from newspapers.

The science presented in newspapers can be of value in the school science curriculum but only if used carefully and critically. In addition, one of the aims of science education should be to develop in students both the will and the ability to read 'newspaper science' with a critical eye and with healthy scepticism. For a number of pupils the only science they will encounter in written form after leaving school will be in the tabloid newspapers – hence the necessity of learning to read with care and purpose. Finally, both newspaper science and the formal science curriculum act as 'media' between the scientific community at one level and the general public at the other (this idea is shown in Figure 12.2). Both contribute in some way to the public understanding of science, although their interaction may not always be productive.

Based on these premises, this section offers notes and suggestions related to the use of news cuttings and printed material from other sources in science lessons.

Why use material from newspapers in science education?

In addition to the general aim outlined above, using newspapers and other printed matter can help to meet the following objectives:

1   To meet general curriculum requirements – for example to enable pupils: to relate science to everyday life, to develop communication skill; to encounter a variety of sources from which they can gain information; to read purposefully an extended range of secondary sources; to engage in the critical evaluation of data; to use secondary sources as well as first-hand observation.

2   To provide material directly related to the content of the formal curriculum. Content analysis of the newspapers has shown that newspaper space is devoted to medical issues, the environment, space, food and diet, energy sources, pollution and waste management, and many other topics that relate to specific areas of science taught in schools. (Wellington 1991).

3   To act as a starter in exploring some ideas about the nature of science, i.e. to distinguish between claims and arguments based on scientific considerations and those which are not; to study examples of scientific controversies and the ways in which scientific ideas change; to appreciate the tentative nature of conclusions and the uncertainty of scientific evidence. Current issues, and those from the recent past such as cloning, BSE and cold fusion, can be used here as a complement to material from the history of science.

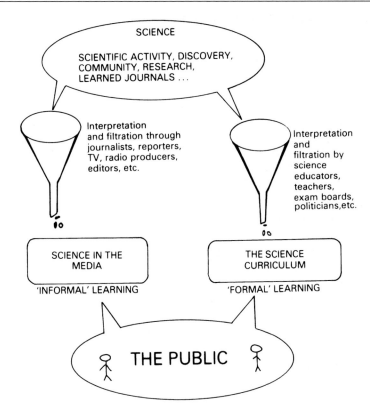

Figure 12.2 Media science and school science as filtering systems.

4 Newspaper material can also be related to cross-curricular themes such as health education, environmental education, citizenship and industrial and economic awareness.
5 To teach pupils to read critically and actively, and to develop an interest in reading about science; to allow group reading, analysis and discussion
6 To raise awareness and interest in current issues related to science, many of which are controversial. By the same token pupils can become aware of some of the values and interests inherent in the development of science, and be enabled to see the limitations of science.

How can they be used?

Newspaper cuttings, and indeed other written material from magazines, super-market leaflets and even pressure groups (such as Greenpeace, Friends of the Earth) can be adapted for classroom use. Table 12.2 provides a list of possible ideas for class and homework which I am sure could be added to.

Table 12.2 Using newspapers in science education

A: *Possible ideas for class work*

1   *Issue raising/introducing an issue*
     for example, controversial issues
2   *Starter activity*
     for example, for a new topic
3   *Prompt/stimulus*
     for example, for discussion/role play; a stimulus to writing
4   *Directed reading*
     for example, comprehension, examining key words
5   *Information/data extraction (and presentation and analysis)*
     for example, making a graph from data in the text; interpreting a graph
6   *Vocabulary/terminology study*
     for example, examining the language in an article; picking out difficult words
7   *Poster making/collage/display creation*
     for example, on the environment; collections of headlines; articles from two papers
     on the same topic

B: *Homework ideas*

1   *Content analysis*
     for example, pupils analyse one week of the paper taken at home (if there is one)
     for its 'science content' – this illuminates their interpretation of what 'science' is.
     Pupils then bring their analysis to the following week's lesson.
2   *Making an activity for others*
     for example, selecting a cutting on science/a scientific issue and devising
     questions/activities on it for other pupils.
3   *Searching for cuttings on a particular topic*
     for example, space, diet, environment, disease, flight, drugs, etc.

(NB: The pupils are probably the best source of newspaper material for the classroom!)

Finally for this section, I would stress the importance of the role of the teacher in encouraging systematic analysis and careful criticism – teachers should not fall into the trap of seeing any of the above as totally independent learning activities.

Which cuttings are best?

I have bought and sometimes reviewed classroom material using news cuttings drawn entirely from the so-called quality press and from *New Scientist*. While such cuttings can give the basis for good classroom activities, they invariably have a reading age higher than the pupils' chronological age and unless heavily edited or used in a very step-by-step, structured way will be unsuitable, even at key stage 4. The quality papers, therefore, need to be handled with care.

This is also true of the tabloids, though for different reasons. I would argue that cuttings from the tabloids (and that includes the *Sun* and the *Mirror*) should be used: first, these are the papers that the majority of school students and adults actually read; second, they present science and scientists in a way which needs to be challenged. Science in the media is so often presented as whiz-bang and dramatic, as certain, as an individual rather than a collective activity, as 'sudden' and unrelated to previous work, as carried out by crackpot and unorthodox discoverers (see Wellington 1991, for a fuller discussion of these points); third, from a purely practical point of view, they are more readable and often shorter and more snappy than the quality coverage, which can sometimes go into inappropriate depth.

How should they be adapted for classroom use?

Certain rules can be followed in choosing and using text:

1   In line with the above comments, the cutting itself needs to be carefully chosen. The total text needs to be fairly brief (perhaps less than half of one A4 side) and, of course, readable. Diagrams, tables, pie-charts and other illustrations will help, especially if one of the aims is to interpret data and look at it critically.

2   If questions are directed at the text, a closed, simple question which merely asks for an item of information or a word from the passage should be placed first. It should be a question which every member of the class can answer. More difficult and perhaps open-ended questions can be left until later. This may seem an obvious point, but how many sets of questions in teachers' worksheets and even in textbooks start off with open-ended, difficult questions which half of a group struggle with and which act as a deterrent to continuing?

3   Questions which ask them to pick out and identify certain words in the passage can be used early on. Once pupils have found and highlighted important words, they can then be set the task of finding out (either from each other, a teacher, a textbook or dictionary) what those key words mean.

4   Open-ended questions which ask for an element of interpretation, discussion and evaluation should be left until the end, once pupils have got to grips with the passage. These questions can go *beyond* the text, and invite speculation and judgement.

To sum up points 2, 3 and 4, questions should be graded from simple to difficult and from closed to open – an obvious rule, but one which is surprisingly often ignored.

5   With more difficult passages, such as from *New Scientist*, teachers may choose to read through an article with a class, and then discuss its main points before embarking on the activities. With other material, teachers may simply let the class work in small groups, or individually, and then bring them together later to compare answers or points from discussion.

In all cases I feel that some teacher intervention is needed to bring out the point behind the activity. This is particularly true in activities aimed at raising questions about the nature of science, such as why do scientists disagree? Are some scientists biased? What counts as a fair test? How are scientists portrayed in the media . . .? and so on.

6   Finally, activities of this kind can very often be used as examples of the presentation of science, for example the way that data and statistics are presented in papers to make certain points or support certain arguments; the way in which science generally is presented to the public. Pupils can thus be encouraged to look critically at the presentation of science by the media – this is surely an essential prerequisite for participation as a citizen in a science-based democracy.

Examples of activities

Over the last ten years I (and others) have produced a number of fairly short simple activities which have been tried out with secondary age pupils. One example is shown in Figure 12.3.

Cuttings which contain surprising stories are worth watching out for. Figure 12.4 shows one example, with a happy ending apart from the demise of the car. A number of questions for individuals to answer, or groups to discuss, could be used with it: 'Why did he survive?' 'Did he reach terminal velocity?' 'How did the "crumpling" of the car help him?' . . . and so on. A short activity like this could make a nice introduction to a dry topic like forces and motion. Older students could take a more quantitative approach: 'What (roughly) would his momentum and kinetic energy have been just before impact?' 'What might (roughly) his rate of change of momentum have been on hitting the car? where did his kinetic energy "go"?'.

Example 2: Interactive science centres

What are interactive science centres?

A 'new generation' of science museums grew up in the 1960s in the USA with initiatives like the New York Hall of Science in 1964 and the Exploratorium in San Francisco in 1969. The principles of the Exploratorium were based on the three Is, put forward by one of the driving forces behind it, Frank Oppenheimer (brother of Robert of atomic bomb fame): *innovation, interaction and involvement*. The new generation shifted museums away from 'objects in glass cases' to a stress on involvement, activity and ideas. Greatly influenced by this shift and by the success of children's museums and galleries, a new breed of stand alone 'interactive science centres' (ISCs) grew up in the 1980s. In 1985 there were none in the UK. A decade later there were over 20, with centres such as the Exploratory in Bristol, and Techniquest in Cardiff leading the way, together

Veggie or not?

IT seems that today more and more people are cutting meat out of their diets. Most people become vegetarians for either health or moral reasons.

The society in which we live makes it virtually impossible to exist in an entirely cruelty-free environment. However, it is feasible to stick to a diet that causes as little suffering as possible. Over 1.4 million people under the age of 16 in the UK have already given up meat and that number is still growing.

Those who eliminate animal produce, meat and fish from their diet for health reasons have plausible grounds for doing so. In extensive medical studies vegetarians were found to eat more fibre, have lower cholesterol levels and, in most cases, be slimmer than the general population.

Not eating meat, especially red meat, can reduce the risk of contracting certain cancers and other of the West's fatal diseases. All the protein, vitamins and minerals required by the body can be found within a vegetarian diet.

There are also environmental reasons for being a vegetarian. Meat is not cheap. The amount of feed eaten by the world's cattle is equal to double the amount of calories required by the world's human population. Yet millions starve.

PESTICIDES

Meat contains approximately 14 times more pesticides than vegetables do; and the biggest pollutants of British waterways are not chemical manufacturers, but meat producers.

Meat production may be inefficient, but marine fishing is even more so. Only 1.5 kg of fish is harvested in each hectare of ocean a year. The fish die from asphyxiation as they are hauled from the sea in huge nets.

The cruelty of marine fishing also affects other sea creatures, such as seals and dolphins, which are caught in the large drag nets used to ensnare tuna.

Forty per cent of the world's catch from the North Sea suffers from lesions and tumours due to pollution and has large amounts of toxins accumulated in the flesh of the fish.

The biggest reason most young people are giving up meat and fish is because they can no longer justify killing animals for food. Most animals are not kept in acceptable or humane conditions and the way many are slaughtered is attrocious.

It's up to both meat eaters and vegetarians to try to improve conditions for animals in the future. Animals have no voice and because of this they are not given the respect they deserve.

Sarah Boxley

Veggie or Not?

This newspaper article appeared in the Sheffield Star on 9 October 1991. Read it carefully and then answer the following questions.

1   What word is used to describe a person who does *not* eat meat?
2   Write down 3 *health* reasons why some people choose not to eat meat or fish?
3   Why does your body need each of these types of food: (a) protein; (b) vitamins; (c) minerals?
4   Give one example in each case of a good food containing: (a) protein; (b) vitamins; (c) minerals?
5   Make a list of 5 things to eat containing 'red meat'.
6   According to this article, what could be a greater risk if you eat red meat?
7   What are the good 'environmental reasons' for being a vegetarian? (You should be able to find three.)
8   Read paragraph 5 again. Why is meat production said to be 'inefficient'?

Additional Questions (9–12)

9   Many fish die from 'asphyxiation' as they are harvested from the sea. What does this mean?
10 What is 'dolphin-friendly tuna'? Why do you think some shops are keen to label their tins of tuna fish this way?
11 According to this article, what is the biggest reason for young people giving up meat and fish?
12 Are you a 'veggie' or 'not a veggie'? What sort of things like parents, friends, adverts etc. have influenced the way you eat? Do you think you'll ever change your mind?

Figure 12.3 An example of a newspaper based activity. [Courtesy of Kathy Mayoh]
Source: Sheffield Star.

Alive! Man who fell 200ft

■ *The tower block where Christopher Saggers fell 220ft.*

A MAN plunged more than 200 feet from a tower block — and survived when a car broke his fall.

Christopher Saggers (26) escaped with little more than a broken elbow and a neck injury after falling from the 22nd floor of flats in Salford, Greater Manchester.

Police said an astonished witness saw Mr Saggers crash on to the roof of the Nissan Micra, lie there for 15 seconds, then get up, brush himself down, and walk away.

The impact almost completely crushed the top half of the car.

A police spokesman said it was a "miracle" Mr Sagger survived.

The car's owner, Salford University student Michael Afilaka, said a friend leaving the flats had told him someone had jumped on his A-registered car.

"I looked out from the window from where the man had fallen and what I saw was unbelievable," he said.

"He had landed bang in the middle of the roof and it had caved in.

"You could open the doors, but it was impossible to get into the car. It was flattened. It must have been a million-to-one chance for him to hit the car right in the middle."

Mr Saggers, Alpha Street West, Seedley, Greater Manchester, was taken by ambulance to Salford's Hope Hospital, where he was yesterday said to be "comfortable".

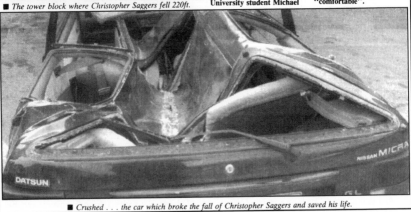

■ *Crushed . . . the car which broke the fall of Christopher Saggers and saved his life.*

Figure 12.4 An unusual newspaper cutting.

Source: Manchester Evening News.

with, in the London Science Museum, a self-contained hands-on centre called Launch Pad. Some of these were attracting up to 200,000 visitors per year and still do. In the next decade, up to 2005, some estimates suggest that a further £1,000 million pounds will have been spent on the ISC movement, largely from support from the UK National Lottery.

Interactive science centres, like elephants, are hard to define – but we all know one when we see one. Perhaps the first distinguishing feature is the general air of noise, enjoyment and activity which greets all those who enter.

Second, they contain activities or 'exploring stations' (McManus 1992) which visitors are invited to touch and do things with, i.e. to interact with. Typically a centre might have between 50 and 200 exhibits, most of which need to be hard-wearing and robust, and at least a few of which will be temporarily 'under repair'. The various centres will have certain exhibits (or 'plores' as they were first christened at the Bristol Exploratory) in common, partly because developers of plores have sold or shared their ideas with others and these have been transferred from one ISC to another. My impression from visiting many of the centres is that most will contain a Bernoulli blower, a rotating turntable with a human on it holding a bicycle wheel, an echo tube, parabolic mirrors and many other exhibits with people doing things on them!

Third, science centres will have 'guides', 'pilots' or 'explainers' (as opposed to a uniformed attendant in earlier generations of museum) circulating around the centre to help visitors in any way, commonly in showing them how to 'interact' with an exhibit although some may attempt to *explain* phenomena (often at their peril, if it involves concepts such as moment of inertia or gyroscopic motion). The key role of the explainer, in my view, is to actually get learners to *engage with an exhibit*, at whatever level. There might typically be four or five explainers 'on the floor', with perhaps about 180 visitors at any one time.

Details of what each centre contains can be found by contacting them directly, often via their web pages (see further reading for details). The centres each have their own distinctive flavour and emphasis, but they all have certain features in common:

• All provide interactive, hands-on learning of science using a range of activities/events/ 'plores' rather than untouched exhibits in glass cases.
• They all emphasise play and enjoyment as an essential element of learning.

The stress is on doing, seeing and experiencing rather than formal understanding and explanation. Although each 'event' carries a short explanation or caption, the evidence is that these are hardly ever read – in addition, the use of formal, structured worksheets in the centres is uncommon, if not discouraged.

How do they relate to the formal curriculum?

My own observations, as an independent observer having visited many of the ISCs in the UK and USA, is that they do relate very closely to many of the areas of the formal school curriculum and even beyond. Some of the concepts being experienced though not explained, such as gyroscopic motion or human perception, extend to the realms of undergraduate science.

In addition, many ISCs can actually fill gaps in the curriculum coverage offered in a school setting. For example, expert demonstrations and 'Science Shows' can show phenomena which are either unsafe or impractical to do in a school lab, e.g. some examples of combustion or other dramatic chemical processes, while at primary level, centres can provide hands-on experiences in an enjoyable, 'free-range' environment which primary schools may not have the resources to offer.

It should also be noted that many exhibits go beyond the straitjacket of a formal curriculum and introduce learners to some difficult, but fascinating and important, topics such as human perception and chaos – the latter using examples from chaotic, unpredictable motion such as spinning magnets, Rott's pendulum, and other pendulum examples which learners are unlikely to see at school.

Learning in science centres . . . and elsewhere

What do we know about learning? At the risk of annoying readers who have a background in psychology, I will attempt to sum up some of the key points about learning which have a bearing on what goes in ISCs and also how teachers can best exploit them. My potted version has three key points.

1   Learning depends on what the learner already knows. Learning is a process which involves interaction between *what is already known and the current learning experience*. For learning to be lasting and meaningful, it must connect with prior knowledge, prior *conceptions* and prior experience – otherwise it becomes rote or parrot-fashion learning. Learners *construct knowledge* on a foundation of what they already know.

2   *Meaningful learning often occurs in a social context* (though perhaps not always). Learners can help each other by talking and interacting – teachers can help learners by supporting, guiding, structuring and *scaffolding* their learning. Learners *construct* their own knowledge, but they often do it best socially. Other people are important.

3   Learning is *a situated process*. All of our knowledge is situated in a certain context or domain. It is often difficult for this to 'travel' or transfer – psychologists have searched in vain for over 70 years for conclusive evidence of transfer of learning or generalisable skills. Knowledge learnt in one context, e.g. a school science laboratory, does not always travel to another, e.g. rewiring your house. The street trader who can add up prices of fruit and vegetables in a jiffy may flounder when asked to do a written arithmetic test with paper and pencil, let alone a Maths GCSE paper.

These three potted points (derived largely from Vygotsky, Ausubel and Bruner) are all important in weighing up the role and the contribution of ISCs and comparing it with the function of formal, school curriculum-based science education. We must recognise that learning in the two contexts is different – formal, school learning can contribute more to some aspects of learning in areas 1 to 3 above than the 'informal' learning in ISCs, and vice versa. It is important to compare and contrast the features of learning in the two contexts, i.e. ISCs and school (see Table 12.1 again).

Learning in formal settings is important. As Paulette McManus puts it:

'In formal educational situations, where you will learn, who you will learn with, whether you are qualified to learn, who you will learn from, what you will learn, how long you will be given to learn it and agreement on what you have learned and your level of understanding are matters largely out of the control of the individual learner. As a result of these restrictions on the individual, formal educational institutions are very efficient, admirable means of communicating knowledge throughout societies for the benefit of those societies and the individuals within them'.

(McManus 1992: 165)

Nevertheless, learning in less formal settings also has a role to play. My argument is that learning science in ISCs is not a substitute for learning in a more formal, school context – but it can be an important complement to it. How?

Assessing the contribution of interactive science centres

My own view is that ISCs make a significant contribution in three areas: the cognitive domain, the affective domain, and the important job of linking science and scientific concepts to real world experiences. I will explain:

1 Firstly, centres contribute *indirectly* to higher-order knowledge and understanding. One way is through what I call the 'rubbing-off' effect of hands-on science. Children visit a centre, and do and see a large number of things in a short space of time. They often see or do something which rubs off and sticks, or 'sparks off' something in their mind which may resurface weeks, months, even years later. In other words, while hands-on science centres may not contribute immediately and directly to deep understanding, their *indirect* effect must not be forgotten.
2 A similar effect occurs through a second area of educational aims: the *affective* domain. This area involves the development of interest, enthusiasm, motivation, eagerness to learn, awareness and general 'openness' and 'alertness'. Interactive hands-on science centres can make a major contribution to the affective area. They may even begin to compensate for the neglect of this area in formal science education. Hands-on science centres generate activity, enthusiasm, adrenalin, excitement and interest. By developing motivation for science and technology they will, in many cases, ultimately contribute to understanding.

3   Finally, 'school science', as those of us who have been through the school system know, seems to have an existence of its own. It has its own *apparatus*, creating a world of conical flasks, test-tube racks, pyrex beakers and all the other bits and pieces which remind adults instantly of school science. It has its own *laboratories* of a kind encountered nowhere else in the universe which by necessity combine working space with learning and teaching space. The world of 'school science' bears little relation to the world outside where science and technology abound. In playgrounds, in kitchens, on sports fields and golf courses, in shop windows, in the back garden or on rubbish tips there is enough science to keep people going for a lifetime. One of the achievements of hands-on science centres has been to relate science and technology to the things that most people (who don't go on to be research chemists) see and use. Lemonade bottles, bridges, incinerators, bricks, lifting jacks and giant see-saws can all be found in interactive centres but rarely in school science labs. Thus hands-on centres can make a major contribution to a broad science education, and therefore scientific literacy, which school science in its unique world would not.

Research carried out in different parts of the world supports my claims. Stevenson (1992), for example, tracked a substantial number of visitors (many from family groups) to Launch Pad at different intervals after their visit. He discussed their memories of the visit as much as six months after the event. He found that family members were able to recall much of their visit in clear detail (how many pupils can do this six months after a school science lesson?). He concluded that a significant number of the memories reported to him showed that *cognitive processing* related to the activities during the visit had taken place. In addition, a substantial body of research conducted in Australia by Léonie Rennie supports the claim that both cognitive and affective learning do occur. She suggests that cognitive learning fades after a time (hardly surprisingly) but that affective outcomes are more resistant and long-lasting.

It seems that ISCs may be one means of providing the excitement and motivation for learners to continue with science post-16 which is clearly needed, given the current depressing statistics on those who choose to follow sciences at advanced level.

In summary

A visit to a science centre is a complement to school learning, not a substitute for it. Science centres can enrich and broaden the formal science curriculum. Each offers a valuable contribution to science education. ISCs work for all ages of learner from 1 to 91 and beyond, and for all kinds of group ranging from the extended family to semi-formal groups such as Guides, Scouts and the Women's Institute. The ISCs have made a tremendous contribution to science education and the public understanding of science on an extremely low budget, with virtually nothing coming from the public purse. They deserve to be supported. Let us hope that the injection of large sums of money will not ruin them, will take account of their roots and will recognise the enormous and unique contribution they have made.

Bringing informal, outside learning into the classroom

We have considered just two examples of how 'informal' sources can be linked with formal science education. There are clearly many others that can contribute. One of the dangers, of course, is to try to over-exploit outside experiences or sources, resulting in what teachers call 'overkill', i.e. trying to make too much of a good thing. Given this qualification, however, there are several ways in which teachers can link the domains of informal, out-of-school learning and formal, structured learning:

- in introducing a lesson or a new topic, such as by starting with the pupils' experiences of that topic;
- in basing a lesson around an out-of-school activity, such as a visit, a TV programme, an advertisement;
- in providing ideas for project work and independent learning;
- by using 'everyday' materials (such as bleach, washing powder, food colourings) to replace or use alongside laboratory materials;
- in overtly valuing children's contributions to classroom discussions and everyday anecdotes about science experience;
- in displaying posters and adverts about the use of science in everyday life, for example plastics, chlorine, drugs;
- in placing practical problem-solving tasks in everyday, relevant contexts.

Looking to the future

One of the founders of the San Francisco Exploratorium, Frank Oppenheimer (brother of Robert), argued more than fifteen years ago for the value of informal learning in promoting science education and science, and against the dominance of formal, certificated education (see Table 12.1):

> '. . . no-one ever flunks a museum or a television program or a library or a park, while they do flunk a course – they do "flunk out of school". Only schools can certify students; only certified students can progress. As a result only schools are conceived as public education. I would like to suggest that the current mechanisms for certification are not only stifling to educational progress but that they are also extraordinarily costly and wasteful. Certification is an impediment.'
>
> *(Oppenheimer 1975)*

Perhaps Oppenheimer was overstating the case for informal, out-of-school education as against the certificated, formal curriculum. But the importance of

264 Enriching science teaching

such learning is certain to grow in the future, not least due to the spread of ICT. Teachers need to be aware of it, to nurture it and to use it whilst avoiding overexploiting it.

References and further reading

Formal and informal learning

Lucas, A.M. (1983) 'Scientific literacy and informal learning', *Studies of Science Education, no.* 10, pp. 1–36.
Lucas, A.M., McManus, P.M. and Thomas, G. (1986) 'Investigating learning from informal sources: listening to conversations and observing play in science museums', *European Journal of Science Education*, no. 8, pp. 41–52.
Schibeci R.A. (1989) 'Home, school and peer group influences on student attitudes and achievement in science', *Science Education, no.* 73, p. 13.

Using 'outside' text or photographs in the classroom

Association for Science Education (ASE) (1991) *Race, Equality and Science Teaching*, Hatfield: ASE. (This contains an excellent section on choosing and using photographs in the classroom with examples that can be taken from newspapers, books, magazines, etc. The aims behind the activities include making science learners into 'critical observers' of the images of people and places presented by photographs.)
Wellington, J.J. (1986a) (ed.) *Controversial Issues in the Curriculum*, Oxford: Basil Blackwell.
—— (1986b) *The Nuclear Issue*, Oxford: Basil Blackwell.
(Both discuss the value of using controversial issues in developing certain skills, and suggest strategies for the classroom. *The Nuclear Issue* also contains examples that can be photocopied for classroom use.)
— (1991) 'Newspaper science, school science: friends or enemies?', *International Journal of Science Education*, vol. 13 no. 4, pp. 363–72 (contains a recent example of content analysis and a review of past news coverage).

Interactive science centres

Griffin, J. (1994) 'Learning to learn in informal science settings', *Research in Science Education*, no. 24, pp. 121–8.
Griffin, J. (1998) 'Learning science through practical experiences in museums', *International Journal of Science Education*, vol. 20, no. 6, pp. 655–63.
McManus, P. (1992) 'Topics in museums and science education', *Studies in Science Education*, vol. 20 (1992), pp. 157–82.
Moffat, H. (1991) 'Museums and the national curriculum', *Museums Journal*, vol. 91, no. 5, pp. 32–7.
Oppenheimer, F. (1975) 'The exploratorium and other ways of teaching physics', *Physics Today*, vol. 28, no. 9, pp. 9–13.
Quin, M. (ed.) (1989) *Sharing Science: Issues in the Development of Interactive Science Centres*, London: Nuffield Foundation/COPUS.
Rennie, L.J. (1994) 'Measuring affective outcomes from a visit to a science education centre', *Research in Science Education*, no. 24, pp. 261–9.
Shortland, M. (1987) 'No business like show business', *Nature*, no. 328, pp. 213–14 (a critical look at 'hands-on' science).

Stevenson, J. (1992) 'The long-term impact of interactive exhibits', *International Journal of Science Education*, vol. 13, no. 5, pp. 521–31.

Wellington, J.J. (1989a) 'Attitudes before understanding: the role of hands-on centres', *Sharing Science*, London: Nuffield Foundation/COPUS.

—— (1989b) *Hands-on Science: 'It's fun, but do they learn?'*, video with notes, Sheffield: University of Sheffield Television Service.

—— (1990) Formal and informal learning in science: the role of the interactive science centres, *Physics Education*, no. 25, pp. 247–50.

Full information on the UK science centres can be obtained from information supplied by the 'British Interactive Group' (BIG) on the Web at http://www.exploratory. org.uk/big/. Complimentary visits for teachers can be arranged to many centres – contact them directly to arrange a visit.

Your own 'nature of science' profile

The aim of the activity that follows is to encourage readers to reflect upon their own view of the nature of science. It is intended to be a way of getting you to think, learn and reflect rather than a valid measurement of your position on some sort of objective scale. So don't worry if, at the end of the activity, your profile is not as you expected. The thing to do then is to consider why – this is an important part of the process.

The 24 statements

Please read each of the statements shown in Table 1 slowly and carefully.

Give each statement a number from 'strongly agree' ($+5$) to 'strongly disagree' (-5) and place it next to the statement. A score of 0 will indicate a balanced view. (For the time being, ignore the initials in brackets.)

Working out your profile

Having 'scored' each statement you now need to work out your own profile. Look closely at Figure 1:

Each statement has at least two letters in brackets after it – for example, PC; some have four – for example, RP, CD. Put your score for each question into the appropriate box or boxes in Figure 1, i.e. some score once, some twice. Note carefully that some scores have to have their sign reversed (i.e. – becomes + and + becomes – before they can be entered into the box).

After you have entered all your numbers into the boxes add up the totals, then transfer the totals from the columns to the correct position on each of the five relevant axes in Figure 2. Join up the five options with straight lines to show your profile of science. Are you a raving relativist? A proud positivist? Or a coy contextualist? What do all these terms mean anyway?

Your nature of science

Many of the terms used may be unfamiliar. In fact, many of them are problematic and a matter of debate. Their meanings change and shift and can

Table 1 The 24 statements

1   The results that pupils get from their experiments are as valid as anybody else's. (RP)
2   Science is essentially a masculine construct. (CD)
3   Science facts are what scientists agree that they are. (CD, RP)
4   The object of scientific activity is to reveal reality. (IR)
5   Scientists have no idea of the outcome of an experiment before they do it. (QD)
6   Scientific research is economically and politically determined. (CD)
7   Science education should be more about the learning of scientific processes than the learning of scientific facts. (PC)
8   The processes of science are divorced from moral and ethical considerations. (CD)
9   The most valuable part of a scientific education is what remains after the facts have been forgotten. (PC)
10 Scientific theories are valid if they work. (IR)
11 Science proceeds by drawing generalisable conclusions (which later became theories) from available data. (ID)
12 There is such a thing as a true scientific theory. (RP, IR)
13 Human emotion plays no part in the creation of scientific knowledge. (CD)
14 Scientific theories describe a real external world which is independent of human perception. (RP, IR)
15 A good solid grounding in basic scientific facts and inherited scientific knowledge is essential before young scientists can go on to make discoveries of their own. (PC)
16 Scientific theories have changed over time simply because experimental techniques have improved. (RP, CD)
17 'Scientific method' is transferable from one scientific investigation to another. (PC)
18 In practice, choices between competing theories are made purely on the basis of experimental results. (CD, RP)
19 Scientific theories are as much a result of imagination and intuition as inference from experimental results. (ID)
20 Scientific knowledge is different from other kinds of knowledge in that it has higher status. (RP)
21 There are certain physical events in the universe which science can never explain. (RP, IR)
22 Scientific knowledge is morally neutral – only the application of the knowledge is ethically determined. (CD)
23 All scientific experiments and observations are determined by existing theories. (ID)
24 Science is essentially characterised by the methods and processes it uses. (PC)

be seen as insults or praise depending on to whom you are talking. Brief definitions for the meanings attached to the five axes in Figure 2 are offered below.

1 Relativism/Positivism Axis

Relativist: You deny that things are true or false solely based on an independent reality. The 'truth' of a theory will depend on the norms and rationality of the social group considering it as well as the experimental techniques used to test it. Judgements as to the truth of scientific theories will vary from one individual to another and from one culture to another, i.e. truth is relative, not absolute.

RP

Statement	Score
1	–
3	–
21	–
12	+
14	+
16	+
18	+
20	+
Total	

ID

Statement	Score
5	–
11	–
19	+
23	+
Total	

CD

Statement	Score
2	–
3	–
6	–
8	–
13	+
16	+
18	+
22	+
Total	

PC

Statement	Score
7	–
9	–
17	–
24	–
15	+
Total	

IR

Statement	Score
10	–
21	–
4	+
12	+
14	+
Total	

Add up the scores in the right-hand columns to give you a grand total for each grid.

N.B. Some statements score positive, some negative.

Figure I

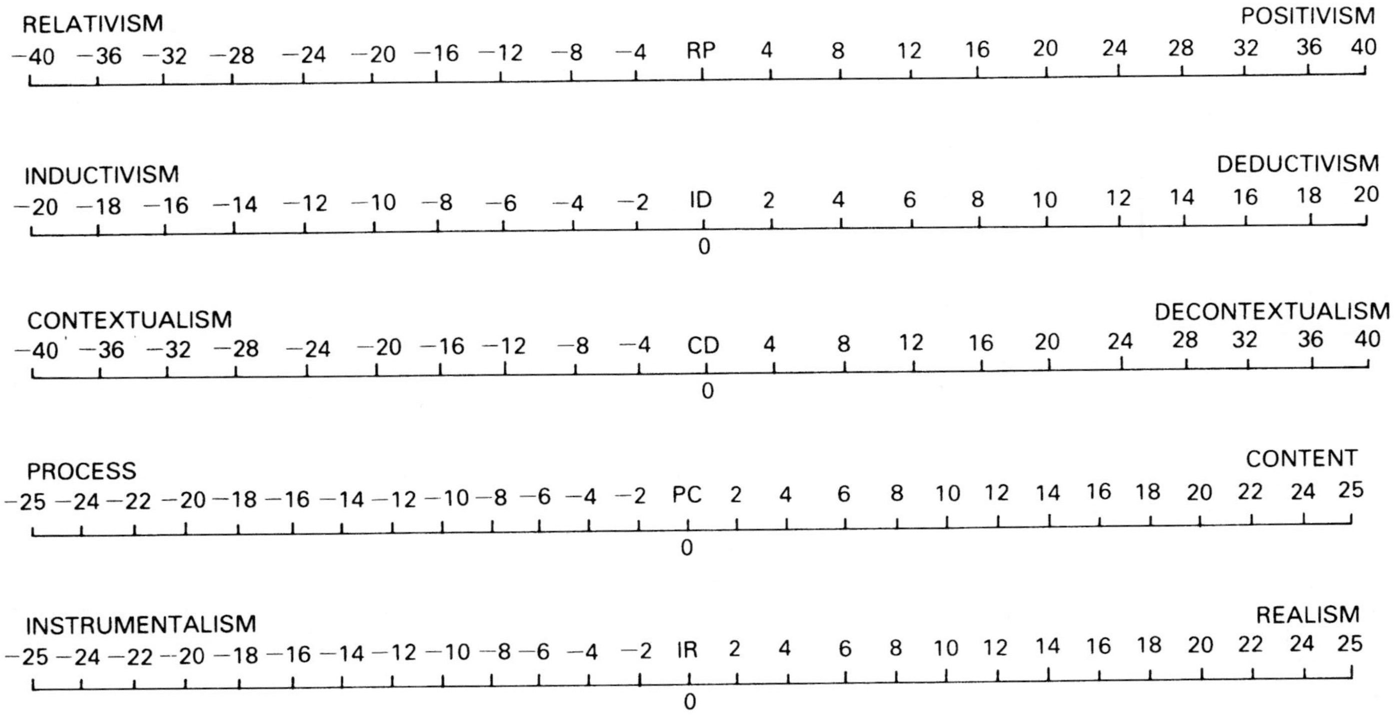
RELATIVISM
POSITIVISM
−40 −36 −32 −28 −24 −20 −16 −12 −8 −4 RP 4 8 12 16 20 24 28 32 36 40
INDUCTIVISM
DEDUCTIVISM
−20 −18 −16 −14 −12 −10 −8 −6 −4 −2 ID 2 4 6 8 10 12 14 16 18 20
0
CONTEXTUALISM
DECONTEXTUALISM
−40 −36 −32 −28 −24 −20 −16 −12 −8 −4 CD 4 8 12 16 20 24 28 32 36 40
0
PROCESS
CONTENT
−25 −24 −22 −20 −18 −16 −14 −12 −10 −8 −6 −4 −2 PC 2 4 6 8 10 12 14 16 18 20 22 24 25
0
INSTRUMENTALISM
REALISM
−25 −24 −22 −20 −18 −16 −14 −12 −10 −8 −6 −4 −2 IR 2 4 6 8 10 12 14 16 18 20 22 24 25
0

Figure 2

Positivist: You believe strongly that scientific knowledge is more 'valid' than other forms of knowledge. The laws and theories generated by experiments are our descriptions of patterns we see in a real, external, objective world. To the positivist, science is the primary source of truth. Positivism recognises empirical facts and observable phenomena as the raw material of science. The scientist's job is to establish the objective relationships between the laws governing the facts and observables. Positivism rejects inquiry into underlying causes and ultimate origins.

2 Inductivism/Deductivism

Inductivist: You believe that the scientist's job is the interrogation of nature. By observing many particular instances, one is able to infer from the particular to the general and then determine the underlying laws and theories. According to inductivism, scientists generalise from a set of observations to a universal law 'inductively'. Scientific knowledge is built by induction from a secure set of observations.

Deductivist: In our definition this means that you believe that scientists proceed by testing ideas produced by the logical consequences of current theories or of their bold, imaginative ideas. According to deductivism (or hypothetico-deductivism), scientific reasoning consists of the forming of hypotheses which are not established by the empirical data but may be suggested by them. Science then proceeds by testing the observable consequences of these hypotheses, i.e. observations are directed or led by hypotheses – they are theory-laden.

3 Contextualism/Decontextualism

Contextualist: You hold the view that the truth of scientific knowledge and processes is interdependent with the culture in which the scientists live and in which it takes place.

Decontextualist: You hold the view that scientific knowledge is independent of its cultural location and sociological structure.

4 Process/Content

Process: You see science as a characteristic set of identifiable methods/processes. The learning of these is the essential part of science education.

Content: You think that science is characterised by the facts and ideas it has and that the essential part of science education is the acquisition and mastery of this 'body of knowledge'.

5 Instrumentalism/Realism

Instrumentalist: You believe that scientific theories and ideas are fine if they work, that is they allow correct predictions to be made. They are instruments that we can use but they say nothing about an independent reality or their own truth.

Realist: You believe that scientific theories are statements about a world that exists in space and time independent of the scientists' perceptions. Correct theories describe things that are really there, independent of scientists, such as atoms, electrons.

Points to reflect upon

Having had a chance to read the working definitions, consider the points below:

- How do you feel about your profile? Has it really 'measured' your views about science?
- Do you feel confident that you understand it all?
- Do you think your views/opinions have been challenged or changed by the exercise? Would you like to go back now and do it again?
- Would you like to try it out on your colleagues?

Whatever the shape of your profile, please do not worry and do not panic! There are many 'natures of science'.

Where do you stand?

This activity is designed to encourage you to reflect on your own views on the two poles introduced above: process/content and integration/separation. First of all, carry out the activity shown in Table 1 – you might find it useful to photocopy that table first (you have permission!).

You should have considered each statement carefully and placed a number from −5 to +5 in the unshaded boxes next to each statement (note that statement 4 has two unshaded boxes beside it). Now you need to add up your scores in order to establish your position. Follow these steps:

1   Add up the scores under each *column*, i.e. P, C, I and S, taking account of the sign of each score.
2   Calculate a value for (P-C) and (I-S), again taking careful account of the sign.
3   Plot your position on a graph as shown in Figure 1. The value of (P-C) gives the x-coordinate; (P-S) gives the y-coordinate.

Look at your position on the graph in Figure 1. You can give yourself a label according to which quadrant you fall into:

• process integrationist: northeast quadrant
• process separationist: southeast quadrant
• content integrationist: northwest quadrant
• content separationist: southwest quadrant

Now is the time to reflect on the activity, and your position on the graph.

• Do you feel that this activity has wrongly placed you – i.e. are you in the right quadrant, according to your intuition? If not, then where do you feel intuitively that your position lies?
• If you are roughly in the right position, why do you feel that you hold such a view? Could you defend it, for example, to other science teachers? What argument should you use to support it?
• Does your view of science agree with that explicit and implicit in the science curriculum which you follow?

Table 1 Where do you stand?

- Consider each statement slowly and carefully.
- Numbers from +5 to −5 will indicate your agreement or disagreement with each statement.
- Place a number from +5 to −5 in the unshaded boxes according to the following scale:

+5	+4	+3	+2	+1	0	−1	−2	−3	−4	−5
agree		agree		don't know		disagree			disagree	
strongly				don't care					violently	

You will be told what to do with those numbers when you have ranked each of the twenty statements.

	Statements	P	C	I	S
1	Each science has its own unique, separate identity.				
2	There is no such thing as 'the scientific method'.				
3	Science education is primarily concerned with transmitting a body of inherited knowledge.				
4	Science has its own unique processes and methods, common to all sciences.				
5	Science processes must be taught *explicitly* by teachers.				
6	Balanced science courses will only achieve status if the separate sciences are abolished.				
7	There is no such thing as a 'true scientific theory'.				
8	The abolution of separate sciences pre-16 would remove freedom of choice, a fundamental human right.				
9	Combined science courses should be taught only to less able pupils.				
10	By abolishing separate sciences before 16 the gender divisions in science education would be removed.				
11	'Processes need to be taught overtly . . . without the encumberance of having to assimilate a body of facts at the same time' (Screen 1986a).				
12	The separate sciences need to be preserved at 14–16 level to maintain standards.				
13	Science teachers should start from the pupils' ideas and build upon them encouraging them to develop their own theories.				
14	The scientific and technological elite needed for future economic growth can only be developed through a separate science curriculum (14–16).				
15	The processes of science can be identified, taught and assessed.				

Statements		P	C	I	S
16	The most valuable part of a scientific education is what remains after the facts have been forgotten.				
17	A good, solid grounding in basic scientifc facts and inherited scientific knowledge is essential before you can go to make discoveries of your own.				
18	An integrated science programme is the only way to achieve an acceptable percentage of science within the overall curriculum.				
19	School leavers and future citizens will only be able to make decisions on scientific issues if they have basic facts at their fingertips.				
20	In the 'information age' all that matters is that pupils know *how* to access information and *where* to acquire the facts.				
		P	C	I	S

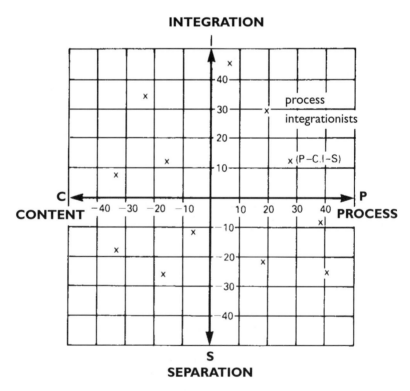

INTEGRATION

CONTENT — C

PROCESS — P

process integrationists

x (P–C.I–S)

S
SEPARATION

Figure 1 Where do you stand? Plot your position on a graph as shown. The crosses show some positions of teachers who have tried this activity.

Index

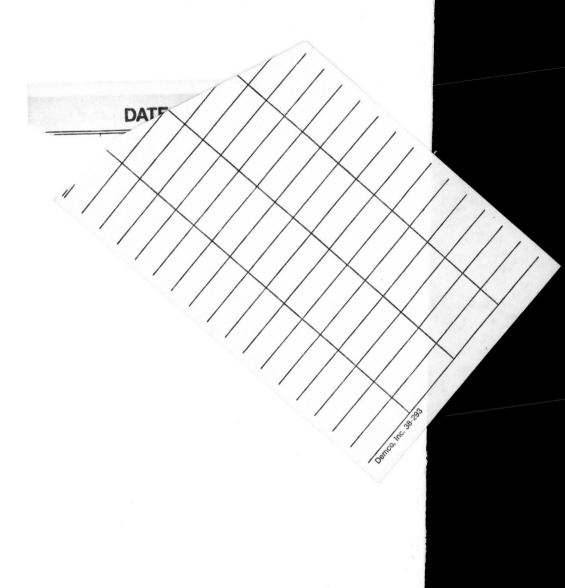

DATE

Demco, Inc. 38-293